U0946852

抗日战争档案汇编

南京永利铔厂战时损失及战后重建档案汇编

2

南京市档案馆 编

中華書局

四、损失调查表、统计清册及相关公文

076 总 秘 077 处 送 存 根

送交总处参考件

REPORT

When the Sino-Japanese War broke out in August, 1937 the Japanese bombers raided our Ammonium Sulphate Plant three times. But the damage was not serious and with our ceaseless repair we kept the whole plant going for several months.

Until the Japanese rushed toward Nanking we were compelled to leave the plant and moved to Chungking with our Government in December of the same year.

It was unfortunate that our hundred percent new plant fell into the Japanese hand. Henceforth the Japs utilized our plant for eight years till the day of their unconditional surrender in August, 1945.

When we took our plant back from Japanese (except the Nitric Acid Department which was removed to Japan in 1942 by the Japs), we did try to start the plant at once, but failed.

After inspecting through the whole plant, we found that all the equipments were ruined and destroyed by the Japs' careless and rough handling during the War Time.

We spent billions of dollars and ten months for repairing the "scrap junk", then we started the plant again in August, 1946. Of course, we can manufacture some fertilizer (ammonium sulphate) for our farmers, but the cost is considerably higher than our original prewar figure and the imported fertilizer price on the present market.

The reason is quite plain that our equipments are too old. Therefore we ought to "shut down" too often for repairing and the production is reduced to about one-third of the original capacity of 150 tons of ammonium sulphate per day. And the power consumption is increased to about 25 percent on account of the equipments being worn out badly.

We are facing the fact, from any point of view, that it is unreasonable to keep on such a chemical plant like this. Furthermore, the life of any chemical plant never lasts ten years. This information has been so claimed by engineers all over the world.

Now the Allied Headquarters has notified the Allied Nations to remove the Japanese industrial equipments for indemnifying their losses in war. Here we enclose a detailed list of our damage-conditions and request our Government to negotiate with the Allied Headquarters to get a complete and good shape of ammonium sulphate plant or a similar one from Japan for indemnification of our loss.

附（一）煤气厂损失表

GAS PLANT

P. 1

ITEM NO.	NAME OF ARTICLE	QUANTITY	DAMAGED PARTS	DESCRIPTION	% DAMAGED	REMARKS
(1)	Skip Hoist and Coke Bin	1	Hoisting Machine, Load Bucket, Coke Crusher, Coke Bin.	Shafts, Bearings, Cable and Motor Ball Bearings badly worn out. Load Bucket rusted. Coke Bin Shell rusted and worn out nearly through.	80%	
(2)	Water Gas Set 14,000 M³/day Generators	2	Steel shell, Water jacket, fire brick lining, Mechanical grate, Speed reducer, Bearings, Lubricating pumps, Motors.	Shells and Water jacket rusted. Fire brick lining cracked and badly worn out. Mechanical grate worm gear and worm, Speed Reducer, Bearings, Shafts, worm out. Check and Automatic Valves leaked and inaccurate. Motors over-heated.	80%	
(3)	Igniters	2	Steel shells, fire brick lining, checker work.	Shells rusted. Fire brick lining and cheker work cracked.	80%	
(4)	Generator's Waste heat Boiler 4'Ø x 10' Pressure 300 lb./in²	1	Steel shells, fire tubes, Drum.	Steel shells, fire tubes and Drum are corroded and pitted badly.	90%	
	Producer Gas Set:					
(5)	Gas Producer	1	Steel shell, water jacket, fire brick lining, Mechanical grate, Bearings, Shafts, Speed Reducer, Motor.	Shells and water jacket heavily rusted, fire brick lining cracked, Mechancial grate worm gears, Bearings, Speed Reducer and Motor Bearings are worn out.	95%	This unit is still under repairing.
(6)	Producer's Waste Heat Boiler	1	Drum, tubes, pipes, gauges, valves, and insulations.	Drum corroded, tubes heavily rusted and corroded on both sides, pipes, valves, gauges disappeared, insulations destroyed.	95%	Still under repairing.

GAS PLANT

P. 2

ITEM NO.	NAME OF ARTICLE	QUANTITY	DAMAGED PARTS	DESCRIPTION	% DAMAGED	REMARKS
(7)	Automatic Control Machines	2	Gears, Shafts, Cylinders, Cams, Motor, Time ralays.	All moving parts worn out in bad shape.	60%	When the Automatic Machine is out of order, we use hand operating, but it's too inconvenient.
(8)	2 - Stage Hydraulic pumps with 10 HP. Motors	2	Casings, Impellers, Shafts, Bearings, and Motors.	Casings scratched in inside, Impellers, Shafts, and Bearings worn out, Motors over-heated.	60%	
(9)	Hydraulic Valves	24	Cylinders, Pistons.	All cylinders and pistons worn out and scratched.	90%	
(10)	790 M^3/hr. Set Blowers with 350 HP. Motors	2	Impellers, Shafts, Bearings, Oil pumps, Irise valves, Motors.	Impellers, Shafts, Bearings and Oil pumps worn out; Motors over-heated.	80%	
(11)	57 M^3/hr. Nitrogen Blowers with 20 HP. Motors	2	Impellers, Shafts, Bearings, Motors.	All moving parts worn out; Motors overheated.	70%	
(12)	Producer Blowers with 10 HP Motors	2	Impellers, Shafts, Bearings, Motors.	Same conditions as Nitrogen Blower(Item 11).	70%	
(13)	Boosters with 15 HP. Motors	2	Casings, Impellers, Shafts, Bearings.	One unit missed and the other one impeller, shaft and bearing nearly useless.	90%	
(14)	Pipes: 54"Ø, 30"Ø, 12"Ø, 10"Ø.	1000 ft.	Cast iron and steel.	All gas, air and steam lines rusted on both outside and inside.	85%	

079

附（二）一氧化碳氧化部门损失表

CO-OXIDATION DEPARTMENT

P. 1

ITEM NO.	NAME OF ARTICLE	QUANTITY	DAMAGED PARTS	DESCRIPTION	% DAMAGED	REMARKS
(1)	5300 M^3/hr. Roots Gas Blowers	2	Casing and Rotors, Shafts, Bearings.	The Casing and rotors worn out, the clearance between them is about ⅛".	80%	Efficiency is decreased by about 30% due to the large clearance.
(2)	200 HP. Steam Engines for Roots Blowers	2	Cylinders, Pistons, Piston rings, Crank Shaft, Bearings, GOvernors, Slide Valves and Lubricating Pump.	All moving parts heavily worn out, Valves leaked, Governors missed.	60%	Steam consumption is 30% higher than before.
(3)	150 M^3/hr. Water Pumps with 30 HP. Motors	2	Impellers, Shafts, and Motors.	The efficiency reduced by 20% due to the impellers shafts, and bearings heavily worn out, motor over-heated.	80%	
(4)	10,000 M^3 - Raw Gas Holder, 5,000 M^3 Converted Gas Holder.	1) 1)	Steel shells, bottom plate, guide rollers.	The steel shells metal become brittle and rusted badly on both inside and outside. The bottom plates cracked and leaked , Guiders are not straight, some Rollers out of contact.	80%	
(5)	Heat Exchangers	4	Shells and Tubes	Shell and tubes rusted on both inside and ouside; about 20% of tubes leaked badly.	90%	We plug up the leaky tubes, so the Heating surface is reduced.
(6)	Converters	4	Steel shells, Grate, and CO-Catalyst.	The steel shells and grate badly corroded, 36 tons of catalyst poisoned.	80%	Owing to the catalyst being poisoned, the efficiency of conversion is very low.

80

CO-OXIDATION DEPARTMENT

P. 2

ITEM NO.	NAME OF ARTICLE	QUANTITY	DAMAGED PARTS	DESCRIPTION	% DAMAGED	REMARKS
(7)	Saturator and Water Heater	1	Shells, Grate, Raschig rings.	½ Raschig rings broken, Grate almost rusted away, shells become brittle and corroded. in inside.	60%	We changed new grate.
(8)	Condenser	1	Shells, Grate, and Raschig rings.	Same condition as Saturator and water heater(Item 7).	60%	We changed new grate and Raschig rings.
(9)	Instruments	7	2-Micromax 6-Flow Meters	2 - Micromax Redorders are out of accuracy. 6 - Flow Meters are out of order.	90%	
(10)	54"ø, 30"ø, 16"ø, Gas & Water lines: 1"ø, 1½"ø, 2"ø, 3"ø, 4"ø, Water, Steam, Air and Gas lines	800 Ft. 1500 "	Cast iron and Steel pipes.	All steel and cast iron pipe lines are rusted badly, and 30% to steel pipes nearly rusted through.	85%	
(11)	Valves: 54"ø, 30"ø, 16"ø, 3"ø, and other different sizes.		Cast iron, Steel, Discs, Stems, Valve seats.	50% valve bodies are in bad shape. 50% valve discs, stems, and valves seats heavily worn out and leaked.	95%	

082

附（三）压缩与合成部门损失表

COMPRESSION AND SYNTHESIS DEPARTMENT

P. 1

ITEM NO.	NAME OF ARTICLE	QUANTITY	DAMAGED PARTS	DESCRIPTION	% DAMAGED	REMARKS
(1)	1500 HP. 300 Kg/Cm^2 Gas Compressors	2	Steam Cylinders, Gas Cylinders, Cylinder liners, Piston, Piston rings, Crank shafts, Main bearings, Cross heads, Connecting rods, Governors, Suction and Discharge Valves, Oil pumps, Base plate.	Steam cylinders, Gas cylinders, Cylinder liners, Piston, and Piston rings are heavily worn out and scratched; Crank shaft, main bearings, Cross heads, Connecting rods worn out badly, lubricating oil pumps check valve leaked, and springs inefficient; Suction and discharge valves leaked, Base plate broken, Governors badly worn out.	85%	These compressors were designed for handling 5,500 cubic meters of gas at the speed 110 R.P.M. each, but now, the maximum speed is limited to 80 R.P.M. due to all moving parts badly worn out; the gas cylinders, pistons and piston rings leaked, so that the capacity decreased to about 40%.
(2)	200 HP. Circulators	2	Steam cylinders, Gas cylinders, Pistons, Piston rods, Piston rings, Crank shafts, Main bearings, Cross heads, Lubricating pumps, Governors.	All moving parts are heavily worn out, mostly like the above mentioned compressors.	80%	
(3)	Intercoolers	2	1st stage to 3rd stage intercooler elements; 4th stage to 6th stage intercooler tubes.	All stages intercooler elements and intercooler tubes badly rusted and leaked.	90%	
(4)	Oil filters	2	Shell head, Upper and lower baffles, Support plates, Raschig rings.	The steel shells, Upper and lower baffle plates, Support plates are rusted, and steel Raschig rings heavily rusted and destroyed.	70%	
(5)	NH_3 Separators	2	Steel shells, Inside parts, Steel gaskets.	Shells rusted, Inside parts corroded.	65%	

083

COMPRESSION AND SYNTHESIS DEP

ITEM NO.	NAME OF ARTICLE	QUANTITY	DAMAGED PARTS	DESCRIPTION	% DAMAGED	REMARKS
(6)	NH_3 Primary Condenser	1	Cooling coils, Mainfold Pipe flanges, Support frame, Weir box, Bolts and Nuts.	The coils are badly rusted and pitted; the support, frames, Weir box, flanges also rusted.	95%	
(7)	NH_3 Converter	1	Steel shell, Upper head, Lower head, Basket, Heat exchanger, Pyrometer tubes, NH_3 Catalyst.	Inter-changer leaked, Catalyst poisoned, Shell, Upper and lower heads, Pyrometer tubes are rusted, Alloy steel basket ruined.	70%	The capacity is reduced to 40%.
(8)	Starting heater	1	Heating coils, Return bends, Pipe connections, Fire chamber.	Heating coils, Return bends, Pipe connections are rusted and joints leaked; Fire chamber cracked.	95%	Now the heating coils stand 150 Kg/Cm^2 only.
(9)	Liquid NH_3 *Storage tanks*	7	Steel shells.	Shells rusted on both inside and outside.	60%	
(10)	NH_3 Storage pipe lines: 82.5/89Ø M/M 51.5/57Ø " 22/30 Ø " 5/7 Ø "	450 ft.	Seamless steel pipes.	All seamless steel pipe lines heavily rusted and corroded nearly through.	95%	
(11)	High pressure and Standard valves	250		All special alloy high pressure and Standard valve bodies, Discs, Stems, Valve seats heavily worn out and leaked.	80%	
(12)	L.P. Steam Buffer tank	1	Steel shell.	The steel shell rusted on both inside and outside.	60%	
(13)	L.P. Steam Regulator	1	Smoot Control.	The Smoot Control is not sensitive enough to pressure changes.	60%	

084

COMPRESSION & SYNTHESIS DEP'T

ITEM NO.	NAME OF ARTICLE	QUANTITY	DAMAGED PARTS	DESCRIPTION	% DAMAGED	REMARKS
(14)	High and low pressure gauges	200		100 pcs. of gauges missed; the other remainders rusted and out of accuracy.	90%	
(15)	Mono-meter and Micromax Recorders	5		All out of accuracy and one of them incomplete.	90%	
(16)	30 tons over head crane 20 tons over head crane	1 1	Gears, Bridge, Beams.	All gears badly worn out, the beam and bridge bent downward.		It can not handle over 20 tons now.
(17)	High and low pressure pipe lines: 110 M. 150/159Ø M/M 30 M. 261/267Ø " 40 M. 412/420Ø " 20 M. 610/620Ø " 10 M. 302/318Ø " 40 M. 180/191Ø " 60 M. 51.5/57Ø " 90 M. 13/32 Ø " 12 M. 100.5/108Ø " 45 M. 82.5/89Ø " 12 M. 25/30Ø " 28 M. 150/159Ø "		Seamless steel pipes.	All the pipings and fittings corroded on both inside and outside and become very thin.	80%	
	20 M. 5/7 Ø " 40 M. 2/6 Ø " 30 M. 25/30Ø " 30 M. 25/30Ø "		Carbon steel pipes.			
			Seamless chrome Vanadium pipe.			
	30 M. 360/368Ø "		Welded steel pipe.			

附（四）纯化部门损失表

PURIFICATION DEPARTMENT

P. 1

ITEM NO.	NAME OF ARTICLE	QUANTITY	DAMAGED PARTS	DESCRIPTION	% DAMAGED	REMARKS
(1)	1600 Tons/hr. 76 ft. head, water pumps with 1000) 590) K.W. synchronous motors and 550 HP. water turbine.	2	Impellers, Shafts, Bearings, Motors, Exciters, Water turbine and motor starting equipment.	Impellers, Shafts, Bearings and water turbine moving parts worn out badly, Motor and Exciters slip rings and commutators 40% worn out; Motor starting equipments are out of order.	85%	These high speed water pumps are shaking as they are running, and the power consumption is 20% to 30% higher th than before, because both the mechanical and electrical parts are badly worn out.
(2)	18 M^3/hr.-Triplex plunger copper solution pumps with 88 K.W. Motors.	2	Cylinders, plungers, crank shafts, cross head, bearings, belts, oil pumps, check valves, and motors.	Cylinders and plungers badly worn out and scratched, crank shafts, cross heads, and bearings, worn out, belt broken, check valves and packing leaked and springs lost their elasticities, motors overheated.	80%	
(3)	15 M^3/hr. Triplex plunger pumps with 20 HP. Motors. Caustic liquor.	2	Cylinders, Plungers, Crank shafts, Bearings, Belts, Check valves and Motors.	Same conditions as the copper solution pumps (Item 2).	80%	
(4)	Air Blowers with 8 HP. Motors	2		Missed.	100%	
(5)	Ice Machines with 200 HP. synchronous Motors.	2	Cylinders, Pistons, Piston rings, Piston pins, Crank shafts, Bearings, Oil pumps, Suction and discharge valves, Motor, Exciters, and Motor starting equipments.	Cylinders and pistons badly worn out and scratched, other moving parts are worn out, oil pumps inefficient, suction and discharge valves and packing leaked, 30% of slip rings and commutators worn out in the motors and exciters. Motor starting equipments are out of order.	80%	

980

PURIFICATION DEPARTMENT

ITEM NO.	NAME OF ARTICLE	QUANTITY	DAMAGED PARTS	DESCRIPTION	% DAMAGED	REMARKS
(6)	Centrifugal pumps	3	Casings, Impellers, Shafts.	Casing corroded, Impellers, Shafts and Bearings worn out.	80%	
(7)	2.5Ø M. x 22M. Water Scrubber	1	Steel shells, Grate, Sprays nozzle, and Raschig rings.	The steel shell rusted and corroded 1/3, grate destroyed ½, spray nozzle worn out nearly useless, Raschig rings ¼ broken.	70%	
(8)	Copper Solution Scrubber 780m/m Ø x 15M.	1	Steel shell, Grate, Separator, Spray nozzle, Steel Raschig rings.	¼ Raschig rings destroyed, shell, separator, grate, heavily corroded.	80%	
(9)	Caustic Solution Scrubber 520 m/m Ø x 15M.	1	Steel shell, Grate, Steel Raschig rings.	The same condition as the Copper Solution Scrubber (Item 8).	80%	
(10)	Copper Solution Filter	1	Shell, Screen, and Insulations.	Shell heavily rusted nearly through, Screen destroyed, Insultion ½ destroyed.	90%	
(11)	1450 m/m Ø x 6240 m/m NH_3 Cooler	1	Steel shell and tubes.	Shell and tubes heavily rusted and corroded on both inside and outside.	80%	
(12)	4'Ø x 12' NH_3 Condensers	2	Steel shells and tubes.	The shells, tubes heavily corroded on both inside and outside.	90%	
(13)	52.5/60 Ø m/m x 7000mm Copper Solution water cooler	1	Coils and Support.	Coils and supports heavily rusted.	90%	30% Cooling Surface decreased, then, the copper solution can't be cooled down to the proper temp. in the Summer time.

087

PURIFICATION DEPARTMENT

ITEM NO.	NAME OF ARTICLE	QUANTITY	DAMAGED PARTS	DESCRIPTION	% DAMAGED	REMARKS
(14)	Reduction Vessles Regenerators Reflex Towers	2 2 2	Stell shells, tubes, Baffle plates, Steam jacket.	Shells, Baffle plates, tubes badly rusted and leaked.	90%	
(15)	Copper Solution Storages Caustic Solution Storages	2 2	Steel shells.	Shells rusted badly and become thin.	90%	
(16)	Pipes: 19M. 399/419Ø m/m. 45M. 210/216Ø " 10M. 512/520Ø " 10M. 311/318Ø " 17M. 610/620Ø " 10M. 412/420Ø " 5M. 302/318Ø " 91M. 203/216Ø " 134M. 150/159Ø " 50M. 100/108Ø " 55M. 825/89 Ø " 30M. 70/76 Ø " 372M. 515/57 Ø " 20M. 25/30 Ø " 38M. 14.7/21.25Ø m/m. 100M. 70/100Ø m/m. 80M. 13/32 Ø "			The Caustic Solution, Copper Solution and gas pipings are rusted and corroded both inside and outside badly.	90%	Those pipings all designed to handle highs pressure liquor and gases. It is very dangerous by using those old pipings as they are getting worse.
(17)	Valves: 25/50Ø m/m. 13/32Ø " 24"Ø, 20"Ø, 10"Ø, 18"Ø, 8"Ø, 4"Ø, 2"Ø, 1½"Ø, ¾"Ø, 6"Ø, 1"Ø.	250	Valve Bodies, Discs, Stems, Valve Seats.	All high pressure and low pressure valves leaked; Discs, Stems, and Valve Seats worn out.	80%	
(18)	Instruments	40	Micromax Concentration Recorder, Water Flow Meter, Pressure Gauges, H.P. Level Gauges, and Thermometers.	All instruments are out of accuracy and some parts missed.	90%	

088

附（五）一百一十二公吨硫酸工厂损失表

112 METRIC TONS SULPHURIC ACID PLANT

P. 1

ITEM NO.	NAME OF ARTICLE	QUANTITY	DAMAGED PARTS	DESCRIPTION	% DAMAGED	REMARKS
(1)	SO_3 Converters	4	Cast iron casing, Electrical heater, Intercoolers, Vanadium catalyst.	Casing and covers cracked and leaked, Electrical heater elements corroded, Intercooler tubes correded and leaked badly. Vanadium catalyst powdered and coated by iron sulphate and dust.	80%	The conversion efficiency is very low due to leakage and poisoned catalyst.
(2)	Sulphur Burner	1	Steel shells, Insulation brick and fire brick work.	Shell metal become brittle and cracked, insulation bricks and fire bricks broken.	90%	After repairing it cracked again.
(3)	Waste heat Boiler	1	Whole set.	Destroyed.	100%	Now we use cooling water spraying over the hot gas pipe to cool down the gas temp. from 1100°C to 400°C instead of waste heat boiler; we can not recover the heat valve which evolved from the oxidation of sulphur by direct burning.
(4)	Sulphur pit and auxiliary equipments	1	Pit, Steam Coils, Sulphur Pumps.	Concrete walls deformed and cracked, rows of steam coils corroded outside and rusted inside nearly through. 2-Sulphur pumps' shafts and impellers worn out, turbine's wheel blades broken.	90%	
(5)	300 HP. SO_2 Blower	1	Casing, Impeller, Bearings, Shafts, Oil Pump, Motor.	Casing inside corroded, Impeller, Bearings and Shaft worn out, Oil pump inefficient. 300 HP. Motor's Rotor and starter clearance not uniform and overheated due to the bearings and shaft heavily worn out.	80%	This high speed Blower is shaking as it is running. The power consumption is 10% higher than before.

11[illegible] METRIC TONS SULPHURIC ACID PLANT

P. 2

ITEM NO.	NAME OF ARTICLE	QUANTITY	DAMAGED PARTS	DESCRIPTION	% DAMAGED	REMARKS
(6)	Absorption Towers Drying Tower	2) 1	Steel shells, Acid-proof brick linings, Acid distributors.	Shells metal become brittle and thin, all three tower shells and acid-proof brick linings cracked and leaked. Distributors worn out by flowing acid.	80%	
(7)	Heat Exchangers	6	Steel shells and tubes.	Shells and tubes badly corroded on both sides; 20% tubes plugged up by iron sulphate.	90%	20% tubes plugged up by iron sulphate as ahrd as stone; we can not take them out, so that the heating surgace decreased and the capacity reduced.
(8)	SO_3 Cooler	1	Steel shells, tubes.	Shells and tubes are in the same condition as the heat exchanger(Item 7).	90%	
(9)	Mixing Tanks	2	Shell, acid -proof brick lining, duriron thimbles.	Shells are all gone, linings cracked and leaked badly, duriron thimbles broken.	95%	One is under replacement, one is under repair.
(10)	Dilution tank	1	Shell, lead and acid proof brick linings, duriron thimbles, piano box.	Whole thing destroyed.	100%	Now we are using Mixing tank instead of dilution tank.
(11)	Spraying Towers	2	Shells, lead and acid brick linings, acid spray nozzle.	Shells leaked, lead and brick linings also leaked, acid spray nozzle worn out.	80%	
(12)	Weak acid Cooler tanks	3	Steel Casing, lead lining and coils.	Steel casings rusted outside and corroded inside nearly through, lead lining and coils leaked.	90%	

060

112 METRIC TONS SULPHURIC ACID PLANT

ITEM NO.	NAME OF ARTICLE	QUANTITY	DAMAGED PARTS	DESCRIPTION	% DAMAGED	REMARKS
(13)	Mist Precipitators	2	Lead shells, electrode, Rectifiers.	Lead shells deformed, lead covered electrodes burst by sparking; Rectifiers rotory discs worn out badly.	90%	The original designed equipments were capable for 75,000 volts, but now, we cut the voltage down to 30,000 volts to prevent the sparking occured on the rotory discs and lead covered electrodes in the precipitators, so that the efficiency is rather low.
(14)	Strong acid pumps Weak acid pumps	8) 3)	Special alloy steel casing, shafts, impellers, packings, 20 HP. Motors.	Casings, Impellers, Shafts, Stuffing boxes, Packing gland worn out, Motor over-heated.	90%	Owing to the shafts and Impellers worn out, so the capacity is reduced.
(15)	105%, 98%, 93%, Acid Cooler	5000 ft.	6"Ø steel pipes for 105%, 6"Ø cast iron pipes for 98%, and 93%.	All 6"Ø steel pipes, elbows, U Bends missed, 6"Ø cast iron pipes, elbows, U Bends rusted on outside, corroded inside nearly through.	100%	
(16)	800Ø M/M, 600Ø ", 400Ø ", SO_2-SO_3 lines	600 ft.	Cast iron and steel pipes.	Outside of pipes rusted, inside corroded by acid.	85%	
(17)	1"Ø, 1½"Ø, 2"Ø, 3"Ø, 4"Ø, 5"Ø, 6"Ø acid, water, air, steam lines:	2000 ft.	Steel and cast iron pipes and fittings.	All pipes corroded inside.	85%	

160

112 M[illegible]TRIC TONS SULPHURIC ACID PLANT

P. 4

ITEM NO.	NAME OF ARTICLE	QUANTITY	DAMAGED PARTS	DESCRIPTION	% DAMAGED	REMARKS
(18)	Different sizes of acid, water, air, steam valves.	250	Steel and cast iron valve Bodies, discs, stems, valve seats.	Valve Bodies, discs, Valve seats, stems, corroded by the flowing acid.	95%	Every valve leaks.
(19)	Herreshoff furnaces and auxiliary equipments.	2	Shells, elevators, screens, shafts, arms, fire bricks, motors.	Some ruined, and some missed.	100%	We bought two complete sets of Herreshoff furnaces for roasting pyrite ore before war, but we did not build them yet except the foundation works.

092

附（六）硝酸厂遭日军洗劫设备表

NITRIC ACID PLANT

(Wholly taken away by Japanese)

P. 1

ITEM NO.	NAME OF EQUIPMENTS	NO. OF PIECES	ITEM NO.	NAME OF EQUIPMENTS	NO. OF PIECES
(1)	Fire Tube Waste Heat Boiler 906 O.D. x 7975 length Accessory Equipments: 2-Safety valves and Y-Connection 1-Combination stop and check valve 1-Feed valve 2-Blow-off valves	1	(8)	50-60% Nitric Acid Pumps with Horizontal motor Capacity: 2 M^3/hr., 15000 mm. head Motor: 3 HP., 1500 R.P.M.	2
(2)	Air Filter(clothe filtering medium type) Capacity: 2200 M^3/hr. 802 wide x 717 high x 1020 length	1	(9)	Variable Stroke Plunger Pumps (vertical single cylinder type) Capacity: 0.34 M^3/hr., 10 Kg/cm^2 head	2
(3)	8" Motor Driven Air Blower (single stage, with 2 motors) Capacity: 1800 M^3/hr. Motor: 20 HP., 2900 R.P.M.	2	(10)	Ammonia Saturator 1020 O.D. x 5765	1
(4)	6" Motor Driven Turbo Blower for Nitrous gases with 1 G.E. motor & blower casing cover, No.2 Centrifugal "OL" type Capacity: 1900 M^3/hr. Motor: 40 HP., 2935 R.P.M.	1 set	(11)	Ammonia Burner 1920 O.D. x 3064 Heater Units 5¼"x3/8" Pyrex sight glass Filter tubes of porous ceramic Micarta tubes 21x24x245 mm. long Micarta washers 25 mm.I.D. x 50 mm.O.D.	1 6 32 139 3 18
(5)	Primary Condensers "A" & "B" (vertical type) 772 O.D. x 6263 high(hood top)	1 set (2)	(12)	Acid Cooler(water-cooling) 83/89 ∅ seamless tubing	1
(6)	0-30% Aqua Ammonia Pump with motors 2" Discharge, 3" suction, 15000 mm. head, Capacity: 25 M^3/hr.	2	(13)	Nitric Acid Storage Tank(Stainless Steel) 2208∅ x 14500 long Capacity: 50 M^3	2
(7)	0-60% Nitric Acid Pumps with 10 HP., 1500 R.P.M. motors Capacity: 15 M^3/hr.	7	(14)	Water Storage Tank 1756 O.D.x1000 Level Tank 762 O.D.x940 Nitric Acid Feed Tank 600 O.D. x 1040 Buffer Tank, 312 O.D.x1052 High Sight Glass Holder, 89 O.D. glass Alloy steel flanges & nuts	1 1 1 1 1 set

093

NITRIC ACID PLANT

(Wholly taken away by Japanese)

P. 2

ITEM NO.	NAME OF EQUIPMENTS	NO. OF PIECES
(15)	Oxidation Towers, 2212 O.D. x 15600 H.	2
	Absorption Towers, 2212 O.D. x 15600 H.	7
	Pyrex Sight Glass, 5¼"∅ x 3/8" thick	8
(16)	Aqua Ammonia Tank, 2012 O.D. x 7000 long	1
	Capacity: 5500 gallons	
(17)	Preheater, 930 O.D. x 3870 H.	1
	Boundom tube pressure gauge, 0.40 Kg/cm2	1
	Water level gauge	1
	Copes feed water regulator	1
(18)	Water Cooler (Double Pipe), 3" x 6000 mm. return bend	1 set
(19)	Nitric Acid Concentrator:	
	High Grade Acid Proof Iron	
	Spare parts, pipe & pipe fittings	
	High silicon material	4 tons
	Victor "Betterweld"	25 lbs.
	Steam Jet & pipe fittings	
(20)	Platinum Gauze, 1870 ∅	1
	Alloy Gauze, 80 mesh	1
(21)	Gauze Wash Pan, 2286 ∅	1
	Gauze Handling Ring, 2035 ∅	1
(22)	Steel Tanks Details, 1200 I.D. wide x 3200 I.D. x 6000 I.D.	1

ITEM NO.	NAME OF EQUIPMENTS	NO. OF PIECES
(23)	Miscellaneous Lead Details:	
	Acid cooling coils	7
	Constant temperature boot	1
	Screen boots	3
	Over-flow outlet	1
	Trough	1
	Plugs	3
	Plug seats	3
	50 ∅ tees	4
	50 ∅ elbow	1
	50 ∅ x 40 ∅ reducers	2
	50 ∅ 25 ∅ reducers	2
	75 ∅ x 50 ∅ reducer with 25 ∅ nozzle	1
	75 ∅ elbows	2
(24)	Bleaching Tower, 362 ∅ x 5600 H.	1
	Acid Heater, 267∅ x 7200 H.	1
(25)	Meters:	1 set
	Single tube monometer with 400 mm. scale	1
(26)	Pyrometer:	
	Micromax temperature recorder	1
	Special thermocouple	1
	Thermocouples	3
	400 meters gauge rubber and spare parts	
(27)	Test Box, 230 O.D. x 500	1
	Acid Cooler, 420 O.D. x 1520	1
	Pyrex Brand Glass Cylinders	2

094

NITRIC ACID PLANT

(Wholly taken away by Japanese)

ITEM NO.	NAME OF EQUIPMENTS	NO. OF PIECES
(28)	Aluminium Piping, 302/314	1
	Floor Drain Pan, 1750 x 4200	1
(29)	Alloy Steel Valves & Cocks:	
	5/8" gate valves, screwed ends	12
	3" gate valves, flanged ends	4
	4" " " " "	1
	6" " " with chain wheel	1
	300 mm. butterfly valve, flanged	1
	½" screwed ends, plug valve	1
	½" " " for 10 Kg/cm^2	10
	½" flanged ends plug valve	1
	1" screwed ends plug valve	1
	1" flanged ends plug valve	10
	1" " " for 10 Kg/cm^2	2
	1½" -ditto-	11
	2" -ditto-	8
	2" -ditto-	3
	3" -ditto-	23
	½" to 1½" Nordstrom valves	6
	2" Nordstrom valves	4
	3" " "	6
(30)	Alloy Steel Piping & Pipe Fittings	
	" " Studs Bolts and Hex. Nuts	
(31)	Type OD Reflex Gages with 4 balls	2
	" " " " " 2 "	1
(32)	Flow Meters and spare parts	1
(33)	No. 25 50% Alloy Steel Pump Motor 7½ HP. 1450 R.P.M.	1
	No. 10 90% Alloy Steel Pump Motor 2 HP. 1500 R.P.M. (Pump to HNO_3 Storage)	1

ITEM NO.	NAME OF EQUIPMENTS	NO. OF PIECES
(34)	Horizontal Acid Pump (For 93% H_2SO_4 Pumps) Capacity: 4M^3/hr.	2
	Motor: 3 HP. 1500 R.P.M.	2
(35)	Exhauster Fan for Nitrous gases	1
	Capacity: 100 M^3/hr.	
	Motor: 2 HP. 3000 R.P.M.	1
(36)	Acid Piping & Assemblies:	
	2" flanged plug valves	2
	¾" screwed plug valves	2
	100 lbs. J/M asbestos paper	2
	2"x20"x50" Banroe blankets	56
	85% magnesia pipe	39'
	85% " "	51'
	450 Kg. J/M asbestos cement	
	675 -ditto-	
	42"x48"x1/16" sheet packing	12
	Chemical Lead	14078 lbs.
	"JOHN CRANE" Packing	28 sets
	Steel Pipes & Steel Forgings	
	50 mm. hard lead straight valves	2
	50 mm. hard lead straight plug valves	2
	Compression type extra heavy brass fittings	
(37)	Steam Jacket & Steel Pipe Details, 300/318 ø x 2715	1 set
(38)	Concentration unit, cast iron details	1 set
	Pyrex Glass Cylinder, 79 I.D. x 89 O.D. x 75 long	4

095

NITRIC ACID PLANT

(Wholly taken away by Japanese)

P. 4

ITEM NO.	NAME OF EQUIPMENTS	NO. OF PIECES
(39)	Asbestos Gaskets, 42" x 48" x 3/32"	46
(40)	Electrodes of Avesta 832 MV	3000 pcs.
(41)	Electrodes of ordinary steel	1500 pcs.
(42)	Hot rolled sheets of stainless steel electrodes	7032 pcs.
(43)	Stainless steel stocks, bars, sheets	
(44)	Different size of Flanges	179
(45)	½" Pipe Plugs	8
(46)	1" Angle Type C.I. Acid Valves	6
	80 mm. Vertical Ball Check "	12
	50 mm. C.S. Ball Check Valves	2
	50 mm. Gate Valves	21
	50 mm. Extra Heavy Gate Valves	3
	50 mm. All Hard Lead Angle Val.	16
	1" All Hard Lead Angle Valves	4
	2" C.I. Angle Valves	8
	2" Globe Valves	50
	3" C.I. Angle Valves	5
	250 mm. Check Valves	2
	80 mm. C.I. Acid Valves	2
	4" Ball Check Valves	3
	4" Gate Valves and Bushings	20
	4" Gate Valves and Handwheels	5
	4" Gate Valves	17
	Hard lead Straight Type Acid Valves	2
	C.I. Lead Line Angle Type Acid Valves	5
(46)	Cont'd;-	
	Ball Check Valves	3
	Lead Line Acid Valves	4
(47)	¾" Steam Trap	1
(48)	1" Bronze Screwed Elbows	12
	100 mm. 90° C.I. Elbows	4
	4" Flanged Elbows	4
	150 ø mm. Elbow	1
	90° Duriron Elbows	9
	Duriron Elbows	6
(49)	Special Tees and Spare Parts	1 set
	C.I. Screw Tees	3
	1½" Extra Heavy Tees	12
	75 x 75 x 50 Tee	1
(50)	Different size of Valve Reducers	52
(51)	Nitric Acid Tank Cooling Pipe	1 set
	No.1 and 2 Acid Cooler Tanks	1 set
	Aqua Ammonia Tank	1
(52)	Double Pipe Cooler and Support	1 set
(53)	Ammonia gas Concentrator	1
(54)	Extra Heavy Filters	7
(55)	3-Ton Overhead Travelling Cranes	2 sets
	Hand Operating Cranes	2 sets
(56)	Handrail Posts	16
(57)	Counter Balance Weights	10

NITRIC ACID PLANT

(Wholly taken away by Japanese)

ITEM NO.	NAME OF EQUIPMENTS	NO. OF PIECES	
(58)	Flow Meter Gauges	8	
(59)	Control Boards	2	
(60)	5" x 10" Crusher	1	

097

附（七）一百五十公吨硝酸铵部门损失表

150 METRIC TONS AMMONIUM SULPHATE DEPARTMENT

P. 1

ITEM NO.	NAME OF ARTICLE	QUANTITY	DAMAGED PARTS	DESCRIPTION	% DAMAGED	REMARKS
(1)	80 tons/day Saturators	3	Steel shells, lead lining, lead coils.	Steel casings are rusted and become very thin nearly through, heavy lead lining deformed and leaked from the pin holes, all lead coils eaten by the hot acid and NH_3 gas, nearly through.	90%	
(2)	150 tons/day Sharples horizontal Centrifuges, with 30 HP. Motors.	2	Casings, Shafts, Bearings, Screen, Lead lining, Oil Pumps, Motors, Automatic Control's pistons, Cylinders, Gears, and Time Relays.	The moving parts worn out; casing cracked inside; Automatic control's cylinder, piston and gears worn out and scratched; Time relay out of order; oil pump inefficient; motor overheated; and driving gear missed.	70%	
(3)	150 tons Conveyor	1	Belt, Idlers, Supports, Motors.	Rubber belt broken into several pieces. Idlers heavily worn out, supports corroded, Motor overheated.	90%	
(4)	Dryer	1	Steel shells, Rollers, Bearings, Gears, Dust Collector, Heater, Elevator.	Dryer, Dust Collector shells and heater heavily corroded on both inside and outside. Shafts, Rollers, Bearings, and Elevator badly worn out.	80%	
(5)	Humidifier Towers	3		Missed.	100%	
(6)	Hot Water Pumps with 5 HP. Motors	3		Missed.	100%	
(7)	50 M^3/hr. Mother liquor pumps with 15 HP. Motors.	3	Casing, Impellers, and Motors.	Acid proof casings, Impellers, Shafts and Bearings worn out.	80%	
(8)	20 M^3/hr. Clear Liquor pumps with 7.5 HP. Motors	3	Impellers, Casings, and Motor.	Same conditions as the mother liquor pumps(Item 7).	80%	

150 METRIC TONS AMMONIUM SULFATE DEP'T

ITEM NO.	NAME OF ARTICLE	QUANTITY	DAMAGED PARTS	DESCRIPTION	% DAMAGED	REMARKS
(9)	3 M^3/hr. Acid pumps with 5 HP. Motors	3	Casing, Impellers, Shafts, Motors.	The same conditions as the other pumps.	80%	
(10)	Air Compressor with 30 HP. Motor	1	Casings and Rotor, Motor.	Piston and Cylinder worn out, Motor missed.	95%	Now the compressed air is supplied by other sources.
(11)	Mother Liquor Tanks Crystal Selectors	2) 3)	Steel shells, Lead Lining.	Shells corroded badly nearly through, lead lining leaked.	95%	
(12)	23 M^3-Acid tanks 18.5 M^3 Setting tanks 13 M^3 Clear mother liquor tanks	2) 2) 3)	Steel shells, Lead lining.	All shells heavily corroded, nearly through, lead lining cracked and leaked.	90%	
(13)	Instruments	40		All pressure gauges, flow meters, for NH_3, H_2SO_4, Air and steam are out of accuracy, and 20 meters badly rusted and useless.	90%	
(14)	Pipe lines and Channels 6"Ø, 52Ø, 4½"Ø, 4"Ø, 3"Ø, 2"Ø, 1½"Ø, 1"Ø.			All lead pipe lines and channels eaten by the acid and become very thin, steel pipes heavily corroded on both inside and ouside nearly through.	90%	

附（八）锅炉房损失表

BOILER HOUSE

P. 1

ITEM NO.	NAME OF ARTICLE	QUANTITY	DAMAGED PARTS	DESCRIPTION	% DAMAGED	REMARKS
(1)	1000 HP. Boilers	3 sets	Drums, Tubes, Valves, Stokers, Superheaters.	Drum body corroded and pitted badly, most rivets not so sound. Tubes corroded and pitted badly. It exploded once soon after restoration. All valves, such as main valves, safety valves, blow valves, and check valves, corroded and leaked badly. Chain grate stokers and worm gear drive mechanism worn out, trouble occurs constantly. Superheater tubes corroded and leaked badly. As the conditions stated above, thses three boilers are about to be scrapped.	85%	Supplied by B. & W. Co.
(2)	Multiple Stages Feed Water Pumps (Electric Drive)	2 sets		All worn out.	100%	
(3)	Multiple Stages Feed Water Pumps (Turbine Drive)	2 sets		Disappeared.	100%	
(4)	Duplex Steam Feed Water Pump	1 set		Worn out.	75%	Made by Worthington Co.
(5)	2-Stage Motor Drive Deaerator Water Pump	1 set	Casing, Impellers, Shafts, Bearings.	Worn out.	75%	Made by GE. & Goulds Cos.
(6)	Feed Water Heaters	3 sets	Casing and Tubes.	Rotten.	90%	Made by Elliot Company

100

BOILER HOUSE

ITEM NO.	NAME OF ARTICLE	QUANTITY	DAMAGED PARTS	DESCRIPTION	% DAMAGED	REMARKS
(7)	Close Type Deaerator	1 set	Casing, Traps, Valves, Pipes, Pipe Fittings.	Dismodified.	75%	Made by Elliot Co.
(8)	Economizer	1 set	Casing, Valves, Tubes.	Corroded and leaked.	75%	Supplied by B.&W. Co.
(9)	Forced DRaft Fans	2 sets	Shafts, Impellers, and Motor Ball Bearings.	Shafts and Impellers corroded. Bearings worn out.	80%	Supplied by B.&W. Co.
(10)	Induced Draft Fans	2 sets	Shafts, Impellers, and Motor Ball Bearings.	One original burnt out, the second one got shaft and impeller corroded. Bearings worn out.	80%	Supplied by B.&W. Co.
(11)	Coal Elevator	1 set	Links, Baskets, Shafts, Drive Gears, Motor Bearings.	Worn out.	75%	Made by Link Belt Co.
(12)	Coal Conveyor	1 set	Rubber belt, Rolling Shafts, Drive Gears, Motor Bearings.	Rubber belt torn to pieces and others worn out.	75%	Made by Robbin Co.
(13)	Superheater	1 set		Disappeared.	100%	Supplied by B.&W. Co.
(14)	Chimney	1 pcs.		It was shortened to avoid air raid. The remainder rusted.	80%	
(15)	Steam and Feed Water Line	80 M.	Valves, Pipes, Pipe Fittings.	Corroded and leaked.	85%	
(16)	Hand Fired Superheater Unit for 3 Boilers	1 set		Disappeared.	100%	

101

附（九）水处理间损失表

WATER TREATMENT HOUSE

ITEM NO.	NAME OF ARTICLE	QUANTITY	DAMAGED PARTS	DESCRIPTION	% DAMAGED	REMARKS
(1)	Water Softeners	3 sets	Tanks, Zeolite, Pipes, Pipe Fittings.	Zeolite poisoned and the rest corroded and leaked.	80%	
(2)	10 HP. Motor Drive Centrifugal Pumps	2 sets	Casings, Impellers, Shafts, Ball Bearings, Motor Bearings.	Corroded and worn out.	75%	Made by GE & Goulds Cos.
(3)	7.5 HP. Motor Drive Centrifugal Pumps	2 sets	Casings, Impellers, Shafts, Ball Bearings, Motor Bearings.	Corroded and worn out.	75%	Made by GE & Goulds Cos.
(4)	Milk Lime Tank and Driving Device	1 piece		Disappeared.	100%	
(5)	Salt Solution Tank	1 piece		Disappeared.	100%	
(6)	Water Line	180 M.	Valves, Pipes, Pipe Fittings.	Rusted and leaked.	75%	

102

附（十）水泵房损失表

WATER PUMP HOUSE

ITEM NO.	NAME OF ARTICLE	QUANTITY	DAMAGED PARTS	DESCRIPTION	% DAMAGED	REMARKS
(1)	250 HP. Motor Drive Centrifugal Pumps	2 sets	Casings, Impellers, Shafts, Ball Bearings, Motor Bearings.	Corroded and leaked.	75%	
(2)	125 HP. Motor Drive Centrifugal Pumps	2 sets	Casings, Impellers, Shafts, Ball Bearings, Motor Bearings.	Corroded and leaked.	75%	
(3)	50 HP. Motor Drive Centrifugal Pumps	2 sets	Casings, Impellers, Shafts, Ball Bearings, Motor Bearings,	Corroded and leaked.	75%	
(4)	30 HP. Motor Drive Centrifugal Pumps	2 sets	Casings, Impellers, Shafts, Ball Bearings, Motor Bearings.	Corroded and leaked.	75%	
(5)	200 HP. Motor Drive Centrifugal Pumps	2 sets		Completely destroyed.	100%	
(6)	20 HP. Motor Degasifying Fans	4 sets		Completely destroyed.	100%	
(7)	Water Line	12 M.	Valves, Pipes, Pipe Fittings.	Corroded and leaked.	80%	

103

附（十一）深井损失表

DEEP WELL DEPARTMENT

ITEM NO.	NAME OF ARTICLE	QUAN-TITY	DAMAGED PARTS	DESCRIPTION	% DA-MAGED	REMARKS
(1)	Deep Wells (500 gals/min. each) and equipments	6	Casings, Pumps, Shafts, Shaft protecting tubes, Motors.	3-deep wells wholly destroyed. 3-deep well casings deformed in bad shape and plugged up by mud and sand in the bottoms. 5-deep well pumps missed. 3-pumps are inefficient due to the impellers, shafts, shaft protecting tubes and bearings being worn out.	90%	The total capacity of 6 wells is 3000 gals/min.. but now it is reduced from 3000 gals/min. to 360 gals/min.(reducing about 88% approximately.)

104

MECHANICAL AND ELECTRICAL DEPARTMENT

P.1

ITEM NO.	NAME OF ARTICLE	QUAN-TITY	DAMAGED PARTS	DESCRIPTION	% DA-MAGED	REMARKS
	Foundry					
(1)	Roots Blower & 20 H.P.Motor	1 set		Disappeared	100%	
(2)	Cupola (2 tons)	1 set		3/8" plate steel shell has been worn out and has been ammended many places. It shrinks and warps up that no brick can be laid. The base plate has been broken beyond repairing.	80%	
(3)	Core Baking Furnace	1 set		The bricks have badly worn out and the top has been rotten.	70%	
(4)	Overhead Crane (10 tons)	1 set		The motor and gears have been so badly worn out that it can not lift 2 tons' weight. It's bridge and beams have been so heavily rusted that it can hardly lift 3 tons.	60%	
(5)	Graphite Crucibles	3 pcs.		Disappeared	100%	
(6)	Patterns	for one complete soda plant		burned	100%	
(7)	Electric Steel Furnace		One transformer, and one switch with one set of automatic control	Disappeared	100%	

105

MECHANICAL AND ELECTRICAL DEPARTMENT

P.2

ITEM NO.	NAME OF ARTICLE	QUANTITY	DAMAGED PARTS	DESCRIPTION	% DAMAGED	REMARKS
(8)	Pig Iron	60 tons		Disappeared	100%	
(9)	Ferro-Silicon	2 "		"	100%	
(10)	Ferro-Maganese	1/4 ton		"	100%	
(11)	Ferro-Chrome	1 "		"	100%	
(12)	Nickel	1/2 "		"	100%	
(13)	Coke	50 tons		"	100%	
(14)	Copper	5 "		"	100%	
(15)	Tin	1/2 ton		"	100%	
(16)	Zinc	1 "		"	100%	
(17)	Phosphour-Bronge	1/2 "		"	100%	
	Machine Shop					
(1)	D. C. Electric Arc Welder (300 Amp.20 HP)	1 set		Disappeared	100%	Motor Generator Type made by G.E.Co.
(2)	D.C.Electric Arc Welder (200 Amp.15 HP)	1 "		"	100%	Motor Generator Type made by G.E.Co.
(3)	-do- (300 Amp.15 HP)	1 "		"	100%	Motor Generator Type made by AEG Co.
(4)	500 Kg. Motor Driven Pneumatic Hammer	1 "		Cylinder worn out and scratched. Motor has been changed. Cylinder and motor become easily overheated.	50%	Bought from Siemsen & Co.

106

[ME]CHANICAL AND ELECTRICAL DEPART[ME]NT

ITEM NO.	NAME OF ARTICLE	QUANTITY	DAMAGED PARTS	DESCRIPTION	% DAMAGED	REMARKS
(5)	Pipe Bending Machines	2 sets		All auxiliary parts missed	40%	Made by Climax Werke A.G. It cannot be used without adding new parts.
(6)	Rolling Machine (1" plate 11' wide)	1 set		Bearings broken and gears missed	80%	Made by Climax Werke A. G
(7)	Punching & Shearing Machine	1 "		Disappeared	100%	Bought from Siemsen & Co. Capacity: Punch 25 mm plate & 25mm hole; Shear 3/4" plate.
(8)	Punching & Shearing Machine	1 "		"	100%	Bought from Siemsen & Co. Capacity: punch 18mm plate & 22mm hole; Shear 1/2" plate.
(9)	D.C.Electric Arc Welder (400 Amp.25HP)	1 "		"	100%	Motor Generator Type made by Lincoln Elec. Co.
(10)	D.C. Elec.Arc Welders (300 Amp. 20 H.P.)	4 sets		"	100%	Motor Generator Type made by Lincoln Electric Co.
(11)	D.C. Elec. Arc Welder (200 Amp. 15 HP)	1 set		"	100%	-do-
(12)	Radial Drill (5 ft.)	1 "		Bombed to pieces	100%	
(13)	Planner (10 ft.)	1 "		-do-	100%	
(14)	Overhead Crane(20 tons)	1 "		The body was bombed out of order and broken in many places. Motor and gears have been out of repairs. Its capacity has been reduced to one half.	50%	

107

MECHANICAL AND ELECTRICAL DEPARTMENT

P.4

ITEM NO.	NAME OF ARTICLE	QUANTITY	DESCRIPTION	% DAMAGED	REMARKS
(15)	Planner (20 ft.)	1 set	Gear worn out. Auxiliary parts missed	80%	
(16)	Lathes Drills and Milling Machines	30-40	They have been used over years and badly out of accuracy.	50%	
(17)	High Speed Steel	400 kgs.	Disappeared	100%	
(18)	Gear Cutters (14½" involute 2 D.P. to 24 D.P.)	17 sets	"	100%	
(19)	Micrometer Calipers(½"-12")	10 "	"	100%	
(20)	Inside Micrometer	5 "	"	100%	
(21)	Files	70 doz.	"	100%	
(22)	Twist Drills(1/16"-3")	20 "	"	100%	
(23)	Elec. Drills (¼" - 1¼")	10 pcs.	"	100%	
(24)	Pipe Threading Dies & Taps (¼" to 4")	10 sets	"	100%	
(25)	Gas Weld & Cutting Torches	25 "	"	100%	
(26)	Jack Screws	28 pcs.	"	100%	
(27)	Chain Blocks (½ to 10 tons)	30 "	"	100%	
(28)	Pneumatic Tools, Grinding Wheels, Oil stone, Levels, Filler Gauges, etc.	2 tons	"	100%	
	Outside Piping				
(1)	Acid Line: 2" 93% H_2SO_4 Pipe Line (Seamless St. Pipe)	270 M.	Rusted on both outside and inside nearly through	60%	

MECHANICAL AND ELECTRICAL DEPARTMENT

ITEM NO.	NAME OF ARTICLE	QUANTITY	DESCRIPTION	% DAMAGED	REMARKS
(2)	3" 93% H_2SO_4 Pipe Line (Seamless St. Pipe)	690 M.	Rusted on both outside and inside nearly through.	60%	
Ammonia Line:					
(1)	2" NH_3 Liquid(Seamless St.Pipe).	650 M.	-do-	90%	
(2)	8" NH_3 Gas (Seamless St. Pipe)	490 M.	-do-	70%	
H.P.Steam Line:					
(1)	2" N.P.Steam Pipe (Seamless St. Pipe)	480 M.	-do-	90%	
(2)	2" H.P. Steam Pipe Insulation	480 M.	Original asbestos cover rotten and replaced with straw ropes.	100%	
(3)	5" H.P.Steam Pipe (Seamless Steel Pipe)	260 M.	Rusted on both outside and inside nearly through.	90%	
(4)	5" H.P.Steam Pipe Insulation	260 M.	Disappeared	100%	
(5)	12" H.P.Pipe (Seamless St.Pipe)	45 M.	Rusted both outside and inside nearly through.	60%	
(6)	12" H.P.Pipe Insulation	45 M.	Original asbestos cover rotten and replaced with straw ropes.	100%	
(7)	3/4" H.P.Steam Pipe for Steam Trap (Seamless St. Pipe)	50 M.	One half missed and the other half rusted.	60%	
(8)	3¼" H.P.Steam Pipe (Seamless Steel Pipe)	30 M.	Rusted on both outside and inside nearly through.	80%	
(9)	3¼" H.P.Steam Pipe Insulation	30 M.	Original asbestos cover rotten and replaced with straw ropes.	100%	
(10)	4" H.P.Steam Pipe (Seamless St. Pipe)	170 M.	Rusted on both outside and inside nearly through.	60%	
(11)	4" H.P.Steam Pipe Insulation	170 M.	Original asbestos cover rotten and replaced with straw ropes.	100%	

MECHANICAL AND ELECTRICAL DEPARTMENT

P.6

ITEM NO.	NAME OF ARTICLE	QUANTITY	DESCRIPTION	% DAMAGED	REMARKS
	L. P. Steam Line:				
(1)	1" L.P.Steam Pipe for Steam Trap (Seamless St. Pipe)	34 M.	Rusted on both outside and inside nearly through.	60%	
(2)	8" L.P.Steam Pipe (Seamless St.Pipe)	145 M.	-do-	70%	
(3)	8" L.P.Steam Pipe Insulation	145 M.	Original asbestos cover rotten and replaced with straw ropes.	100%	
(4)	12" L.P. Steam Pipe (Weld Steel Pipe)	450 M.	Rusted on both outside and inside nearly through.	70%	
(5)	12" L.P.Steam Pipe Insulation	450 M.	Original asbestos cover rotten and replaced with straw ropes.	100%	
	Raw Gas Line:				
(1)	5" Raw Gas Seamless Pipe	120 M.	Rusted on both outside and inside nearly through.	70%	
(2)	2" Raw Gas Seamless Pipe	50 M.	-do-	70%	
	Compressed Air Line:				
(1)	1¼" Compressed Air (wl)	120 M.	-do-	80%	
(2)	2" " " (W.2.)	180 M.	-do-	80%	
(3)	3½" " " (w.l.)	180 M.	-do-	80%	
(4)	5" " " (w.l.)	450 M.	-do-	80%	
	Water Line:				
(1)	2" Feed Water, Well water and cooling water (Seamless st. pipe and w.l.)	850 M.	Rusted on both outside and inside nearly through. One third of it cracked by freezing due to lack of cover in Winter.	80%	
(2)	3½" Feed Water (Seamless st. pipe)	30 M.	Completely rotten.	100%	

110

MECHANICAL AND ELECTRICAL DEPARTMENT

ITEM NO.	NAME OF ARTICLE	QUANTITY	DESCRIPTION	% DAMAGED	REMARKS
(3)	8" River Water, Well Water (w.l.)	250 M.	Rusted on both outside and inside nearly through.	60%	
(4)	10" Cooling Water (w.l.)	250 M.	-do-	60%	
(5)	20" Cooling Water (w.l.)	450 M.	-do-	60%	
	Sewer Line:				
	5" to 20" sewer pipes (C.I. & Concrete)	2,200 M.	All rotten and clogged.	100%	
	Pipe Supports:				
(1)	Single column pipe supports	130 pcs.	Rusted	30%	
(2)	4 column pipe supports	37 pcs.	Rusted and inclined by bombing.	30%	
	Expension Joints:				
	12" L.P.Steam Pipes	18 sets	Mostly rotten and destroyed.	80%	
	Steam Traps:				
(1)	H.P.Steam Traps	7 sets	Destroyed.	100%	
(2)	L.P.Steam Traps	8 "	"	100%	
(3)	Bolts and Nuts	10,000 pcs.	Rotten.	100%	
	Pipe Roll Stand:				
(1)	12" Pipe roller stands	80 sets	"	100%	
(2)	8" pipe roller stands	80 "	"	100%	
	Electrical Department				
(1)	350 H.P. Oil Switches	2 sets	Current carrying parts burned.	40%	
(2)	250 H.P. Compensators	2 "	Current carrying parts burned and relays out of order.	45%	111
(3)	200 H.P. Compensator	1 set	Current carrying parts burned.	45%	

M[illegible]ANICAL AND ELECTRICAL DEPARTM[illegible]

ITEM NO.	NAME OF ARTICLE	QUANTITY	DESCRIPTION	% DAMAGED	REMARKS
(4)	Centrifugal Oil Purifier	1 set	Mechanical Parts destroyed.	100%	
(5)	Air Compressor (100 working power with one 200 HP. driving motor Size: 20/12 14)	1 set	One 1/2 H.P.Motor missed, Piston ring, feather valves and bearings worn out. Cylinder-head cracked.	40%	Made by Worthington Co.
(6)	Steel Angle-Towers	6 sets	Badly rusted.	40%	
(7)	20 H.P. Gear Motors	2 "	Main parts destroyed.	60%	
(8)	1000 KVA Transformers	5 "	Casing rusted nearly through	30%	
(9)	500 KVA "	2 "	-do-	30%	
(10)	75 KVA "	3 "	-do-	30%	
(11)	50 KVA "	3 "	-do-	30%	
(12)	60 H.P. Motors	4 "	Windings and bearings burned.	60%	
(13)	300 Amp. air circuit breaker	1 set	Destroyed.	100%	
(14)	Electric Siren (1½ H.P.)	1 "	Disappeared.	100%	
(15)	4000 volts Synchronous Automatic Starter (590 K.W.)	1 "	Parts worn out and meters disappeared.	60%	
(16)	-do- (1000 K.W.)	1 "	-do-	60%	
(17)	300 Amp. Siemens Air Circuit Breaker	1 "	Burned out.	80%	
(18)	15 H.P. Motor	1 "	Disappeared.	100%	
(19)	100 H.P. Motors	2 sets.	"	100%	
(20)	Single Core Lead-coverrd Cable (91/10 S.W.G.)	180 M.	Insulation breaks down.	90%	

112

MECHANICAL AND ELECTRICAL DEPARTMENT

ITEM NO.	NAME OF ARTICLE	QUAN-TITY	DESCRIPTION	% DA-MAGED	REMARKS
(21)	Single Core Lead-covered Cable (61/12 S.W.G.)	180 M.	Insulation breaks down.	90%	
(22)	3 Core lead-covered cable (37/13 S.W.G.)	40 M.	-do-	90%	
(23)	Motor Starters (for whole plant)	200 sets	Due to lack of proper maintenance in the past years, they can not function properly.	30%	
(24)	Motors (for whole plant)	200 sets	Worn bearings cause rubbing between rotor and starter, therefore over-heated easily.	40%	
(25)	Manual Telephone Switch Board for 30 subscribers	1 set	Disappeared.	100%	

113

附（十三）土木工程损失表

DEPARTMENT: CIVIL ENGINEERING

P. 1

ITEM NO.	LOCATION	QUANTITY	DAMAGED PARTS	DESCRIPTION	% DAMAGED	REMARKS
(1)	General Office	1 Building		Floor and floor support destroyed...... Wall destroyed.......... Windows and Glasses broken and destroyed...... Tiles destroyed...... Galvanized iron channels rusted......	100% 60% 30% 10% 100%	Area 240 M^2
(2)	Ware-house	1 "		Galvanized iron sheet roof all destroyed...... Brick wall destroyed...... Doors and windows glasses either broken or destroyed......	100% 20% 40%	Area 2000 M^2
(3)	Machine, foundry, and forge shops.	1 "		Steel trusses heavily rusted...... Galvanized iron sheet roof rusted...... Wall destroyed...... Windows glasses broken......	40% 30% 40% 50%	Area 5200 M^2
(4)	Three floors Staff's domitory building.	1 "		Doors and windows destroyed...... Glasses broken...... Wall destroyed......	40% 50% 20%	Area 720 M^2
(5)	Workmen dormitory building	32 Rows		Doors and windows destroyed...... Tiles broken...... Door and windows glasses all broken......	100% 10% 100%	Area 4158 M^2
(6)	Third Village: Employees family residences	123 Rooms		Doors and windows and glasses broken...... Wall destroyed......	100% 100%	
(7)	First Village: High Staff's domitory	4 Buildings		Floors, windows, and doors destroyed...... Glasses broken......	20% 40%	
(8)	Second Village: Staff's family residences	31 "		Floor and floor supports destroyed...... Doors, windows, and glasses destroyed...... Wall...... Galvanized iron sheet water channels and pipes rusted......	40% 40% 20% 40%	

114

DEPARTMENT: CIVIL ENGINEERING

ITEM NO.	LOCATION	QUANTITY	DAMAGED PARTS	DESCRIPTION	% DAMAGED	REMARKS
(9)	Gas Plant	1 Building		Galvanized iron sheet walls destroyed................................. Steel trusses rusted........................ Windows glasses broken....................	80% 30% 40%	Area 660 M^2
(10)	CO-oxidation	1 "		Windows, doors, glasses broken..........	40%	Area 100 M^2
(11)	Compression, Purification and Synthesis	1 "		Galvanized iron sheet wall heavily rusted and leaked..................... Window glasses............................ Street trusses rusted.....................	100% 30% 30%	Area 1740 M^2
(12)	Sulphuric Acid Plant	1 "		Roof leaked................................. Glasses destroyed.......................... Steel trusses rusted........................ All concrete pipes leaked and broken under ground..........................	20% 40% 30% 100%	Area 600 M^2
(13)	Boiler Room	1 "		Wall destroyed............................... Doors and windows destroyed............ Glasses broken..............................	20% 10% 50%	Area 350 M^2
(14)	Water Treatment Department	1 "		Doors and windows destroyed............ 60% doors and window glasses broken....	40% 60%	Area 250 M^2
(15)	Pump House	1 "		Glasses broken.............................. Wall destroyed..............................	50% 10%	
(16)	Cooling Water Tower	2 Buildings		Wood walls destroyed..................... Cooling water frame destroyed..........	50% 80%	Area 900 M^2
(17)	Catalyst Plant	1 Building		Doors and windows destroyed............ Glasses broken..............................	20% 20%	Area 540 M^2
(18)	Laboratory	1 "		The roof's wooden frame and tiles destroyed.................................. Wall destroyed.............................. Glasses broken..............................	80% 50% 20%	Area 450 M^2

15

DEPARTMENT: CIVIL ENGINEERIN

P. 3

ITEM NO.	LOCATION	QUANTITY	DAMAGED PARTS	DESCRIPTION	% DAMAGED	RAMARKS
(19)	Electric Department	2 Buildings		Roof's wooden frame destroyed.......... Doors and windows destroyed........... Glasses broken.........................	10% 20% 50%	Area 500 M^2
(20)	Civil Department	1 Building		Roof's wooden frame and tiles destroyed. Glasses broken.........................	30% 60%	Area 200 M^2
(21)	Nitric Acid Plant	1 "		Whole building deformed and destroyed by Japanese bombs in 1937 August.......	90%	Area 360 M^2 3 Floors
(22)	NH_3 Storage Department	1 "		Roof leaked............................	40%	Area 450 M^2
(23)	Substation	1 "		Roof leaked............................ Doors and windows and glasses destroyed.	10% 40%	
(24)	Hospital & Reception	2 Buildings		Roof leaked............................ Doors, windows and glasses.............	10% 80%	
(25)	NH_3 Sulphate Plant & Packing Room	1 Building		Steel trusses rusted................... Roof leaked............................ 80% glasses broken.....................	30% 60% 80%	Area 2000 M^2
(26)	Whole Plant Underground Concrete Pipes	3000 Ft.		40% destroyed 30% leaked	70%	
(27)	Wharfs	3	Steel Pontoon Bridges Supports & Plateform	Steel Pontoon Missed................... Wood Supports, Bridges, and Plateforms destroyed.............................	100% 70%	
(28)	River Bank Stone Pavement			Destroyed..............................	60%	Area 8000 M^2

116

GENERAL

ITEM NO.	NAME OF ARTICLE	DAMAGED PARTS	DESCRIPTION	% DAMAGED	REMARKS
			all Furnitures, stationeries, etc. ~~wholly taken away by Japanese.~~ disappeared.	100%	

117

附（十五）商店和仓库损失表

STORES AND WARE HOUSES

ITEM NO.	NAME OF ARTICLE	DAMAGED PARTS	DESCRIPTION	% DA-MAGED	REMARKS
			all machine tools, & other ~~appara~~ supplies MATERIALS ~~AND SUPPLIES~~ ~~wholly taken away~~ by ~~Japanese~~ disappeared	100%	

118

LABORATORY

ITEM NO.	NAME OF ARTICLE	DAMAGED PARTS	DESCRIPTION	% DA-MAGED	REMARKS
			all Instruments, apparatus, chemicals, etc. wholly ~~taken away by Japanese~~ disappeared	100%	

119

五、民营事业申请价配日本赔偿物资办法、赔偿要点

《战害赔偿法》要点（抄件）（一九四七年一月一日）

「戰害賠償法」要点

查上次歐戰後，各國多於停戰Armistice簽字之後，和會開幕之前，公佈關於戰害賠償之法律。如法國一九一九年四月十七日法律即是。關於戰害賠償問題，首須決定賠償之責任，次究賠償項目，往後規定請求權之行使及賠償之方法。茲分別述之於後。對日和會不久開幕，我國自亦應有此項法規之訂立。

（一）戰害賠償之責任

凡爾賽條約第二三一條宣言德國及其同盟，應負担協約國及其人民所受一切戰害。因此協約國政府得向德國要求損害賠償。關於賠償當時計有兩說：一說為戰爭為國與國之事，人民所受戰爭損害為不可抗力之損害，政府對人民損害並無賠償義務。是以人民僅有接受救濟而無權要求賠償。另一說則主張戰害應由全國人民共同負担，是以國家應有其責，而人民對國家而有其要求權。此兩說中後者為一般所接受，是以各國戰後對之佈法律規定戰害賠償。而國家再以其對於人民所負之賠償總額加上國家直接損害，向戰敗國要求賠償。

但上述僅就合法行為所致損害而言，倘敵國在戰爭形式中違

144 2.

及國際法規定時，其所給予人民損害均屬不必要或出於掠奪者，則又當別論。違法行為為違法徵用、徵收現金，非戰略上之必要而毀壞人民私產，毀壞文化，掠奪物資等，則無論其開始戰爭目標之正當與否，均應負賠償責任。

(二)賠償項目

蘇說法國一九一九年四月十七日法律中規定五種賠償項目，例舉如左：得認為戰害應受賠償者，為下列各種損害：

(A)敵人在佔領期間以徵用 Requisition、徵役 Requisition of Service、徵收現金 Contribution 名義所強索之物資、金錢或人力所受之損失。

(B)被掠奪物資，被妨害之收穫，被損傷之牲畜或樹木，被掠奪之證券票據，無論在本國或在外國。

(C)房地、森林、工廠及其一切設備所蒙受之損害。

(D)在戰地內，由軍事上攻守所受之破壞，無論係本國軍隊所為者，亦包括在內。

(E)船舶之損害。

(三)請求權之行使

請求賠償，在向本國政府提出，協助本國政府對其人民付償。至政府對於侵向戰敗國要求乃另一問題。……是政府對敵國要求賠償系以人民所受損害為根據。英美觀念，人民戰害賠償，得由政府代表要求，但係政府行為，所得賠償系政府財產，政府得自行指定分配應以賠償人民合法之要求。美國於一九二八年以前 Settlement of War Claim Act，規定極詳。

(四)賠償之方法

……此次盟國政策決定以日本工業設備賠償，於去年二月下旬在日盟軍總部間附設 Reparation Branch 研究此項問題。一九四六年一月二十日對日政府訓令保持工業現狀。但是否賠償只限於工業設備？按波茨坦宣言第十一條之「日本得保持工業使其經濟足以支撐且得從而榨取公正之物資賠償，但不使其能重整軍備以作戰……」云。"Japan shall be permitted to maintain such industries as will sustain her economy and permit the exaction of just reparation in kind, but not those which would enable her to rearm for war ……"。所謂「物資賠償 reparation in kind」者，並不指定以日本工廠賠償，此點規定，而不以戰後一次賠償為限。該條之意義容許日本繼續有相當工業，但聯盟國照以公正估計賠償之額，自其工業供其產取其物資。此次賠償物資兼包括各種日用品，材料，機器原料

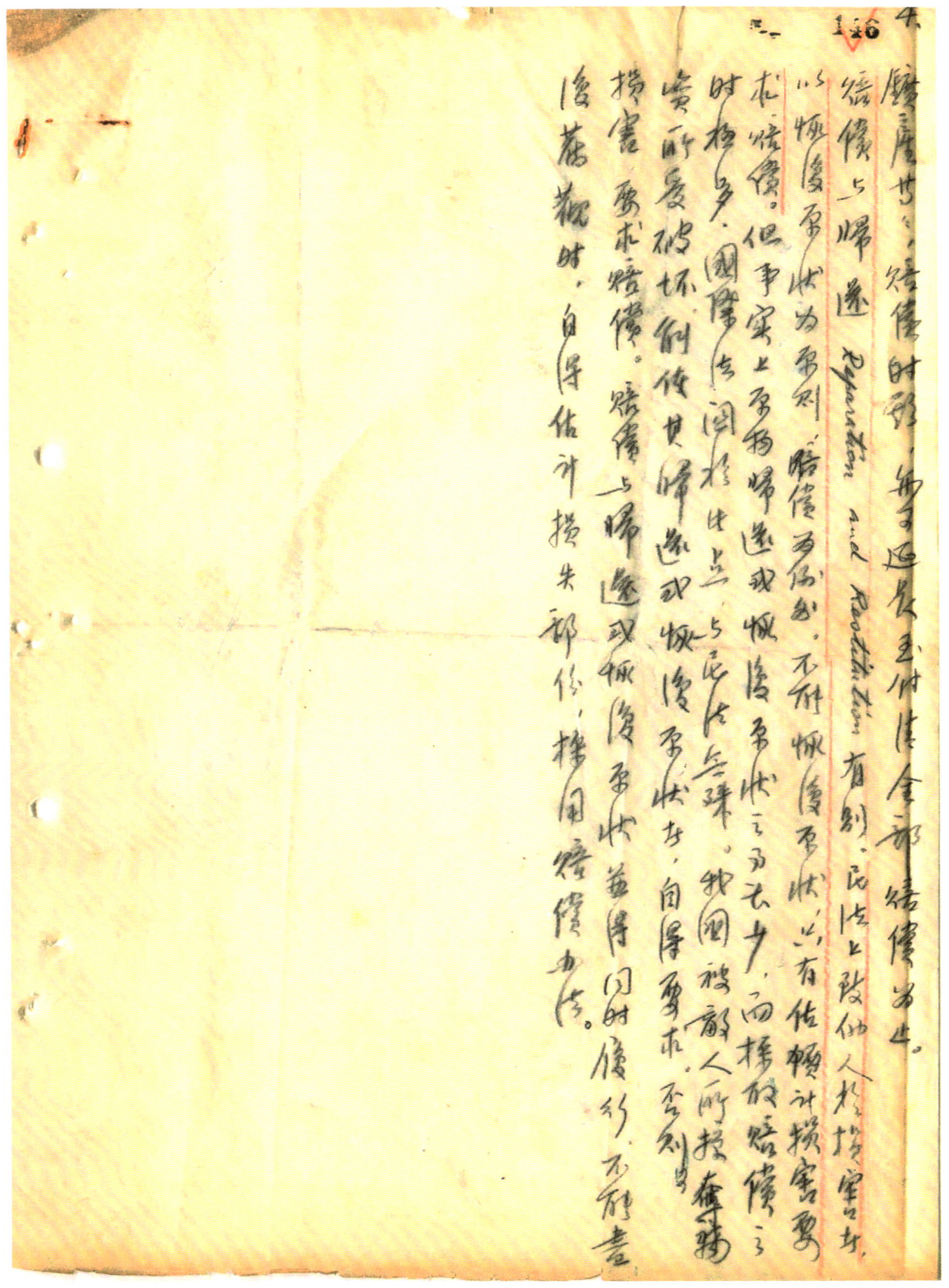

失。鳞庵节之赔偿时期，如予过长，则至付清全部赔偿为止。

赔偿与归还 Reparation and Restitution 有别。民法上致他人于损害者，以恢复原状为原则，赔偿为例外。不能恢复原状，只有估价计损害要求赔偿。但事实上原物归还或恢复原状之可能者少，而采取赔偿之时极多。国际公法於此点与民法无殊。我国被敌人所掠夺物资所受破坏，倘使其归还或恢复原状者，自得要求。否则当损害要求赔偿。赔偿与归还或恢复原状并得同时履行。不能尽复旧观时，自得估计损失部份，采用赔偿办法。

民营工厂承办日本赔偿酸碱工厂办法（抄件）（一九四七年二月二十四日收）

存根

159

民营工厂承办日本赔偿酸碱工厂办法

一、配交民营之日本赔偿酸碱工厂三厂，由经济部择由办理该项工业著有成绩之工厂永利化学工业公司、久大盐业公司、天原电化厂、天利氮气厂及中国火柴原料厂等五厂主持办理，并由各主持工厂分别邀集国内各酸碱工厂及火柴工厂联合投资共同经营。

二、前项主持办理之五工厂经指定：

（一）永利化学工业公司、久大盐业公司及其他酸碱工厂为一集团。

（二）天原电化厂、天利氮气厂及其他酸碱工厂为一集团。

（三）中国火柴原料厂及其他火柴厂为一集团。

三、全国各酸碱工厂及各火柴工厂应各就本厂财力物力人力情形向主持之五工厂接洽投资、共同经营之办法，其不愿投资者听其不参加投资。

四、各酸碱工厂及各火柴工厂之投资，除已足额外，该主持之五厂不得拒绝接受。

五、投资比率，在每一厂中，其主持之工厂得占总额百分之三十至四十五，其余每一厂之投资不得超过该主持工厂之股数。

六、前项投资如遇不足时，该主持工厂及其他各厂得按已投资之比例增加投资。

七、各厂集资数额，包括设备价值、拆迁及运输该项设备费用、修置设备费用、购置厂地及建筑厂屋等费用，装置设备费用以及开工经营该厂所需之营运周转费用在内，其总额除价值设备费用由评价委员会评定外，其余各项由主持之工厂按照实际需要斟酌拟定。

八、配交民营之酸碱三厂设备，依照赔偿委员会第二次委员会议决议「可供民营之设备可以价配使用」之规定，应由承办该三厂之工厂备价领用。

九、前项价款之交付，或以现款，或以公债，或以赔偿损失费抵抵，应俟行政院赔偿委员会决定后再行依照办理。

十、拆迁该酸碱三厂设备事务，由盟军总部主持办理，但每一厂所由我国派遣督导拆迁人员二人，由各承办之厂推选之，而有经验、通晓英语之高级人员数人，由经济部遴派或指派。

160

十一、運輸該廠機器之事務，自日本港口運至我國口岸，由交通部負責籌運，所需費用由承辦工廠照所運數量分別備款歸墊，其自我國口岸運至建廠目的地，由承辦工廠自行籌劃，所需運輸工具，除儘自備外，得請交通部協助辦理。

十二、承辦工廠於接到經濟部交辦該項工廠文件後，應於五日內派遣負責代表來部商洽進行事項。

十三、承辦工廠於決定承辦該項工廠後，應即擬具建廠計劃書，送部審定俾照辦理，

十四、關於投資建廠以及進行中各項事務，應由承辦工廠與本部在該廠所設之工商輔導處切取聯繫，商洽進行。

六合县政府为转发民营事业申请价配日本赔偿物资办法给永利铔厂的训令（一九四七年八月二十八日）

事由：為轉發民營事業申請價配日本賠償物資辦法令仰知照由

六合縣政府訓令

府建字第　號

中華民國三十六年八月二十八日

令永利化學公司錏廠

案奉

江蘇省政府卅六府建四字第八三九六號訓令内開：

「案奉　行政院卅六經字第二六三六三號訓令内開：查民營事業申請價配日本賠償物資辦法業經本院本年七月一日第十次會議決議通過，並由賠償委員會依照儘量價配民營以減輕國庫負担及對彼方條件具備地方予以適量分配兩原則，再將價配民營總噸數及分配各地區物資之類别與數量詳為擬訂呈院核定，除由院公布暨分令外，合行抄發該項辦法，令仰知照。此令。等因，附民營事業申請價配日本賠償物資辦法一份。奉此，除分行外，合行抄發原辦法一份，令仰知

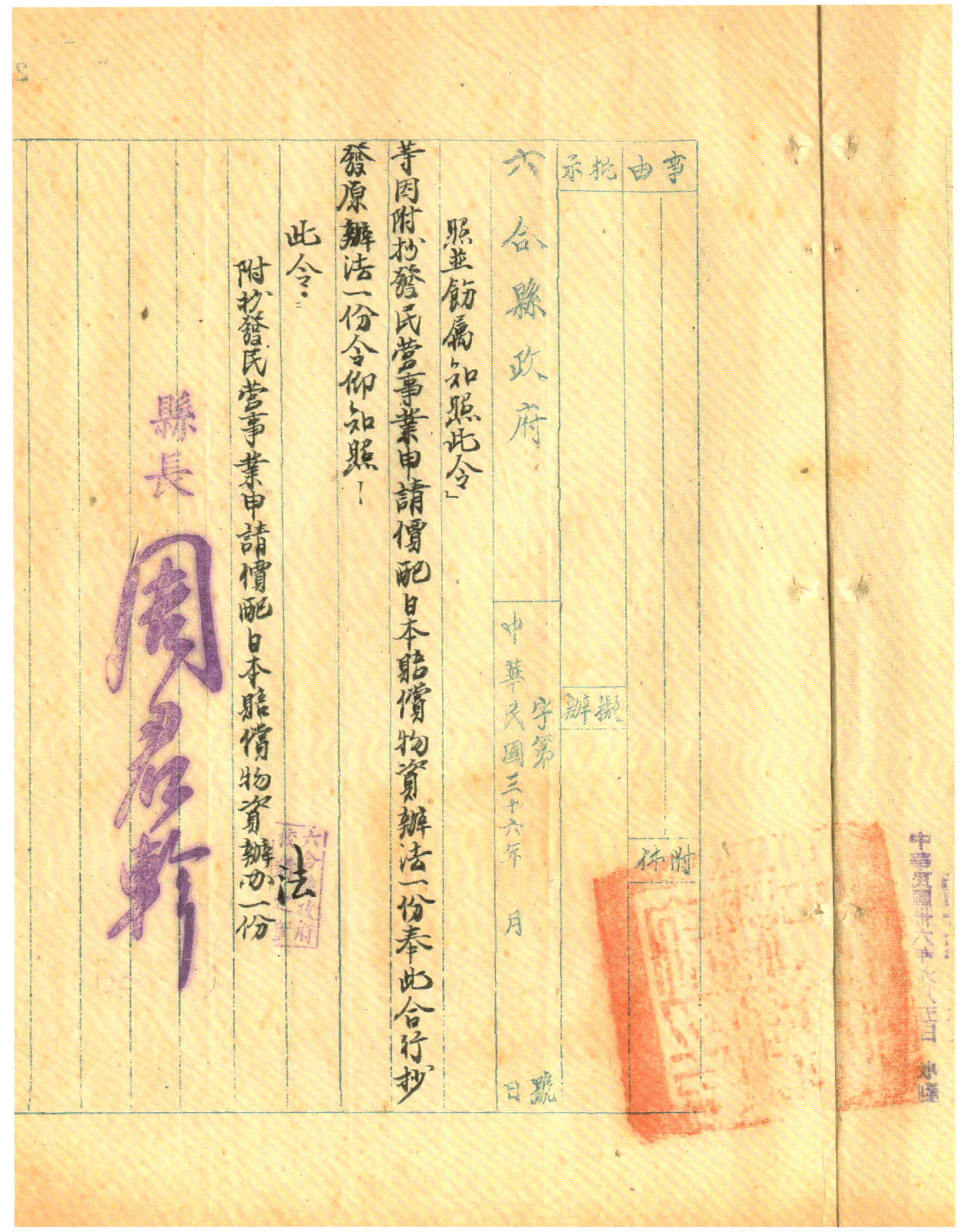

事由
批示
六合縣政府
照並飭屬知照此令」
等因附抄發民營事業申請價配日本賠償物資辦法一份奉此合行抄
發原辦法一份令仰知照！！
此令。
附抄發民營事業申請價配日本賠償物資辦法一份
縣長 周厚軒
中華民國三十六年 月 日
字第 號
擬辦
附件

民營事業申請價配日本賠償物資辦法

第一条 凡中華民國人民出資經營事業（以下簡稱民營事業）申請價配日本賠償物資依本辦法辦理。

第二条 民營事業申請價配日本賠償物資應以行政院核定分配民營事業部份為範圍

第三条 民營事業申請價配日本賠償物資應填具申請表及建廠或補充廠計劃書呈由經濟部核轉行政院賠償委員會審定後分別配售賠償委員會於必要時得採用標售方式出售前項書表之款式另訂之

第四条 民營事業申請價配日本賠償物資其審核標準如左：

一 申請人曾對本業經營著有經驗及成績者

二 組織健全足以勝任者

三 計劃完善確實可行者

四 集資數目確能達到計劃者

合於前項各款由民營事業並具有左列情形者得優先價配之

一 在抗戰期間曾申請配購之物資確有重大損失並有事實證明者

二现在業務具有急切補充之需要經政府核定者

三對申請配購同類之工礦業物資其本業曾在後方確有重大貢獻者

第五条 配售民營事業之日本賠償物資由經濟部會同有關機關及全國性人民或工商團體代表組織評價委員會估定公平價格送由行政院賠償委員會審定由承受物資之民營事業依照備款領用

前項評價委員會之組織及評價辦法另定之

第六条 民營事業於核定配售物資時應向國庫或代理國庫之銀行先繳納全部價款（約估數）百分之五之保証金於物資由日起運時補繳全部價款百分之二十五俟全部物資到達中國口岸時再補繳全部價款百分之二十其餘於兩年內分期繳納其詳細辦法另訂之

第七条 償配民營事業之日本賠償物資其運輸事項依左之規定

一自本港口至中國口岸之運輸由交通部代办所需費用由購受物資之民營事業按批照付不得在價款內計算

二自我國口岸運抵目的地之運輸由購受物資之民營事業自辦但得洽請交通部協助其運費由購受之民營事業自行籌付並應儘速轉運

经济部关于赔偿物资分配方法事给永利化学工业公司的通知（抄件）（一九四七年九月二十三日）

永利化學工業公司
YUNGLI CHEMICAL INDUSTRIES, LTD.

No. 294　年　月　日

寄鹽廠

抄

經濟部通知　京卅六字第[illegible]號
中華民國三十六年九月廿三日

通知　永利化學工業公司

案准行政院賠償委員會三十六年九月十日京(卅六)二字第二一九〇號函以准駐日代表團報告盟軍總部對賠償物資分配方法最近又決定將原擬由各國提出申請改爲分批抽籤等情經邀集有關部會商以日本賠償物資清單尚未作最後確定將來我方抽得物品種類數量與前擬申請者自不免發生差異又抽得之物資是否合於民營民營願否承受以及有否承受之力量事前均難確定爰商定每次抽得之物資由接收委員會迅即報告賠償委員會召集有關部會共同洽商分配辦法將來可能提出之物資撥交價配民營除報院并分函有關部會外請查照等由到部查我國應獲取之日本賠償物資前經依照申請拆遷辦法按諸我國應獲取之比率分批提出申請其第一批擬請拆遷之物資業經開具種類數量連同理由提請拆遷并就該批物資中可能供給民營使用者儘量價配民營當經本部就價配民營部分之該項賠償物資斟酌各種情勢分配各地設廠通知該公司主持承辦酸鹼各廠并邀集同業各廠商集資共同經營在

. 7. 4,000

九月廿七日收到

永利化學工業公司
YUNGLI CHEMICAL INDUSTRIES, LTD.

No.……　　　　　　　　　　　　——295

——年……月……日

案兹准前由美日本賠償各盟國物資既經盟軍總部決定改為分批抽截其抽得之物資種類數量自不能与原擬提出申請者相同將來價配民營事業之日本賠償物資種類數量應俟分批抽得之物資經逐次會商決定後由本部斟酌按次通知各地辦理惟該項物資雖未確定然於每次抽截後即須從事拆遷進行設廠為免民營事業籌備不及有誤進行起見所有前此通知籌備各廠其已成立籌備會者應仍舊進行以便該項價配物資確定奉到通知後即可依照「民營事業申請價配日本賠償物資辦法」第三條之規定申請價配核轉審定其尚未成立籌備會者亦應早日成立報部俾將來克以同樣申請又民營事業承辦各廠派員赴日監督拆遷事項前定由各地工業協會推薦人員再由部遴選派遣現以物資分配未定其任務無從確定應暫停推薦除分函各省市政府并令行本部各工商輔導處及通知各有關工商團体廠商知照外特此通知

36. 7. 4,000

六合县政府为转发民营事业价配日本赔偿物资各种办法给永利錏厂的训令（一九四八年三月十三日收）

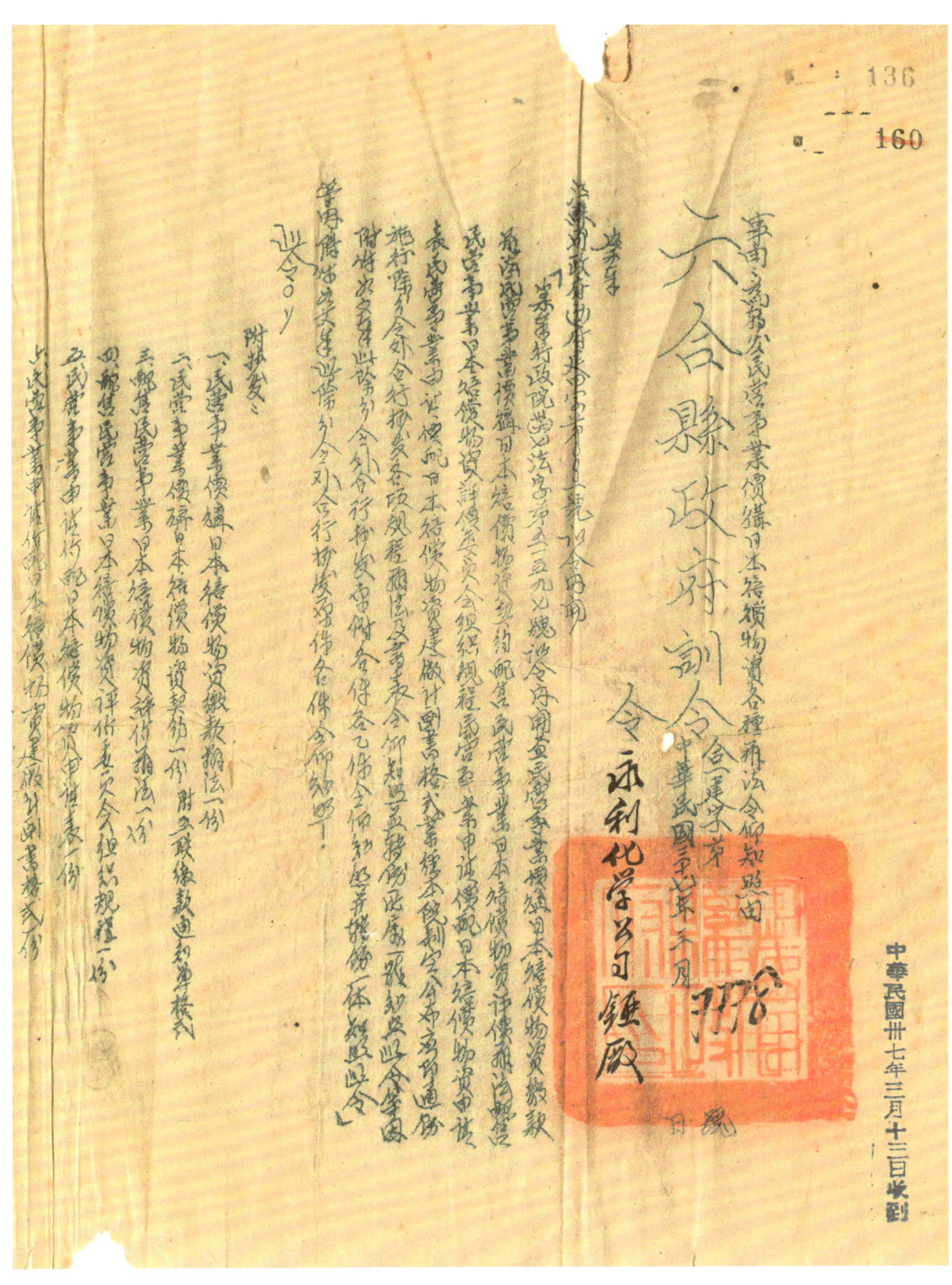

中華民國卅七年三月十三日收到

六合縣政府訓令

事由：為轉發民營事業價購日本賠償物資各種辦法令仰知照由

令永利化學公司錏廠

附（一）民营事业价配日本赔偿物资缴款办法

縣長周昱彰

民營事業價購日本賠償物資繳款辦法

第一條 凡申請價領日本賠償物資之民營事業於核定價領時應由經濟部訂立交貨繳款契約其承領物資之價格應依照民營事業申請價配日本賠償物資辦法第五條之規定辦理如該物資價格僅能於事後估計而未評定者應先繳納相當於估全部價款百分之五保證金及於物資由日本港口起運而未全部抵達我國港口期內繳納相當於估全部價款百分之二十五於物資自日本全部運抵我國港口後以該項價款及保證金同時繳納

前項價款繳納後仍由經濟部填發繳款通知書規定限期在評價未審定以前仍照前項價款繳納其繳納在審定以後照評定價格繳納與繳納全部價款或評定價款百分之二十其餘百分之八十得在兩年內分期繳之

所繳保證金及第一次價款如與評定價款有出入時由經濟部通知承領人於繳納第二次價款時補繳或在應繳價款內扣除之

第二條 前條應繳價款百分之八十應自經濟部正式通知接收單發出之日起每六個月為一期分別繳納計第一期繳納未付價款百分之二十第二期百分之二十第三期百分之二十五第四期百分之三十五每期應繳價款得提前繳納之

第三條 應繳價款繳納手續依照左列規定辦理之

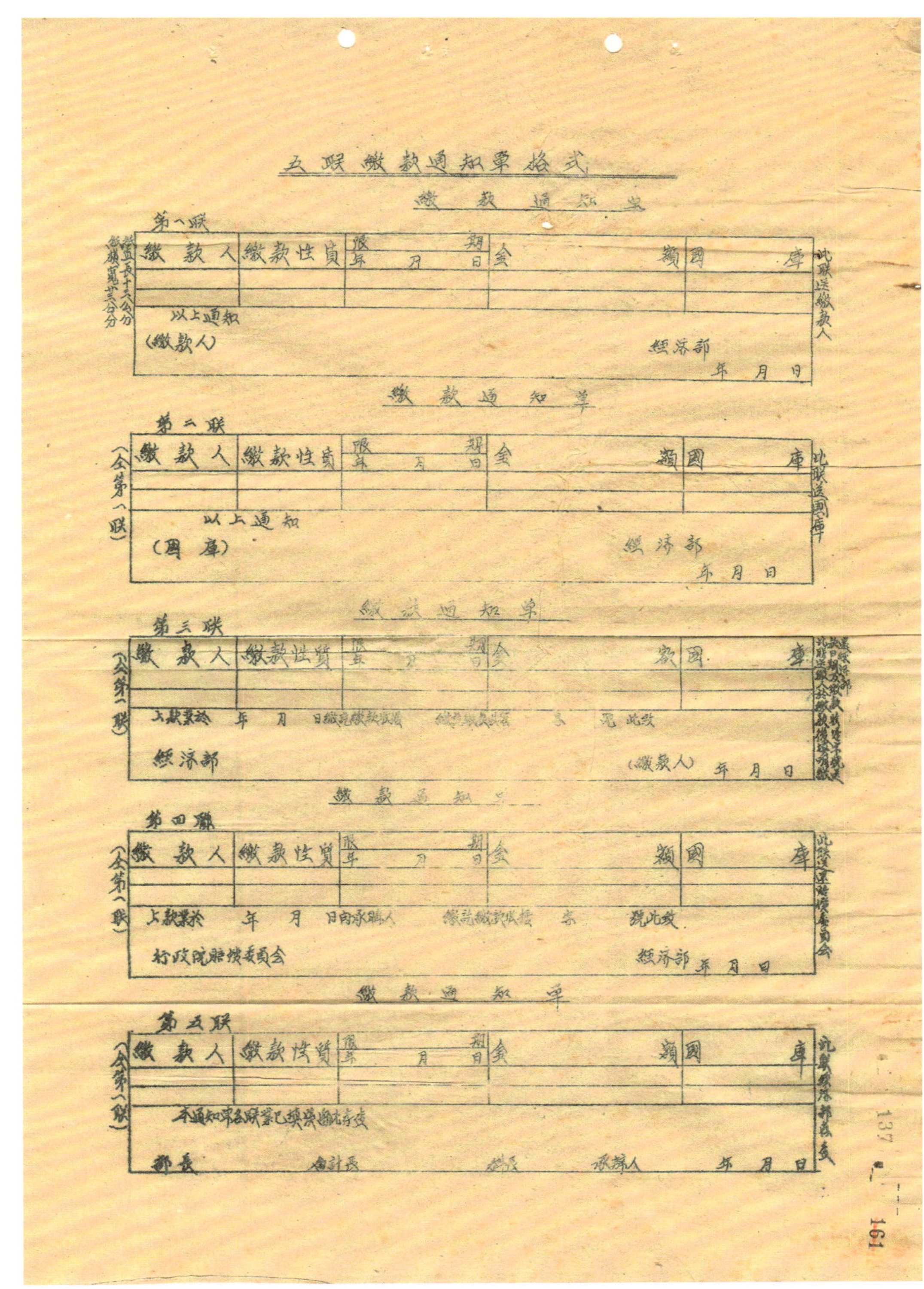

五联缴款通知单格式

缴款通知单

第一联

（纸直长十六公分 纸横宽廿三公分）

缴款人	缴款性质	限期 年 月 日	金额	国库

以上通知

（缴款人）

经济部

年 月 日

此联送缴款人

缴款通知单

第二联

（仝第一联）

缴款人	缴款性质	限期 年 月 日	金额	国库

以上通知

（国库）

经济部

年 月 日

此联送国库

缴款通知单

第三联

（仝第一联）

缴款人	缴款性质	限期 年 月 日	金额	国库

上款业於 年 月 日缴讫缴款收据 [illegible] 字 号 此致

经济部

（缴款人） 年 月 日

此联送缴款人於缴款後送经济部[illegible]

缴款通知单

第四联

（仝第一联）

缴款人	缴款性质	限期 年 月 日	金额	国库

上款业於 年 月 日向承赔人 缴讫缴款收据 字 号 此致

行政院赔偿委员会

经济部 年 月 日

此联送还赔偿委员会

缴款通知单

第五联

（仝第一联）

缴款人	缴款性质	限期 年 月 日	金额	国库

本通知单各联业已填发备此存查

部长 会计长 科长 承办人 年 月 日

此联经济部存查

162

138

一、缴款缴纳前由经济部填具五联缴款通知单（格式一）以第一联及第三联送缴款人（即承购物资之民营事业）第二联送国库第四联送赔偿委员会第五联存部备根

二、缴款人接到第一第三两联缴款通知单后即填具五联缴款书（格式六）缴国库照章依限将应缴款项连同缴款书缴送指定之国库

三、国库收到前项缴款书时应即将经济部所送第二联缴款通知书核对无误后将缴款书收据联盖具报库收讫戳记后送还缴款人以缴款书报查联送经济部查核

四、缴款人取得国库盖发之收据后即将第三联缴款通知单填注款项缴讫情形呈送经济部备查

五、经济部收到国库之缴款书报查联及缴款人送到之第三联缴款通知单核对无讹后以缴款报告联转送财政部存查第四联缴款通知单送赔偿委员会

第四条 偿额之价款以美金为计算单位但承受之民营事业每期缴款时得按中央银行挂牌市价折合法币缴付

第五条 承受物资之民营事业所缴全部价值百分之五保证金俟第四期应缴款内扣除

第六条 民营事业对于物资由日本港口运至本国港口交付之运输费用於物资全部交接完毕后（收运缴经济部转交赔垫

第七條 民營事業對於物資運達我國港口及所需設備、保管及保險等費用，其由經濟部代付者，應於提貨前分繳交經濟部歸墊。

第八條 本辦法自公佈日施行。

民營事業價購日本賠償物資契約

立約人（承購日本賠償物資民營事業全名）（以下簡稱甲方）、經濟部（以下簡稱乙方），茲因甲方奉准價購日本賠償物資，除依照「日本賠償物資［illegible］辦法」規定辦理外，關於承購該項物

資之接收及繳付價款等，訂定條款如次：

一、本契約所價購之物資（以下簡稱物資），甲方應依民營事業申請價購日本賠償物資辦法之規定繳納全部價款。甲方如或於［illegible］時受有損失，不得要求乙方賠償，其未來之［illegible］應由價貨款內扣抵。

二、甲方價購之物資，其詳細清單以在東京盟軍總部發表拆遷之設備中所列者為準；該項物資之名稱、種類、式樣規格、大小及數量為準。

三、甲方價購之物資於物資運抵我國港口時，即在船邊交由甲方負責接收，甲方並應預先準備存放該項物資之倉庫。

四、自我國港口起運所需費用由甲方自行負擔。

五、如甲方對第三第四兩項未經準備存放該物資之倉庫并報關保險等事務，得由乙方代為辦理，但所有各該項費用概由甲方按照乙方已代付之款數，於提取物資時一次繳納乙方歸墊。

六、自日本港口運抵我國港口之該項物資所需費用，如已由乙方付完畢，應由甲方於［illegible］日內備款一次送交乙方繳納歸墊。

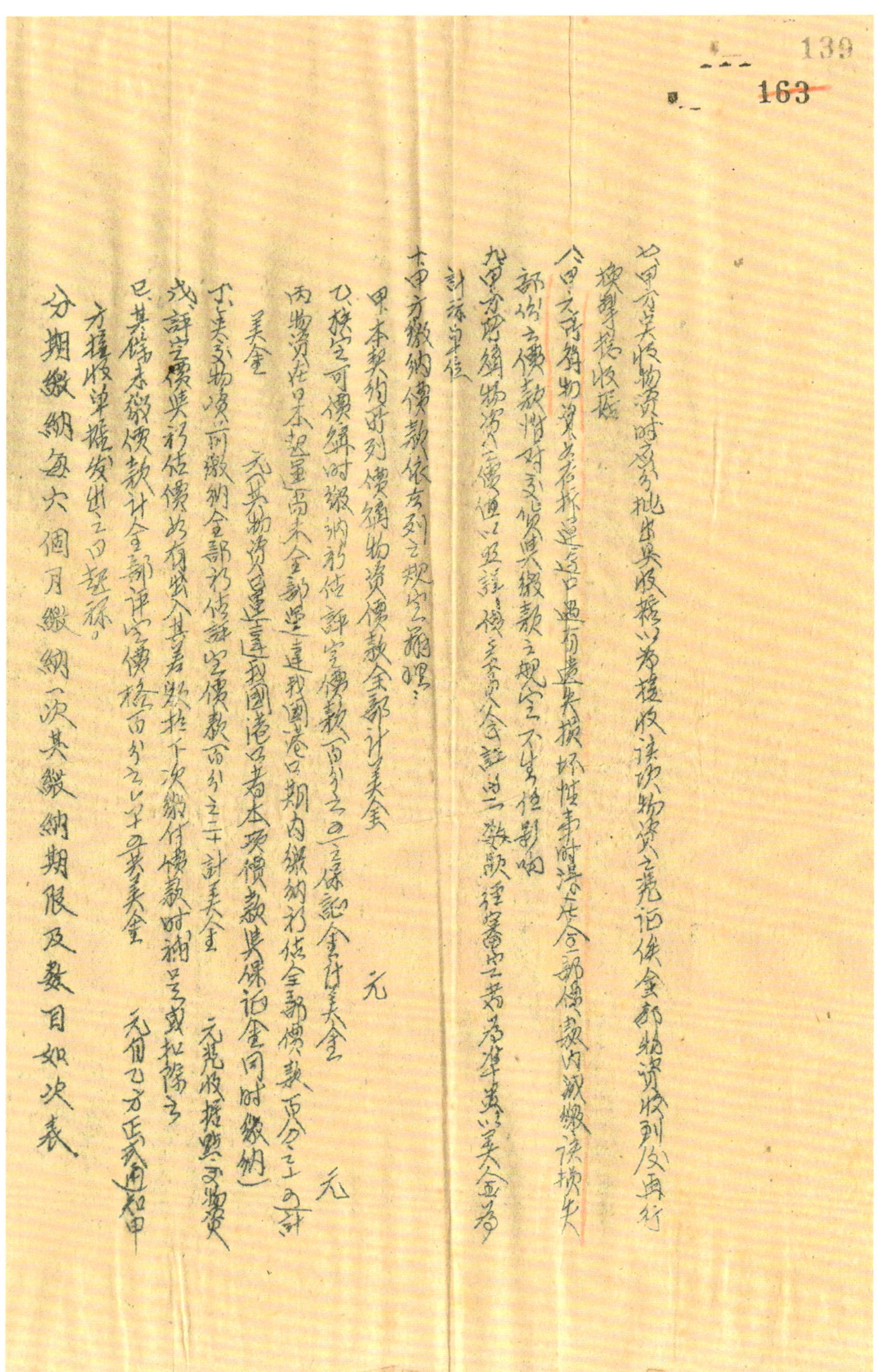

139

163

七、甲方交收物资时，应分批出具收据，以为接收该项物资之凭证，俟全部物资收到后再行换掣总收据。

八、甲方所购物资若在拆运途中遇有遗失损坏情事，得由全部偿款内减除该损失部份之偿款，惟对于乙方缴与缴款之规定不生任何影响。

九、甲方所购物资之价值以美金计算，其各项之价值另以详细清单开列数款，种类需要若干若干美金，以美金为计算单位。

十、甲方缴纳偿款依左列之规定办理：

甲、本契约所列偿购物资偿款全部计美金　元

乙、核定可偿解时缴纳于估评定偿款百分之四十之保证金计美金　元

丙、物资在日本起运前未全部运达我国港口期内缴纳于估全部偿款百分之五十四计美金　元（其物资已运达我国港口者，本项偿款与保证金同时缴纳）

丁、其余物资以前缴纳全部于估评定偿款百分之二十计美金　元，凭收据照交物资

戊、评定偿与于估偿如有出入，其差数于下次缴付偿款时补足或扣除之

己、其余未缴偿款计全部评定偿格百分之六十四共计美金　元，由乙方正式通知甲方接收单据发出之日起算。

分期缴纳每六个月缴纳一次，其缴纳期限及数目如次表

期别	到期年月日	金额	約佔全数百分比
第一期		計美金　元	約佔評定 10%
第二期		計美金　元	約佔評定 20%
第三期		計美金　元	約佔評定 15%
第四期		計美金　元	約佔評定 10%
附注	第四期应缴款项以实际全价应缴尚缺之价款全部交清		

由前償債時已經繳納約佔評定價百分之五之保證金款計美金　元在第四期應繳償款內扣除

十一、前項價款繳付時按當時中央銀行掛牌美金之市價以東折合法幣繳付

十二、乙方對於應繳償款不得拖延，如逾期未繳時其應繳未繳之款應由甲方及其保證人連帶負責清償，乙方遇有必要時亦須依民營事業申請補配日本賠償物資辦法第九條之規定處理之，甲方放棄先訴抗辯權

十三、本契約一式四份除由甲乙雙方及保證人各執一份外，其餘一份由經濟部轉送財政部備查

立契人甲方（承購物資民營事業全名）

負責人

地址

乙方經濟部

負責人

甲方保證人（名稱）

負責人

地址

中華民國　年　月　日

附（二）民营事业申请价配日本赔偿物资申请表

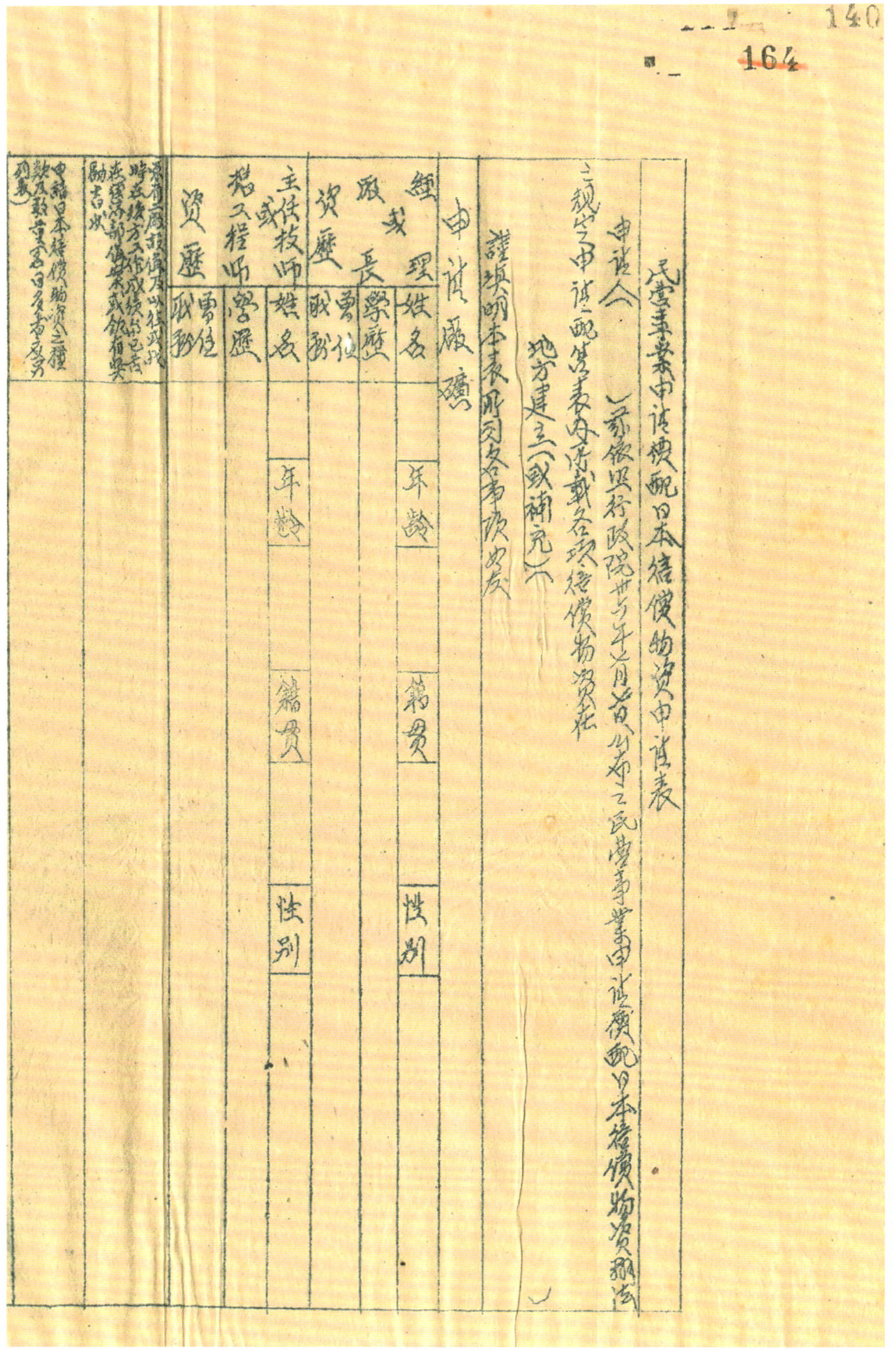
164

140

民營事業申請價配日本賠償物資申請表

申請人（　　）茲依照行政院卅六年六月廿四日公布之民營事業申請價配日本賠償物資辦法之規定申請配售表內所載各項賠償物資在

地方建立（或補充）（　　）

謹填明本表所列各事項如左

申請廠礦

經理或廠長資歷	姓名	年齡	籍貫	性別
	學歷			
	曾任職務			
主任技師或總工程師資歷	姓名	年齡	籍貫	性別
	學歷			
	曾任職務			
現有之廠設備及以往或戰時在後方工作成績以已否派遣參加部份事業或飲有經驗者狀				
申請日本賠償物資之種類及數量需要原因（另列表）				

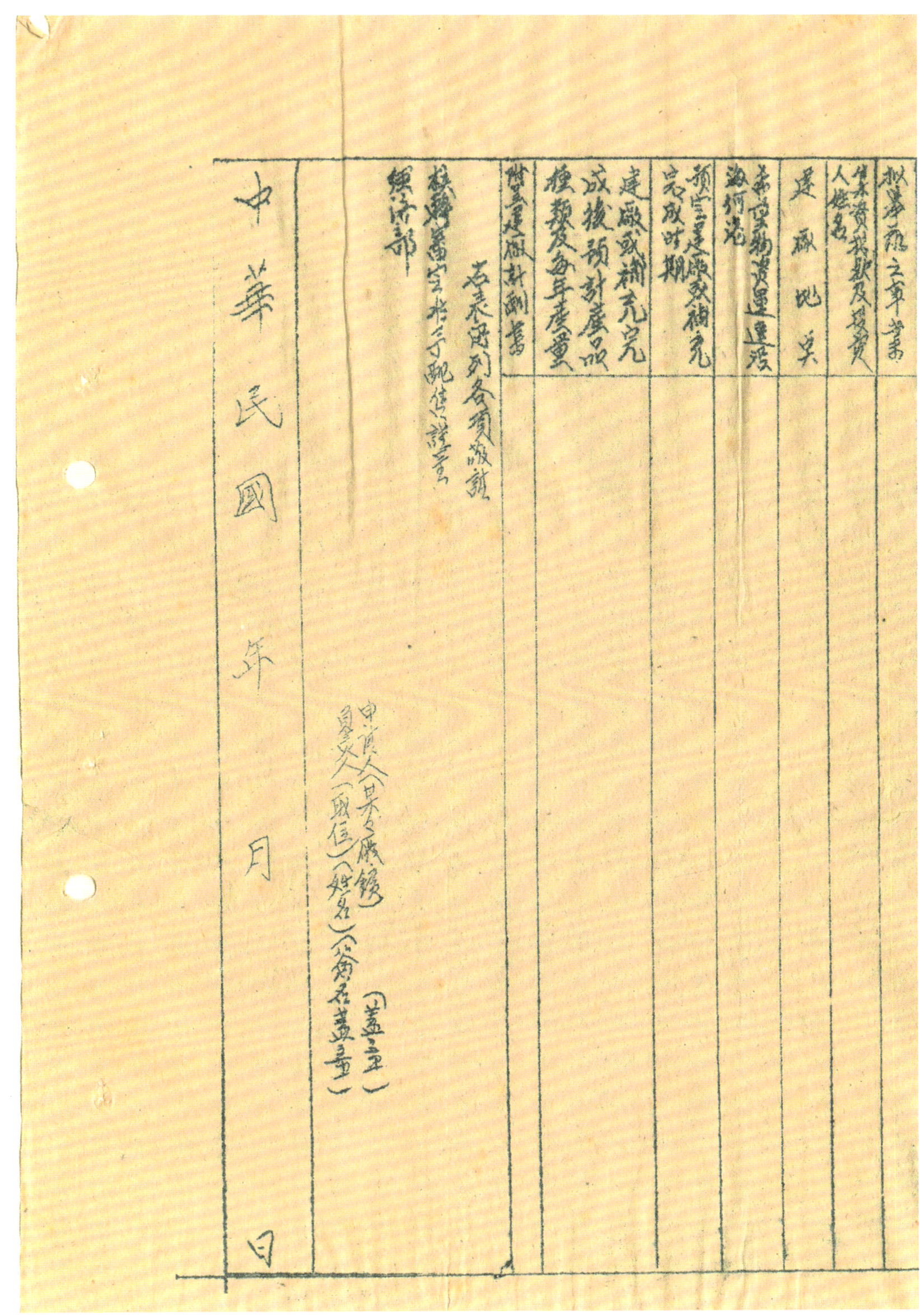

擬籌辦之事業	集資款及投資人姓名	建廠地點	希望物資運達海河港	預定建廠或補充完成時期	建廠或補充完成後預計產品種類及每年產量	附呈建廠計劃書

右表所列各項敬請

核轉當局予以配售為禱

經濟部

申請人（某某廠號）

負責人（職位）（姓名）（簽名蓋章）（蓋章）

中華民國　　年　　月　　日

附（三二）配售民营事业日本赔偿物资评价办法

配售民营事业日本赔偿物资评价办法

第一条 本办法依民营事业申请价配日本赔偿物资办法第五条之规定制定之

第二条 本办法评价之物资以行政院核定价配民营部份之日本赔偿物资为限

第三条 评价价配民营之日本赔偿物资其价格暂估价参照盟军总部所列该物资之价值估定之

第四条 物资运达我国港口后另行斟酌其当时品质并依照现况照市价并参酌盟军总部所列价格予以评定之

第五条 同式或同类物资在二件以上照盟军总部所列价值仅有总数未予个别列价者应就各件物资斟酌其新旧性能等项比照市价分别评定之

第六条 在运输途中受有损害之物资应就损害程度评定其价格

第七条 本办法自公布之日施行

配售民营事业日本赔偿物资评价委员会组织规程

第一条 配售民营事业日本赔偿物资评价委员会（以下简称评价委员会）依民营事业申请价配日本赔偿物资办法第五条之规定组织之

第二條 評價委員會置委員九人，其名額之分配如左：

一、經濟部代表三人 二、財政部代表二人 三、全國性人民之商團體代表四人

前項工商團體代表由經濟部指定之

第三條 評價委員會置主任委員一人，由經濟部部長在經濟部代表內指定之

第四條 評價委員會設於經濟部內

第五條 評價委員會開會由主任委員召集並任主席

第六條 評價委員會辦理會務所需人員由經濟部部長在部內職員中調充或另聘用臨時人員

第七條 評價委員會評議價格時得征詢各該物資之工商專家之意見或聘請該工商專家列席

第八條 評價委員會評議價格依評價辦法辦理

第九條 評價委員會評定之價格由經濟部送達行政院賠償委員會審定之

第十條 本規程自公布之日施行

附（四）民营事业申请价配日本赔偿物资建厂计划格式

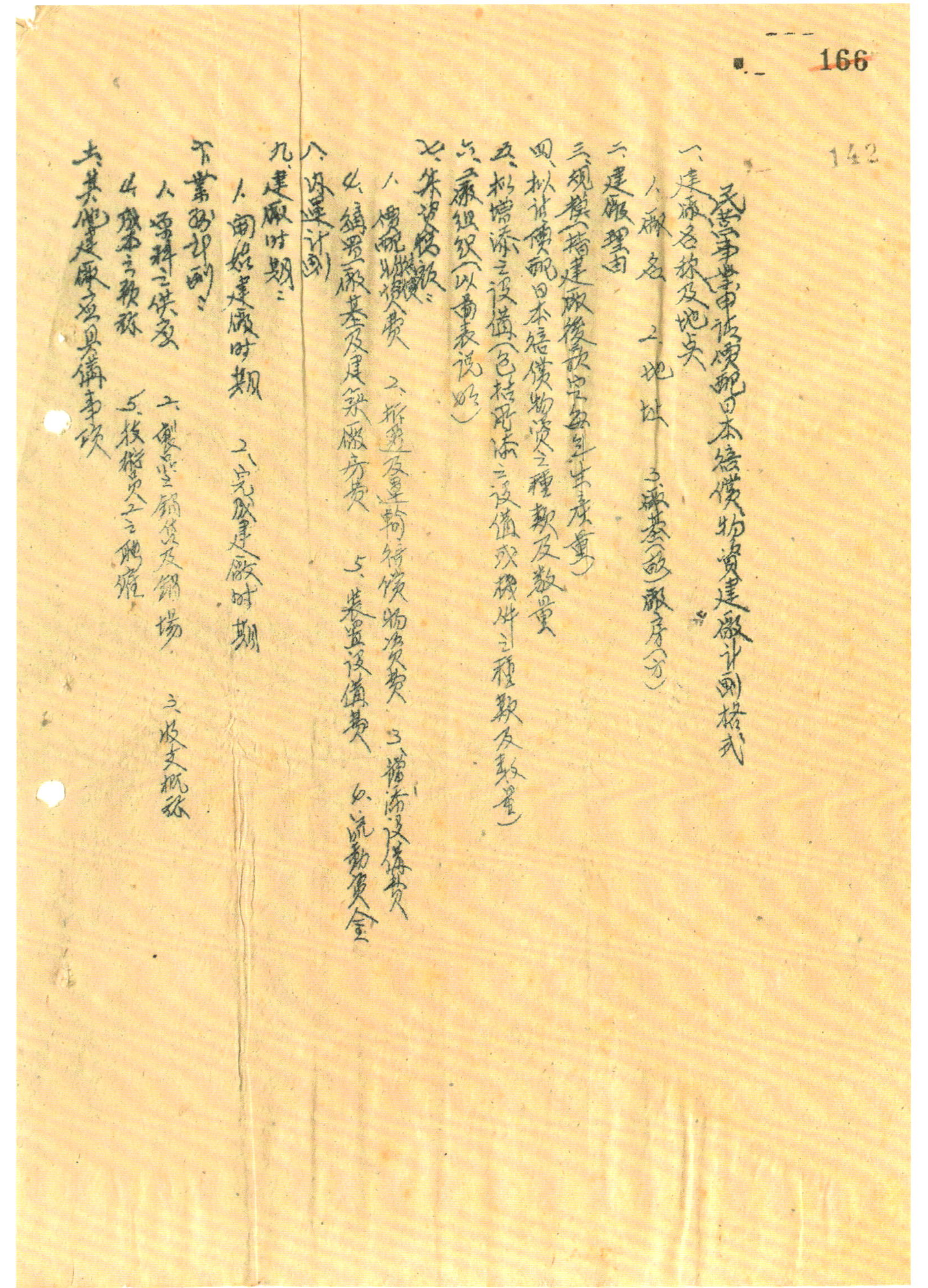

166

142

民营事业申请价配日本赔偿物资建厂计划格式

一、建厂名称及地点

1、厂名 2、地址 3、厂基（或）厂房（分）

二、建厂理由

三、规模（指建厂后预定每年生产量）

四、拟请价配日本赔偿物资之种类及数量

五、拟增添之设备（包括自添之设备或机件之种类及数量）

六、厂组织（以图表说明）

七、集资情形：

1、价配物资费 2、拆迁及运输该项物资费 3、增添设备费

4、购置厂基及建筑厂房费 5、装置设备费 6、流动资金

八、兴建计划

九、建厂时期：

1、开始建厂时期 2、完成建厂时期

十、业务计划：

1、原料之供应 2、制品之销售及销场 3、收支概算

4、成本之预算 5、技术人员之聘请

十一、其他关于建厂应具备事项

六、机器设备、物资及存款赔偿

永利化学工业公司关于接收工作事呈经济部特派员办事处的报告（一九四五年十月三十一日）

永利化學工業公司信箋

接收工作報告第七號

十月十六日至十月三十一日

一、清理蒸氣發生爐部鍋爐三座内有一部尚完好，餘部待修理并需配備零件。

二、煤氣部趕修藍煤氣發生爐。

三、高壓部將大壓縮機整理後試車一次。

四、硫酸部　礦鉄爐經日人使用數年損壞甚多，計非兩個月不能修理竣工。

五、硫酸錏部　現以多數技工趕修其大離心機及乾燥機中和罐等設備，均已試車，情形良好。

六、鉄工製造部趕造備件。

七、木工部清理木模業已完畢。

八、電工部整理完畢。

九、醫院、工人宿舍、職員宿舍大體均已佈置。

十、擬十一月五日開始復工。

謹呈

經濟部特派員辦事處

永利化學工業公司呈

十月三十一日

民國　年　月　日

永利化學工業公司寄

重慶總辦事處：保安街一百一十號

上海辦事處：梅白格路九十三號

南京通訊處：

永利化学工业公司关于硫酸铔厂硝酸设备被日本人拆卸运走恳祈追还事呈经济部苏浙皖特派员文及经济部批复

（一九四五年十一月十四日至十二月七日）

永利化學工業股份有限公司 呈 經濟部蘇浙皖特派員

事由	擬辦	批示	備考
呈爲硫酸錏廠内硝酸設備被日人拆卸運走懇祈追還由			
附件			

字第　號　年　月　日　時到

收文　字第　號

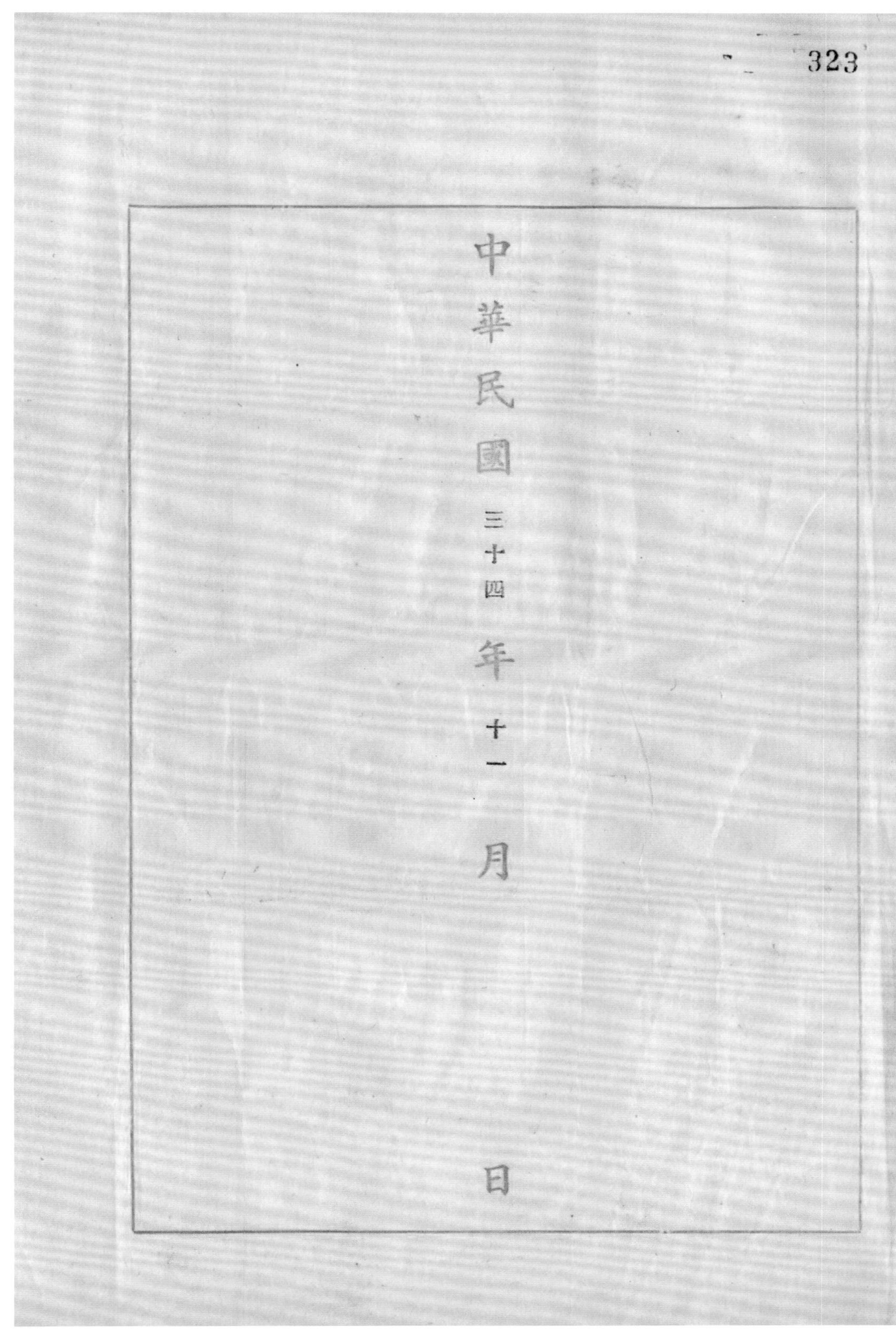
323

中華民國三十四年十一月日

325

呈爲硫酸錏廠內硝酸設備被日人拆卸運走懇祈追還事竊敝公司在

江蘇省六合縣卸甲甸硫酸錏廠會奉

鈞署令派人接收除接收情形當俟整理完畢另行呈報外玆據侵佔敝

廠之「永禮化學工業株式會社」負責人玉置豐助氏云：

「原有硝酸製造設備會於民國三十年一月間經日本駐華軍部大

使館日本國內之設備營團與當時之南京僞政府實業部四者協議

後命敝社在原狀之下全套拆卸運往日本九州大牟田市東洋高壓

會社（該社郎永禮股東之一）因此遂於同年三月間拆卸完畢裝

箱委託日本軍用艦船陸續運往指定地點該項搬運直至同年八月

方始完竣貲款之數依據當時審定合日幣四拾壹萬餘元上述設備

因戰時曾受飛機轟炸之影響及無人管理期間竊盜之損害並非完全無缺者運日以後業經修復完善迄最近消息聞該設備在東洋高壓工場連續工作每日生產量達二十噸云

如上所陳貴公司如欲收回該項裝置設備尚希及早與大牟田工場開始談判因聞三井近被解散東洋高壓會社既爲三井傍系公司之一恐一旦逸失時機將來不易收回也」

等語查該項硝酸設備本爲敝廠之一部兹既查明下落自應原物收回惟目前交通狀況運回該項機器非短期内所能辦理今當三井解散之時而東洋高壓會社又爲三井傍系公司之一理合呈請

鈞署轉呈

324

經濟部與駐日盟軍總部接洽先行備案俟交通狀況許可時再行拆卸
運回所有一切費用以及機件損害應保留向日索還賠償之權此呈
經濟部蘇浙皖特派員張

具呈人 永利化學工業股份有限公司
上海辦事處代表人李偶夫
地址：上海梅白格路九三號

錏廠

317

經濟部批（卅四）工字五五九〇六號
卅四年十二月七日

事由：根據永利硝酸廠設備爲敵拆運日本情形一案批復知照由

具呈人：永利化學工業公司

卅四年十一月廿一日呈一件爲公司硫酸錏廠內硝酸廠全套設備被日人運走經查明事實補陳埈核

允賜追索收回原物由

呈悉。查此案已據本部蘇浙皖區特派員呈報業據該公司呈

請經轉呈陸軍總司令部轉飭日本聯絡總部負責查取歸

還並電駐日盟軍統帥部查照保全該項設備以便運回應用等

情，仰即知照。至關於機件損害及運回費用應保留向日索取賠償

之權一節，准俟另案辦理。此批。

经济部苏浙皖区特派员驻京办事处主任徐肇基关于永利化学工业公司硝酸部分请求追回失物保留赔偿一案致该公司的训令（一九四五年十一月十九日）

事由：奉特派員辦公處令為本處前呈永利公司硝礦部份請求追回失物保留賠償一案已分呈何總司令暨翁部長核辦令仰知照由

附件

擬辦

決定辦法

年　月　日時到

經濟部蘇浙皖區特派員駐京辦事處訓令　文別

訓令

訓字第　號

中華民國三十四年十一月十九日

令永利化學工業公司

案奉

特派員辦公處發字第一二七二號指令內開呈悉查本案已據該永利化學工業股份有限公司上海辦事處呈同前情經分呈何總司令暨翁部長核辦矣仰即知

收文　字第　號

照此令等因奉此查此案前據該公司呈報到處當經呈請在案茲奉前因合行令

仰知照此令

主任 徐澤基

资源委员会关于永利化学工业公司部分设备被日本人移设日境事给外交部的函（抄件）（一九四六年七月十日）

271

抄件

案准资源委员会六月七日资秘文字第五七号函开：

「案准外交部转驻日盟军五月三十一日电内开：『南京永利硫酸铔厂一部份设备被日人移设日境，请通知该厂速即抄录详单附说明书寄盟军以便交涉驻日盟军』等由，相应录转原电即希查照迳洽为荷。」

等因；查敝公司硫酸铔厂自二十六年冬沦陷，工厂全部为敌侵占，原有硝酸厂机件设备，于三十八年被日人搬运至日本九州福冈县大牟田东洋高压工业株式会社之横须工场，最近综合各方报告及敌遗留东洋高压工场事业概览之记载，知该工厂地点即在大牟田市新开町六番地，而其本店则设在东京市日本桥区室町二丁目一番地。此案于去年敌投降后，敝公司即经呈请经济部转请陆军总司令部饬日本联络总部负责查取归还，并电驻日盟军统帅部查照，保全该项设备，以便运回在案。兹奉钧部驻日盟军电示，用特将敝公司原有硝酸厂设备被日移设日境各机件开列详单，并陈明办理经过，敬祈

鉴察照办，迅赐追查运还，以便安装复旧，制造硝酸，以充兵工农肥原料，无任感幸。谨呈

外交部部长王

谨呈

三十五年七月十日发出

永利化学工业公司和外交部关于硝酸设备赔偿事的电文（一九四六年八月一日）

263

抄件

永利化學工業公司錏廠

外交部收電

收電第5111號　第1頁

發電者：代表團

地名：東京

譯電者：王醒民

發電：35年8月1日12時0分

收電：35年8月2日9時40分

南京外交部請譯轉浦口永利化學工業公司硝酸設備經多次接洽總部已同意交辦約一月以後即可拆遷在日本海港交貨請預先準備船隻等為盼代表團徑引

中華民國　年　月　日

字第　號第　頁

廠址：江蘇省六合縣卸甲甸　通訊處：南京西華門三條巷六合里二號　電報掛號：四五三四南京

日本东洋高压株式会社归还硝酸制造设备契约书及译文（一九四六年八月二十四日）

276

契約書（草本）

東洋高圧工業株式会社（以下単ニ東圧ト称ス）ハ硝酸製造設備ノ建設ヲ産業設備営団（以下単ニ営団ト称ス）ノタメニ請負ヒタルニヨリ之ガ建設ニ要スル未完成ノ装置（以下単ニ装置ト称ス）ヲ永禮化学工業股份有限公司（以下単ニ永禮ト称ス）ヨリ買受クルニ付契約スルコト左ノ如シ

第一条　東圧ハ永禮ヨリ其ノ所有ニ係ル装置ヲ金四拾万八千参百参円（中華民國維新政府現物出資評価額）ニテ買受クルモノトス

第二条　装置ノ引渡シニ要スル解体・荷造・運送其ノ他一切ノ費用ハ東圧ノ負担トシ現地ニ於テ東圧永禮ノ代表者立会ノ上現品ヲ授受スルモノトス

第三条　永禮ハ装置ノ引渡シニ当リ其ノ上ニ存スル他人ノ一切ノ権利ヲ永禮ノ計算ニ於テ消滅セシムルモノトス引渡シ後ニ於テ之ガ判明シタル場合永禮ハ

中華民國卅五年八月廿四日簽印

第四条 第一条ノ売買代金ハ装置全部ノ引渡シ完了後本公司ヨリ永礼ニ支払フモノトス

第五条 装置ノ解体・荷造・運送其ノ他引渡シニ要スル手続ハ凡テ本公司ニ於テ手配シ永礼公司之ニ協力スルモノトス

第六条 営団ニ於テ本件装置ヲ含ム硝酸製造設備ガ不用トナリタル場合永礼ガ設備ノ全部又ハ一部ノ買受ヲ希望スルトキハ本公司ハ之ガ売渡シヲ営団ニ対シ斡旋スルモノトス

第七条 売渡シ価格ハ売渡スベキ設備ノ取得原価ヨリ償却金ヲ控除シタル金額トス但シ売渡シノ時ニ於ケル時価ガ其ノ金額ヨリ低キ場合ハ時価ニヨル

償却金ハ営団ニ於テ前条設備ノ貸付ニヨリ得タル既往ノ貸付料金累計額ヨリ取得原価ノ既往迄利息累計額ヲ控除シタル金額トス

278

前二項ノ外売渡シニ関シ其ノ物件ノ受渡シ方法其ノ他必要ナル事項ハ別ニ協定スルモノトス

昭和拾七年　月　日

東洋高圧工業株式会社

代表者　高島基江

永礼化学工業股份有限公司

代表者　玉置豊助

右承諾候也

昭和拾七年　月　日

產業設備営団

代表者　藤原銀次郎

右契約ノ証トシテ本証書参通ヲ作製シ各自其ノ壹通ヲ保有スルモノトス

一、永利化学工業股份有限公司ヨリ賠償受クベキ酒精醸造設備

機械名	型式能力	数量	備考
醱酵設備			
1. 醱化器	径 一、八七〇粍 高サ 三、〇五四粍	一	
2. 白金故網	—	一	
3. 白金備洗皿	深サ 一五五粍 径 二、三八五粍 厚サ 五粍 径 一、〇二〇粍	一	
4. サチュレーター	—	一	
5. エセースキルター	厚サ 一八粍 径 八九〇粍 高サ 四、〇〇〇粍	一	
6. 豫熱器	厚サ 一二粍 径 九〇〇粍 高サ 七、三五〇粍	一	
7. 醱酵汽罐	厚サ 五粍 七七〇粍 高サ 五、五〇〇粍	〇 一	
8. 一次瓦斯冷却器		二	
9. ステンレス製ブースター	圧力 四三五	一	
10. 吸收設備	△ 一封度/一平方吋		
11. 吸收塔	厚サ 五粍 径 六、三〇〇粍 高サ 一五、〇〇〇粍	九	
12. 仝右附屬磁製リング	径 五五粍 長サ 七五粍	三三[illegible]立方米 Cubic meter	

280

番号	名称	数量
13	水準調節タンク	一
14	[illegible]塔	一
15	アミノドヒーター	一
16	アミノドクーラー	一
17	[illegible]	一
18	[illegible]槽	二
19	[illegible]タンク	一
20	[illegible]タンク	一
21	[illegible]プラットフォーム	四

番号	品名	寸法	容量・重量	数量
22	揮発油 42 [illegible]			二
33	濃硫酸 [illegible]			一
24	苛性曹達 アイードタンク	三尺径 三尺高(?)	二九又七三一 〇〇 kg〇 入	一
25	硫酸 アイードタンク	三尺径 三尺高(?)	四九又 〇〇 四〇 kg〇 入	一
26	ニンヂンサー		一	二
27	遠心[illegible]デ[illegible]ー		一	二
28	脱ミンセントレーター		一	二
29	蒸発 [illegible] 塔		一	一
30	濃縮 [illegible] 塔 タンク		一	二
31	[illegible] タンク		一	一
32	ドリップパン	三尺径	一二〇〇 二〇〇 kg入	二
33	[illegible]		一	一
34	コンデンサー [illegible]	三尺高 径	四一 七〇〇 八〇〇 kg入	
35	高[illegible]			
36	ステンレス [illegible]		三尺 [illegible]	一 二 三 一二〇〇 七二 米

282

二吋 二四〇米
一吋半 二〇四米
一吋四分ノ一 四五米
一吋 一〇〇米
二分ノ一吋 九〇米

37 鋳鉄製ストップ瓣 口径 四分一吋及四分三吋 四
38 鋳鋼製ストップ瓣 口径 四分ノ一吋〃三吋 五
39 鋳鉄製スリース瓣 口径 二吋〃一〇吋 一二
40 鋳鋼製スリース瓣 口径 一吋二分ノ一〃三吋 二
41 ステンレス製スリース瓣 口径 八分ノ五吋〃六吋 一八
42 ステンレス製コック 口径 二分ノ一吋〃三吋 五一
43 鋳鉄製減圧瓣 口径 二分ノ一吋〃二吋 一
44 鋳鉄製直角瓣 口径 二分ノ一吋〃三吋 一
45 鋳鉄製安全瓣 口径 三吋 一
46 鋳鉄製逆止瓣 口径 三吋 一
以上

契約書譯文

東洋高壓工業株式會社（以下簡稱東壓）因已承受該事業設備營團（以下簡稱營團）之委囑，担任建設硝酸製造設備用，特向永禮化學工業股份有限公司（以下簡稱永禮）借用其在文末尾所載前項建設必需之裝置（以下簡稱裝置），茲訂立合同如左：

第一條 東壓按照中華民國維新政府現物出資評價額以日金肆拾萬捌仟叁百零叁圓正向永禮收買其所有之裝置。

第二條 關于引渡該裝置所需費用及拆卸、裝捆、搬運等一切統由東壓負担之。該裝置應于現地由東壓、永禮兩方代表人會同辦理交割。

第三條 該裝置引渡時他方對於該物上存在之一切權利，永禮應負責使之消滅（該裝置引渡時如牽涉他方權利，永禮應負責清理以[illegible]東壓無涉之意）。引渡以後，查明有他人權利時，亦同。

第四条　第一条所载货款应在装置一引渡完毕后由东压交付承礼

第五条　关于该装置之拆卸包装搬运及其他一切必要手续统由东压办理但承礼须予以协助

第六条　营团他日不需用包括本装置在内之硝酸制造设备时承礼如有意购买其设备之全部或其一部者东压应居间向营团请其卖予承礼

上述情形之下东压居间前来斡旋以营团必须同意优先售予承礼

第七条　前条（译者加）装置之价值应于收进原价中减去纯折旧额后作为售价但售出当时时价低于价值时应照当时时价计算之

所谓纯折旧额者系指上述设备出租所得之既经租金总数减去收进原价之经过利息总数后之余额而言　前两项以外关于买卖物件授受方法及其他必要事项另行之

昭和拾柒年　月　日

東洋高壓工業株式會社

代表人　高島基江

永禮化學工業股份有限公司

代表人　玉置豐助

以上各條款均予同意

昭和拾柒年　月　日

產業設備營團

代表人　藤原銀次郎

右契約本文共叁份各執壹份為憑

永利化学工业公司为硝酸设备退还一案给外交部亚东司的函（抄件）（一九四六年九月七日）

259

抄件　由滬處交謝先生

茲據本部駐日代表團本年八月廿六日來電內開：「永利化學公司硝酸設備退還一案，原則上已商妥，曾於八月一日電請轉告該公司準備船隻，迄未奉覆，乞再轉催該公司妥謀運輸辦法及起運日期，並派一專人以本團職員名義來日主持洽收事宜等語，查該團八月一日來電，略稱：「永利化學工業公司硝酸設備經多次接洽，總部已同意交辦，約一月以後即可拆遷在日本海港交貨，請預先準備船隻等語。」經即抄同原電轉達在案，迄未見復，相應再行函請查照，以速準備船隻，並派專人前來本部亞東司面洽赴日主持洽收事宜為荷。此致

永利化學工業公司

外交部亞東司啓

卅五年九月七日

经济部苏浙皖区特派员驻京办事处关于永利化学工业公司被占厂产机件器材等特准担保先予发还事给该公司的文（一九四六年九月九日）

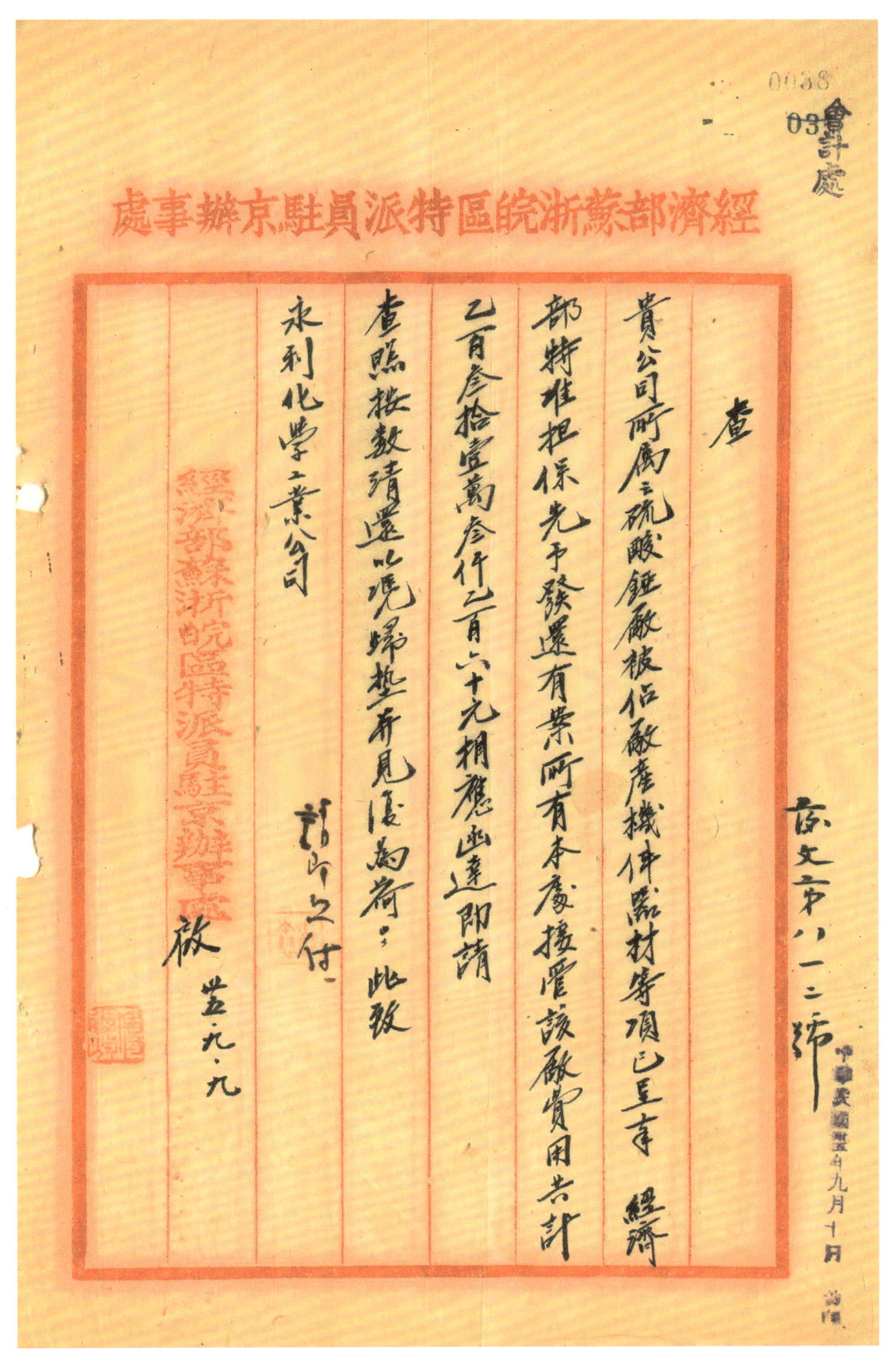

0038

03

會計處

經濟部蘇浙皖區特派員駐京辦事處

京文字第八一二號

中華民國卅五年九月十日

查

貴公司所屬之硫酸錏廠被佔廠產機件器材等項已呈奉 經濟部特准担保先予發還有案，所有本處接管該廠費用共計乙百叁拾壹萬叁仟乙百六十九元，相應函達，即請

查照按數繳還，以憑歸墊，並見復為荷。此致

永利化學工業公司

經濟部蘇浙皖區特派員駐京辦事處 啟

卅五·九·九

永利化学工业关于向日本收回硝酸厂机件设备应付运费请转商由日方照付或暂准记账收回赔偿后缴还事呈经济部文及经济部对此问题的回复（抄件）（一九四六年十一月八日至三十日）

肯铔廠　呈經濟部　文

207

呈為公司向日本收回硝酸廠機件設備應付運費請轉商由日方照付或暫准記賬俟收回賠償後繳還由

中華民國卅五年十一月八日發出

案奉

鈞部卅五年十月廿四日京工字第一四四八二號通知內開：

「前據該公司卅五年九月五日呈為本公司硝酸廠設備被日刼去懇轉商以運兵赴日回國船隻運回一案，當經本部函請國防部核辦並批示在案。茲准聯合勤務總司令部卅五年十月十五日運水字第一一四五五號刪代電，以奉國防部交下該公司硝酸機器由日本裝運回國，俟有船時當可代運，惟此項運費應由該公司自行結付，囑查照轉知等由，仰即逕洽辦理，特此通知」

等因；奉此，查公司硝酸廠設備被日人掠刼以去，原應由日本負責運回，照舊安裝，恢復戰前生產情況，方屬合理，祇以目前運輸困難，

208

貴令運回，恐非短期內所能辦理，不得不自行設法，趕緊運回，恢復舊觀，茲蒙

鈞部商准聯合勤務總司令部俟有船時即為代運回國，仰見關懷國防化工生產之重要，曷勝銘感。惟應付運費飭令公司自行結付一節，公司在喪亡之餘，收復工廠，整理開工，艱難應付，已感竭蹶，此時實無力籌措此項運費，擬請

鈞部再為轉商駐日代表團，責由日方照付，設因礙於規定，不便照辦，懇准暫予記賬，容俟向日方收回賠償，即行繳付。

鈞部維護工商權益，無微不至，用敢瀆呈，仰乞

鑒察轉商批示祇遵。謹呈

209

經濟部

永利化學工業公司　謹呈

地址：上海四川路四一〇號

寄
錏廠
182

永利化學工業公司

抄經濟部批　京工川字第一七七一八号　卅五年十一月卅日

具呈人永利化學工業公司

三十五年十一月八日呈一件，為本公司向日本收回硝酸廠機件設備，應付運費，請於日本照付或暫准記帳，俟收回賠償後繳還由

呈悉，業予據情函請外交部轉洽矣。此批。

字第　號第　頁　民國　年　月　日

中華民國三十五年十二月五日

上海四川路一〇號四樓　電話一五一六七　電報掛號八八八七

永利化学工业公司关于为硝酸厂机器被日敌拆卸运走应责令赔偿新机并装置完善保证开工事呈经济部文（一九四六年十二月十七日）

寄 203
錏廠

謝爲杰先生
趙如晏先生
章懷西先生
劉本慈先生

呈為硝酸廠機器被日敵拆卸運走應責令賠償新機并
裝置完善保證開工由

中華民國卅五年十二月拾七日發出

竊公司江蘇六合縣卸甲甸硫酸錏廠原有製造硝酸設備，在抗戰時期被日
敵與南京偽政府勾結將其全部拆卸，運往九州大牟田裝置使用。公司
曾迭呈
鈞部備案，請求向日敵索賠，嗣奉
外交部轉來駐日代表團來電，略示，硝酸設備，總部已同意交還，即
可拆遷在日本港口交貨，請預先準備船隻，等語；旋公司又呈請
鈞部轉咨
國防部令知運兵赴日船隻回程記裝公司全部硝酸機器，嗣奉
批「已予據情函請國防部查照核辦」，并奉
通知「准聯合勤務總司令部代電以奉國防部交下該公司硝酸機器由日

204

本裝運回國俟有船時當可代運惟此項運費應由該公司自行結付」等因在案；本應靜候國防部派船裝運回國，毋庸多瀆，惟據公司新由美來華之美籍化學專家德利君稱：「凡化學機器若擱置不用必致腐蝕其速度較之使用時尤快該項硝酸設備因日人發動侵略戰爭停止製造乃十年前事其腐蝕情形可想而知再依普通商業習慣利息折舊每年按百分之十計算則此項損失已等於原來全部價值今雖能由日本運回然因上述情形復經過兩次拆卸搬運實已等於廢鐵其價值實屬微乎其微故此項硝酸機器其舊有者只能作爲廢鐵估價應責令日人賠償相等於原來產量之新機器包括廠屋地脚在內并負責建築安裝直至正常出貨時爲止」等語；查德利君係化學專家，其所稱不爲無見，理合呈明

205

鈞部所有公司硝酸設備，應併入賠償案內，責令日人照樣賠償新機器及廠屋地脚，并負責建築安裝，保證出貨，至將來由日本運回之舊硝酸設備，只能作爲廢鐵估價，於賠償案內剔除之，是否有當，伏候

鈞裁。此呈

經濟部部長王

永利化學工業公司謹呈

地址：上海四川路四一〇號

已登記

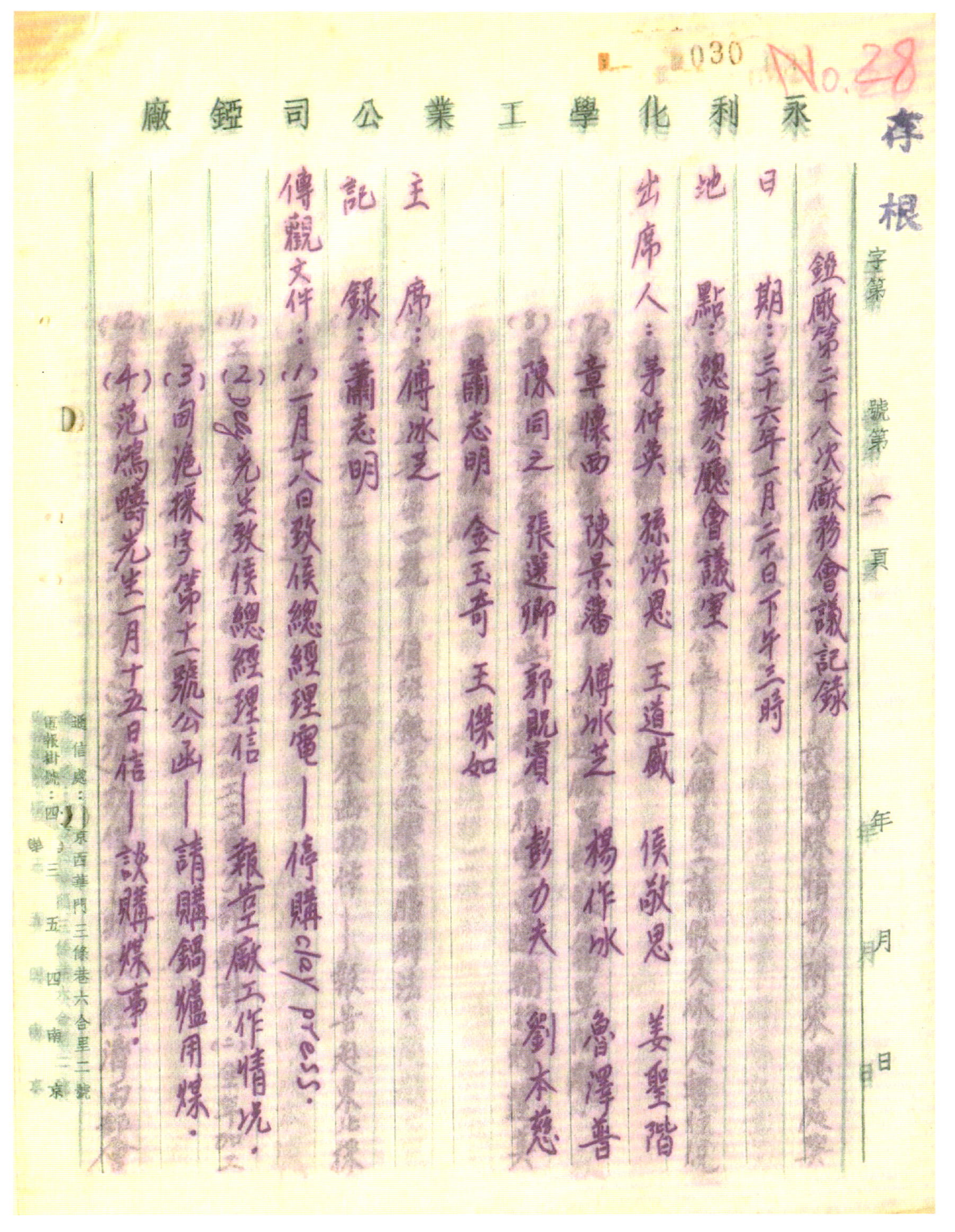

030 No.28

存根

永利化學工業公司錏廠

字第　號第　一　頁　年　月　日

錏廠第二十八次廠務會議記錄

日　期：三十六年一月二十日下午三時

地　點：總辦公廳會議室

出席人：茅仲英　孫洪恩　王道威　侯敬思　姜聖階　章懷西　陳景藩　傅冰芝　楊作冰　魯澤普　陳同之　張選卿　郭覲賓　彭力夫　劉本慈　蕭志明　金玉奇　王傑如

主　席：傅冰芝

記　錄：蕭志明

傳觀文件：(1)一月十八日致侯總經理電——停購clay press.

(2)Dey先生致侯總經理信——報告廠工作情况.

(3)向滬採字第十一號公函——請購鍋爐用煤.

(4)范鴻疇先生一月十五日信——談購煤事.

通信處：南京西華門三條巷六合里二號

電報掛號：四二五四南京

永利化學工業公司錏廠

字第　號第 二 頁　年　月　日

(5)滬司採(36)字第四號公函——談購煤情形，附來總處與中興往來函底各一份。

(6)滬司總(36)字第七號公函——公佈員工請假及休息暫行規則，附規則二份。

(7)滬司運(36)第三號公函——談運廠器材裝箱單問題。

(8)向滬運字第三號公函——報告總豐昌運輸行轉運美國機器抵廠。

(9)本廠通告第四號——值班飯堂改變用膳辦法。

(10)李悦言先生一月八日及一月十五日來函抄件——報告赴東北採購美善之經過。

(11)工訓部統計表格三份——(一)工友加工工資分部統計，(二)全年加工統計，(三)各部工友人數旬報。

(12)外交部批文(美36字第0534號)抄件——財政、經濟兩部會

通信處：南京西華門三條巷六合里二號
電報掛號：四三五四 南京

永利化學工業公司錏廠

032

28

字第　號第三頁　年　月　日

主席報告：印保証單，已經美大使館轉送美大進出口銀行。

(13) 京(36)字第一二號公函副本——領回浮碼頭事，附保証書。

(14) 滬司總(36)字第5號公函——談聯總55病床設備事，附聯總衛生業務委員會來函一件。

(15) 南滬總字第4號公函——復滬司總(36)字第5號公函，報告病床交涉原委。

(16) 日本供賠償工業情形一覽表（摘抄）一份。

(17) 中央日報一份（一月十七日及十八日）——拆運日賠償物質問題。

(18) 湖南湘潭、湘鄉兩縣煤礦清表（抄件）一份。

(19) 向脊辰先生一月四日來信——希望工廠產量增高，成本減低，以利農民。

(20) 沽鎮經理處一月一日公函——報告恢復營業。

(21) 三十五年度華北區全年營業報告一份。

通信處：南京西華門三條巷六合里二號
電報掛號：四二五四 南京

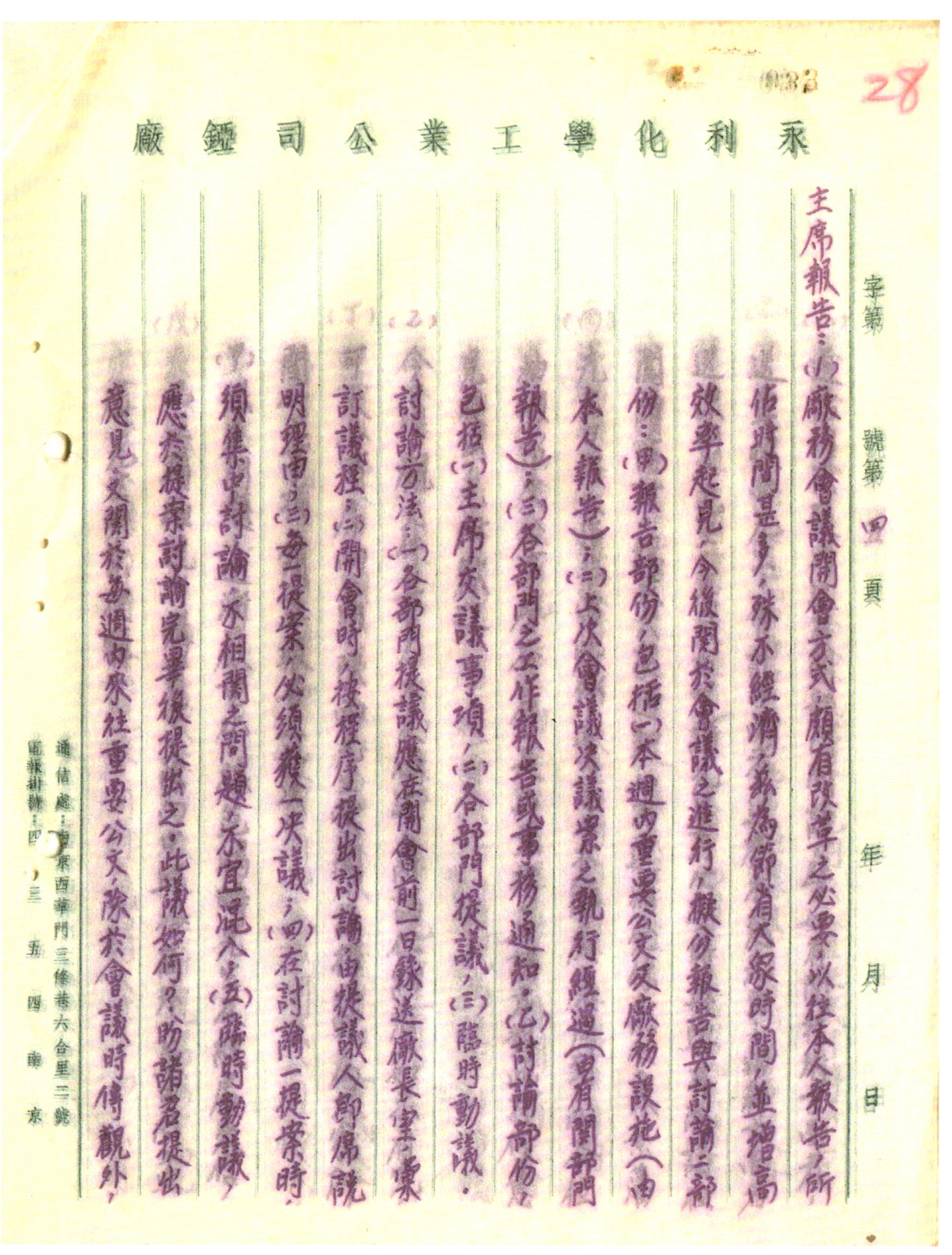

永利化學工業公司錏廠

字第　　號第四頁　　年　月　日

主席報告：（1）廠務會議開會方式，頗有改革之必要。以往本人報告，所佔時間甚多，殊不經濟，兼為節省大家時間，並增高效率起見，今後關於會議之進行，擬分報告與討論二部份：（甲）報告部份，包括（一）本週內重要公文及廠務設施（由本人報告），（二）上次會議決議案之執行經過（由有關部門報告），（三）各部門之工作報告或事務通知。（乙）討論部份，包括（一）主席交議事項，（二）各部門提議，（三）臨時動議。討論方法：（一）各部門提議應在開會前一日錄送廠長室，彙訂議程；（二）開會時，按程序提出討論，由提議人即席說明理由；（三）每一提案，必須獲一決議；（四）在討論一提案時，須集中討論，不相關之問題，不宜混入；（五）臨時動議，應於提案討論完畢後提出之。此議如何？盼諸君提出意見。又關於每週內來往重要公文，除於會議時傳觀外，

通信處：南京西華門三條巷六合里二號
電報掛號：四一三五四 南京

永利化學工業公司錏廠

字第　號第五頁　年　月　日

（乙）通常均係隨時送有關部門閱讀，譬如有關技術方面者，送章懷西先生；會計方面者，送劉本懋先生；物料方面者送謝同之先生。意自希望諸先生有必要時再與有關諸位閱讀商討，總求大家週知，如有遺漏，必係無心。陳景藩

（丙）先生日常工作非常忙碌，實際上亦難處處周到，盼各位抽暇常來公事房查看，是為至要。如諸君對此有何意見提出，尤所歡迎。

（乙）今日傳觀文件甚多，不及備述，請諸位細看，如未看完，

（丁）可來公事房向蕭、陳兩先生索閱。茲擇比較為大家所關心之事項，簡單報告之於次：

（甲）煤炭問題，逐漸嚴重化，據范鴻疇先生及總處來信，

（戊）已在積極進行購買中，除向中興洽商外，並由周子孟庵先生來京接購。

通信處：南京西華門三條巷六合里二號
電報掛號：四，三五四 南京

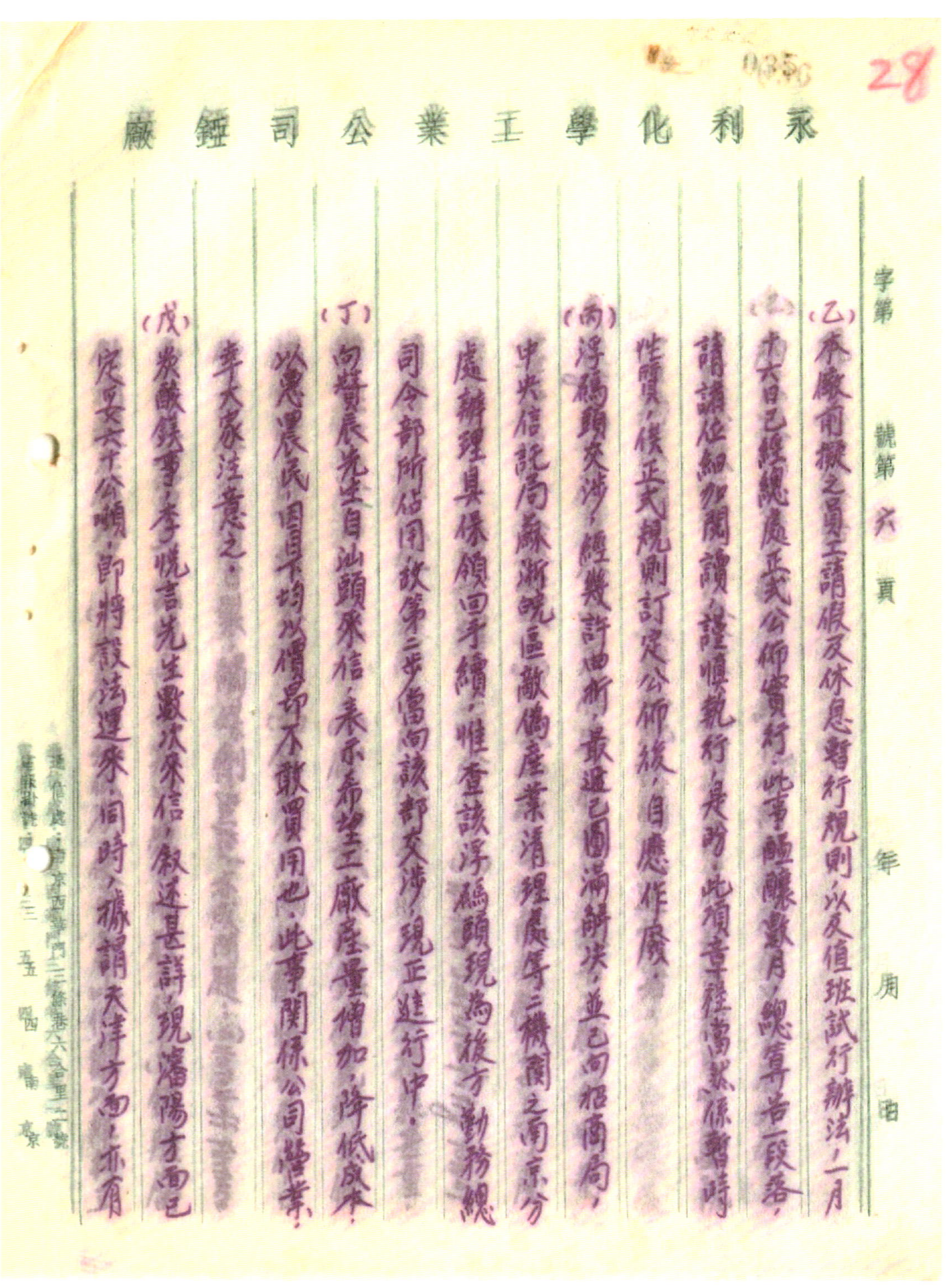

永利化學工業公司錏廠

字第　號第六頁

(乙)本廠前擬之員工請假及休息暫行規則，以及值班試行辦法，一月十六日已經總處正式公佈實行，此事醖釀數月，總算告一段落，請諸位細加閱讀，謹慎執行，是盼。此項章程當然係暫時性質，俟正式規則訂定公佈後，自應作廢。

(丙)浮碼頭交涉，經幾許曲折，最近已圓滿解決，並已向招商局、中央信託局蘇浙皖區敵偽產業清理處等三機關之南京分處辦理具保領回手續，惟查該浮碼頭現為後方勤務總司令部所佔用，故第二步當向該部交涉，現正進行中。

(丁)向贊辰先生自汕頭來信，表示希望工廠產量增加，降低成本，以惠農民，因目下均以價昂不敢買用也。此事關係公司營業，希大家注意之。

(戊)炭酸鉄事，李悦言先生數次來信，敘述甚詳，現瀋陽方面已定妥六十公噸，即將設法運來，同時，據謂天津方面亦有

年　月　日

通信處：南京西華門三條巷六合里二號
電報掛號：二三五四 南京

永利化學工業公司錏廠

字第　號第 ㄨ 頁　年　月　日

現貨，正在接洽。

(己)病床設備交涉，衛生實驗院合約仍在考慮中。另有50床已由行總蘇寧分署撥發，現暫存京小處，將來衛生實驗院

(辛)一百病床領到後，該廳此種設備送還該署。

(庚)Sayre先生本月十八日曾有信寄侯先生，報告工廠工作情形甚詳，内容大致如次：(1)一氧化碳氧化觸媒劑每日可產二百公斤，不久當可增至三百公斤；(2)Water saturating tower待修；(3)硫酸錏大粒結晶問題已獲解決，但錏損耗甚重；擬裝一四寸10x Scrubber；(4)壓縮機氣缸鑲套覓到三個備用件，即可換裝一套；(5)錏氣合成觸媒劑情形惡化，白貨不佳，勢須自製，觸媒劑Basket亦成問題；(6)Herreshoff Furnace已裝置妥當，且已試燒一二星期內，應可順利工作；(7)鍋爐腐蝕問題在研究中；(8)焦炭質地低劣，使氫氣比例難以維持正

通信處：南京西華門三條巷六合里二號
電報掛號：四二五四南京

037

永利化學工業公司錏廠

字第 號第八頁 年 月 日

常）（9）錏液每日産十九至二十噸。

（辛）本人上週去京，在經濟部抄來「日本供賠償工業情况一覽表」，該表内容甚雜，本人只就酸鹼兩項摘録，其中所示數字，殊足供吾人參考，盼大家多予注意，並盼發表意見，俾綜合向總處提出。此事關係公司大局甚大，同人萬勿忽視。中央日報十七、十八兩日，對於日償物資首批五十九萬餘噸拆遷我國之運輸辦法及次序均有詳細記載，今特提付傳觀。其中化工佔二萬四千噸，内容已畧見本人上次廠務會議之報告，茲不再贅。據經濟部工業司吳承洛司長對本人表示，將來接收日本碱廠時，願欲我公司表示意見，或竟官商合辦亦可。官方此種表示，亦頗值得吾人注意。至於錏廠請求賠償一事，已請總處進行交涉，不過政府方面似僅注重盟軍總部批准拆遷之物資，賠償問題，一時恐不會有何結論耳。此外，

通信處：南京卸甲甸郵政信箱第一號
電報掛號：四一五五四南京

永利化學工業公司錏廠

更有一點，吾人亦應牢記，即吾人請求賠償，應着眼全局，職廠方面，亦不宜放鬆，以後大家如獲得何種消息，均盼提出，供大家研究。

(3) 今日有兩事提出討論：

(甲) 前日周亞庵先生到廠，於歡迎閻幼甫先生席上，談起一事，謂范故總經理夫人與其嫂范靜生先生夫人現在滬上，無處安身，暫時寄住金城銀行宿舍，非常不妥，其嫂身體不好，就醫亦深感不便，以范先生生前對公司之功勳，身後遺族乃蕭條至此，實不合理。當經楊運珊先生提議於本廠廠址內建築范公紀念堂，附設住宅，使范公遺族永有安身之處，在座同人，全體鼓掌贊成。本人對於此一建議，亦甚贊成，惟紀念堂之建築乃永久紀念，非請專家設計不可，萬不宜草率從事，最好與籌建銅像事併案

039

28

永利化學工業公司錏廠

字第　號第十頁　年　月　日

辦理，倘汜夫人急不及待，不妨先於二村添建甲種住宅一所，將一村住房騰出一幢，請汜夫人暫行遷入，將來紀念堂成立之後，再作長久打算，不知諸位意見何如？據土木部估計，如款項籌妥，兩個月內即可完工，本人已請王道咸先生前去測量地址矣。如無異議，即可動手。

（乙）本月十七日中央日報載有焦作中福煤礦即將恢復生產之消息，並謂該礦現有存煤約十萬噸，將由燃料管理委員會收購，以濟京滬一帶之煤荒，現道清鐵路即可通車，煤運困難不復存在云。此雖係一好消息，本人已函傅曼雲先生即去燃料管理處調查，後悉該礦所產質屬無烟煤，用燒鍋爐，似不合宜，惟經查「中國礦業紀要」知其品質甚好，灰份為5.19%，硫磺為0.70%，揮發份為5.[illegible]%，固定碳則高達8[illegible]%，且亦有鍋爐砟一種，顧名思義，當可

通信處：南京西華門三條巷六合里二號
電報掛號：四二五四 南京

用於鍋爐，至少可與烟煤摻和而燒，不知諸位有何意見否？此

彭力夫：此種煤炭，火焰甚短，且多屬大塊，恐不好用。若必須使用，則除非將三座鍋爐同時開動，改開慢車，或可維持。

章懷西：以前塘沽鍋爐，曾以大同「紅煤」與烟煤混合燃燒，情形甚好。對

陳同之：中福公司之鍋爐，全係使用無烟煤，但其鍋爐烟筒下裝有風扇。又該礦所產亦多碎煤，恒佔40%以上。

劉本懋：無烟煤價格，在上海每噸九十七萬元，恐即使能用，亦非我廠財政所許可。

楊運綱：依本人看見，即使有錢去買，恐亦終不能用。據本人所知，燒焦炭末之鍋爐，構造迥異，其爐條必須離水管甚近，燒無烟煤與燒焦炭相似，我廠鍋爐，係依烟煤燃燒情形而設

計，恐即同時開用三座鍋爐，或再多，亦無濟於事。如萬一不得已，亦不妨以鍋爐一試，其[illegible]，平心而論，台灣煤炭質

通信處：南京西華門三條巷六合里二號
電報掛號：四二五四南京

永利化學工業公司錏廠

字第　號第十二頁　年　月　日

地雖不甚佳，但購買碓尚便捷，以目下情形度之，亦只有此路可走，不過，總處諸公似已對台灣不感興趣，為搶救煤荒計，吾人仍應有以鼓勵之。

彭力夫：湘廠開煤礦，既屬事在必行，何不趁川廠煤礦產煤無法利用之時，將人力物力移湘加緊進行？此乃解決煤荒之根本辦法，不知可向總處建議否？

主席：此事楊仲子先生已在籌劃，為救急起見，一方面可向總處建議，再購台煤若干；一方面對於中福無烟煤，應設法利用。本人耳聞首都電廠鍋爐因有Pulverizer設備，幾乎各種煤炭均能使用，關於此事，擬請楊運珊先生負責與S.T.Lee先生一談。

侯敬恩：本人因三天前電壓又有跳動，曾往訪首都電廠，經再三調查知該廠並未發現此種現象，其主要病源乃在浦口配電所。

通信處：南京西華門三條巷六合里二號
電報掛號：四三五四 南京

永利化學工業公司錏廠

最近由總綫分電供給浦鎮機廠，故我廠電力受其影响，當經本人提議於該支線上安裝O.C.B.設備，最近已恢復正常，該廠表示，願我廠速將長途電話裝妥，以便保持聯絡，此議實甚重要。又該廠近來亦飽受煤炭之恐慌，其現存貨質地極壞，且夾雜石塊甚多，工作頗難維持云。

又近來Delly與G.T.Lee兩先生在工作上時有見解不同之處，機械部同人每苦無所適從，屢需本人從中為其緩衝，方便進行工作。

楊運珊：Delly先生人甚好，易於接近，G.T.Lee先生則脾氣稍嫌固特，即以Herreshoff furnace點火工作而言，彼即不顧Specification之規定，堅持己見，(譬如規定上載明，此種火磚砌成之爐灶，必須撤火緩燒，徐徐增加溫度，歷二三十日，始可正式開用，但G.T.Lee先生則謂所用火磚堆存已久，內部已乾，毋需緩燒，主張三兩日

通信處：南京西華門三條巷六合里二號
電報掛號：四二五四 南京

28

043

永利化學工業公司錏廠

字第　號第十四頁　年　月　日

即可正式使用之）本人既無法反對彼之意見，而章魯兩君又碰彼之釘子，故祇好聽其自然，或者彼之主張有良好之結果。

章懷西：應將二人之工作劃分清楚，明白告知，以免衝突。

主席：工作早已經侯先生分派清楚，Daly先生主持設計及操作，G.T.Lee先生則主持安裝與建造。兩位先生或因對公司感情甚好，急於求功，遂不免稍有抵觸耳。吾人應居中善為應付，俾得發揮所長，為我廠用。

金玉奇：茲有一小事報告：查廢曆年初，廠外菜販將停市三天，農場方面，擬於明日配給每戶（不分員工）蔬菜八斤，附葱一束。收價一千五百元。

主席：此舉甚善。

通信處：南京西華門三條巷六合里二號
電報掛號：四三五四　南京

永利化学工业公司关于錏碱各厂损失惨重恳予拨给日本拆卸之厂机器以资复兴事呈经济部文（抄件）
（一九四七年一月二十七日）

抄件

299

永利化學工業公司錏廠用箋

總番第8號第一頁

抄呈經濟部文

事由：呈為公司錏碱各廠損失慘重懇予撥給日本撤卸之廠以資復興由

竊公司錏碱各廠，自抗戰軍興，即遭淪陷，向人東國存與存之大義，毅然西撤，損失慘重。勝利復員，曾蒙鈞部令將原有各廠先後發還，并由公司將接收經過情形呈報各在案。惟兩廠等被敵人佔據八年之久，粗濫使用，毁壞之慘，目不忍睹，雖經半年以上之努力修理，舉債累累，勉強開工出貨，而其產量仍不及戰前之半，實已無法恢復舊觀，祇有靜待　政府於向日本索回賠償時，償還現金，或於日本撤卸工廠，撥給工廠，以謀補充擴展，重建化學工

中華民國36年1月27日

廠址江蘇六合卸甲甸　通信處南京頤和路廿三號　電話三三九九六、電報掛號四三五四

300

永利化學工業公司錏廠用牋

第　號第二頁

業之助。據聞「關於日本賠償案内民營事業概歸經濟部核辦」等情，逖聽之下，不勝興奮。現日人金錢賠償，既時不可期，而撤卸工廠以爲賠償損失之用，又經明令規定，則國内被日人佔據損毁之廠，似有接受此撤卸工廠以爲賠償損失一部分之機會。公司事業，素賴鈞部維護，用敢據情申請，懇於此次日本撤卸工廠，撥給永利錏碱工廠各一，并盼於工廠拆運時，能允公司派員參加，俾對於機件之取捨，得以權衡，免致虚耗噸位，公私兩益。遍切陳請，敬候鈞裁，賜予逾格成全，無任厚幸。謹呈

經濟部

永利化學工業公司謹呈

中華民國36年4月27日

廠址江蘇六合縣卸甲甸　通信處南京頭和路廿三號　電話三三九九六　電報掛號四三五四

经济部工业司关于永利化学工业公司硫酸铔厂硝酸设备被日劫去使用已逾龄洽令日方赔偿新机事给永该公司的函（抄件）（一九四七年二月二十日）

165

硝酸厂专卷

中华民国卅六年二月廿四日收到

抄经济部工业司二月廿日来函

前奉 交下

贵公司来呈一件以本公司硫酸铔厂之硝酸设备前被日劫去使用业已逾龄请转洽令日方赔偿新机一案业经由部函请外交部转洽并批知在案兹原呈

附需壹份即希

查照补送以便应用为荷此致

永利化学工业公司

经济部工业司启

谢为杰、赵如晏关于赔偿问题致傅冰芝的函（一九四七年三月十日）

144

照抄卅六年三月十日謝為杰趙如晏兩先生由東京來函

冰芝賜鑒：尊函二月廿四、廿六兩函及玫芝致我芝（UF-51）函均奉悉。

（一）如晏及杰於二月十二晚乘車去九州，三月六日回到東京，在外廿二天，除詳查硝酸廠設備外，尚參觀硫酸、肥料有關之工廠，茲將簡報如下：

（a）硝酸廠設備，日人由我廠取來，多半殘缺不全，且有放置不用或使用破損者。彼等需有日本軍部式之硝酸廠四套，工作簡單，效力甚低下。我廠設備取來修改，用Burners, Coolers及towers，仍照軍部式方法，添配Blowers, Pumps, Air filter and one extra tower，並日式之濃硝酸塔一套，換言之日出十五噸之濃硝酸，現在原來四套尚在工作中，此後來之一套，已被美軍點封，留待我方解決。如晏與杰將我方設備按圖一一詳點，回東京之後，數日內將整理打字，成為詳表，再赴美軍討論。

（b）交涉歸還，此點恐尚多口舌，因美軍方面甚注重原則，即歸還物資，當為原來劫去之原物為限。至原物之損壞及一切交通、營業等之損失，將仍劃入賠償項內。美軍歸還與賠償，係分開兩機關辦理，手續非常麻煩認真。如晏與杰希望能設法交涉，先將東洋高壓之日本式一套（即中間有我廠設備及日本設備之15噸廠）能先交與我廠，運回裝起，以便開工出貨，同時其他硝酸廠之一切損失，一一提出要求賠償。賠償手續即使拖長，而不大影響硝酸出貨。此點等已多次與我國駐日代表團各專家（法律、歸還等專門人員），加以討論，準備充份材料與理由後，再前往與美軍交涉，結果如何，誠難預料，惟有努力為之。本團內國際法專家龔錢博士，編有《戰害賠償法要點》，特抄呈以供參考，此為未發表之文獻，只供團內參考，請抄一份寄總處參考。

（c）此次除清查硝酸廠設備外，尚多方設法乘此外出機會，多多參觀研究日本之酸鹼及有關工廠。在此前呈函中，未曾提及一字參觀工廠事，因美軍檢查信件甚嚴，如事前提及，則出外行動極不自由，故如晏與杰在未出發之前，曾與三井、三菱作種種接洽，以為参觀之廠之準備，以不至『出麻煩』為原則，多處参觀，本函係託與人帶上海報部，故得詳為報告，来函請不必提及此事。（據團內往返信件，分兩種辦法：(一)普通每星期一次或兩次，由美軍用機運遞報部，(二)特别函件託團中要人，有機會時，親帶上海報部，此種特帶信件，機會較少）。此次参觀工廠，有不同方法之合成錏廠四個，硫酸錏廠四個，硫酸廠六個，蘇爾維鹼廠三個，煉焦廠及副產三個，以及V_2O_5觸媒廠，硝酸廠，硝酸錏廠，人造汽油，玻璃廠，水泥廠等等，及三井鑛山之每日出產一萬四千噸之煤鑛，人造尿素，木酒精，福麿林，有機染料等等。因在南京時，Dely君對於煤氣廠之氣去硫問題，(desulfurization of Raw Gas)及硫酸錏之結晶及V_2O_5之Catalyst之自製各問題，欲加以研究，故吳與杰對於此各點，特别注意，並与各廠技術人員詳細討論，而於時對機件親為察看，並索有圖樣、工作報告、方法等。製碱方面，對於滷水中Mg^{++} Ca^{++}之設備及方法，及各母液之成份，炭酸塔之作用与效能，及副產之製造，($CaCl_2$, $NaHCO_3$, $NaOH$等)，亦特别加以注意，收集材料、圖件、筆記等，均盡力詳細條成報告，以應我公司各廠之参考。大略言之，日本之製錏工業，皆模倣歐美各國之方法；製碱則一方採襲Solvay，一方自行改良。吳與杰（所采工廠，三井系統与三菱系統均不同，分述如下：

(I) 大牟田方面：(1) Dupont Co.'s Claude Process Synthetic NH_3 (1000 atm.), (2) Synthetic Methanol (3) Monsanto Process H_2SO_4 (4) $(NH_4)_2SO_4$, (5) Electrolysis NaOH, (6) Coke Oven & By-Product of German Process, (7) Low Pressure HNO_3, Japanese Mulilling (?) Process (8) German Fisher's Process Synthetic Gasoline, (9) Dupont's NH_3 & CO Catalysts (10) Synthetic Urea (11) Coal Mine (12) Zn & Products (13) Organic Dyes & Chemicals，均係三井系。

(II) 八幡之牧山及黑崎各廠：(1) 旭硝子之Glass (2) Solvay Soda & By-Products, (3) I. G. Farben Process之Synthetic NH_3 (300 atm.) (4) $(NH_4)_2SO_4$ (5) H_2SO_4 日本(的)式法 (6) Kopper's Process Coke Oven & By-products (7) Organic Dyes & Chemicals.

以上均為三菱系。

146

三頁

(Ⅲ) 下関港曹達工廠：(1) Dupont, Synthetic Methanol & NH_3 Combine Process Plant（中间CO作成甲醇精），(2) H_2SO_4，(3) $(NH_4)_2SO_4$，(4) Urea，(5) Synthetic Formalin，(6) Urotropin (Hexymethalme tetramine)，$ZnSO_4$ & By-Products（三井系）。

(Ⅳ) 宇部方面：(1) 宇部 Solvay Process Soda，(2) Fanser's Process Synthetic NH_3 (Italian Process) 300 t/m.，(3) H_2SO_4，(4) $(NH_4)_2SO_4$，HNO_3 Acid Pressure Type，57 #/D，Italian Process，(5) NH_4NO_3（宇部曹達系）。

(Ⅴ) 德山方面：(1) 德山 Solvay Process Soda，(2) By-Product Cement Plant（利用蒸馏废液），(3) Ca、Mg及錫蠟之精製，(4) 研磨之磚石粉混，日產1000吨之設備。

(Ⅵ) 大阪方面：(1) 錦武之工場 Catalysts，(2) 前田工廠。

以上各廠，均擬作詳細報告，整理資料，以供參考，實深厚重。

(二) 日本各地沿鐵路線之各大城市之工業區，除京都奈良兩處外，均被美軍轟炸，美軍投彈，似均有目的而且精確。大略言之，与軍火有關之軍械、軍火、飛機廠，用炸彈全毀之。一般工業區用燒夷彈，燒毀民房及木製倉房，使彼時失去工作能力，而將來仍有用並似預知必登陸佔領日本，故對於肥料工廠、交通鐵道等均予以保留，則佔領時有許多方便之處。

(三) 日本城市之敵人受最苦，工人次之，而農村則仍富足。農民漁民，比戰前更為有利：(1)日元不值錢，舊債容易還清，(2)有實物可出售，(3)房舍未受轟炸，衣物食物糧食，(4)美軍鼓勵農漁生產，無內戰之虞，環境安定，市區与交通稍繁，缺乏年少強壯軍士再盡力改善中，与我國有同處，有不同處。我國戰勝國，農村尚不如被戰敗國也。

(四) 工業方面，原料極感缺乏，尤以煤之質与量為最。美軍鼓勵肥料、鐵、煤生產，凡以上工人，均得特別之配給，工廠方面，亦有特別之協助，原料、交通，亦儘力優先，多廠均作三年再建計劃，逐步實行。在此情形之下，工作自多方便，較中國又多不同之處。

(五) 關於書籍方面，東京因大炸之後，書籍較少，京都舊書店中購到(1)植物分類地理一書，昭和十九年，京都帝大，北村四郎氏編，又購到(1)日滿支工業年鑑，昭和16年，(2)滿洲工礦總覽，(3)輕金屬年鑑等書，而回時均帶回。

(六) 廠內煤炭問題如何？經濟問題最近如何？至為懸念，請隨時示知為禱。專此敬請

鈞安

職 謝為杰 謹上

硝酸廠自製機件

品名	件數	價值（戰前價）
天車	2	CN$ 749.56
鏈鹵桶	1	816.36
人力天車	2	1,700.34
各種機械零件	——	74,873.28
		CN$ 78,139.54

经济部关于永利化学工业公司请求拆迁日本铔碱工厂各一以充赔偿本公司之损失事给该公司的批复（抄件）

（一九四七年三月十七日）

附：清单一份

301

抄經濟部批

京工(36)字第三六七七一号
中華民國卅六年三月十七日

具呈人 永利化學工業公司

卅六年一月廿七日呈一件為請拆遷日本錏鹼工廠各一以充賠償本公司之損失由

呈悉。查日本賠償各盟國之物資據盟軍總部提出日本初步可提供賠償之工業設備清單僅有機器鋼鉄冶煉輕金屬軋製酸鹼造船及火力電廠等六大項其中我國應獲得之種類及數量業由行政院賠償委員會按照我國應分得之比率擬定提請拆遷並由該會就我國可能獲得該項賠償設備之總額內按其性質分別配交國營或民營其配交民營之設備經由該會第二次委員會議決議「可供民營之設備可以價配使用」等語各在案經查酸鹼一項其配交民營者計有硫酸廠一廠年產量一萬一千噸廠設大沽口燒鹼廠兩廠其一廠年產量四千八百噸廠設海南島其另一廠年產六千六百噸廠設海州該三廠既經配交民營其關於建廠及拆遷等項自應早為準備惟該項酸鹼工廠僅有三廠而國內經營該項工業之同業頗多應由該業同業聯合共同經營並由本部核定將該三廠交由辦理該項工業著有成績之工廠永利化學工業公司久大鹽業公司天原電化廠天利氮氣廠及中國火柴原料廠等五廠主持辦理並分為一、永利化學工業公司久大鹽業公司及其他同業工廠為一集團二、天原電化廠天利氮氣廠及其他同業工廠為一集團三、中國火柴原料廠及其有關各火柴廠為一集團即由各主持之工廠分別邀集國內各酸鹼廠及各火柴廠參加投資共同經營如有其他化學工廠願意參加投資者並可准其參加經營至各工廠所受戰事損失之賠償事項應俟行政院賠償委員會統籌全局決定辦法後再行辦理除檢發日本賠償之酸鹼工廠三廠清單及民營工廠承辦日本賠償酸鹼工廠辦法分行各主持工廠立即進行並通知中華化學工業會轉知各化學工廠外茲檢發該項清單及辦法各一份仰即依照於奉到本批後五日內派遣負責代表來部洽商進行辦法為要此批

附發清單及辦法各一份

303

COPY

ELECTROLYTIC CAUSTIC SODA PLANTS

Plant No.	16	18
Company (Factory)	Nippon Soda K.K. (Kyashu) 九洲	東亞合成化學工業 Toa Gosei Kagaku Kogyo K.K. (Takaoka) 高岡
Location City	Karitamachi 苅田町	Takaoka 高岡
Prefecture	Eukuoka 福岡	Toyama 富山
Number & Type cells Diaphram	125 Nankano Bititter 中野	360 Allen-Moore
Designed NaOH	4,800 tons	6,600 tons
Capacity $CaCl_2$ (Metric tons per year) ? CaCl(OCl)	15,000 tons	
Liquid Cl_2 (Metric tons per year)	2,880 tons	

Detailed information not received.

LIST OF FACTORIES WITH CONTACT SULFURIC ACID SETS TO BE TAKEN INTO CUSTODY AND CONTROL

No.	Company	Construction Date	Factory	Location	No. of sets	Design capacity
13	Nihon Jukagaku 日本重化學	1939	Amagasaki 尼崎	Amagasaki, Hyogo 兵庫	1	11,000 T.

Company: Nippon Jyukagaku Kogyo Co. Ltd.
Factory: Amagasaki Factory.
Capacity of Sets 30ton/day
Type osame

EQUIPMENT IN CONTACT SULPHURIC ACID PLANT

Quantity	Item	Type	Capacity
2	Furance	Herreshoff Style H.19.6 foot. Col.8 vol. 1169m^3	20 T/day
1	Dust collector	Osame style 4.6m/m Vol. 86.8 m (each one 2.3 mxx3m separated in two room)	7000m^3/h.
-	Hot cottrell		-
1	Mist cottrell	Osame style 6.6m 9.4m Vol.10.5m Pole 49 (each one 3.3m 4.7m separeted in two room)	6000m^3/h
2	Drying tower	diam. 1.5H.6 lm Vol. 15.6m^3	
1	Scrubbing tower		
1	Gas cooler	Diam 1.4m. 5.8m	4000m^3/h
1	pre-heater	Diam 1.65 h 4.5	2000m^3/h
1	Pre-heater furnace	2m x 2m H. 5m.	150 Kg/h Provided. coke 6.500 Cal. up
1	Heat exchanger	1.6 m x 4.5 m	
1	Heat exchanger	1.4 m x 4.5 m	
1	Converter	No. 1 Diam 2.34m H. 1.372m	95%
1	"	No. 2 Diam 2.34m H. 2.56m	95%
1	Absorption tower	Diam. 2m h 6m Vol. 22.1 m^3	
1	Oleum tower	Diam. 2m H. 6m	

305

SECRET

2	Turbo-blower	Hidachi style air pressure 1.25 Kg/cm 50 HP.	4500 m^3/h
1	"	Ebara style air pressure 1.25 Kg/cm 50 HP.	5000 m^3/h
1	Blower for gas coller		2000 m^3/h
2	Circulating acid storage tanks	2m x 2m	
2	Gauge tanks	1.5m x 1.5 m	
2	Surge tanks	1.5m x 1.5m	
2	Storage tanks	169.7 m^3	
1	Storage tank	166.2 m^3	
1	Storage tank	50.2 m^3	
2	Pumps	Vertical pump 35 HP diam 125 mm	65 m^3/h
2	"	10 HP Diam 75mm	15 m^3/h
4	"	7.5 H 65mm	15 m^3/h
3	"	Groundless 7.5 H made of lead	15 m^3/h
2	"	Groundless 7.5 H (made of acid proof iron)	

Irrigation cooler pipe method.

1 set	65 mm 750 mm (for 98% acid)	65 M^3/h
1 set	65 mm 140 mm (Oleum)	15 M^3/h

范鸿畴和傅冰芝关于赔偿问题的往来信函（抄件）（一九四七年三月二十六日至二十七日）

309

照抄傅廠長卅六年三月廿六日致范鴻疇先生函底原文

永利化學工業公司錏廠用牋

第　號第一頁

鴻疇兄台鑒　昨來京偕本懋同之兩兄往訪經濟部工業司吳司長吳君笑謂限
五日內來決定辦法然乎　弟則告以並非負責來作決定不過願聞詳情且盼保
留至侯先生回才作決定而已吳君表示允諾據該部擬以硫酸廠交永久集團辦
地點在大沽口而以海州燒鹼廠交天原集團海南燒鹼廠交火柴廠集團如表
同意可派人至日本親查各該廠何項機器須拆將來即據所要機件估價
公家包運至上海設廠地點可考慮變通每一集團祇能擔任資金百分之三十
乃至四十五其餘未詳之點可協商解決燒鹼廠在日應附有動力設備云云關
於辦廠種類　愚　意以燒鹼廠為上硫酸廠次之蓋戰前旭公即欲與民生公司
在川合辦三十噸燒鹼廠派同事兩位去鞏縣兵工新廠實習值戰事發而罷
侯先生去年出國前曾有在塘沽或青島設立電解燒鹼廠之擬議　弟意侯

廠址江蘇六合縣卸甲甸　通信處南京頤和路廿三號　電話三三九九六　電報掛號四三五四

310

永利化學工業公司錏廠用牋

第　號第二頁

先生回對於燒鹼廠或仍有興趣至於日本硫酸廠亦係鈀觸媒法與我廠相似如歸我辦自屬駕輕就熟不過此時錏廠有百一二十噸硫酸之設備儘足敷出產百五十噸硫酸錏之用單獨出售硫酸恐未必有如許市場其獲利未必有燒鹼之厚究竟電解燒鹼是否較硫酸為更合乎需要且更可獲利弟在此未能臆斷聊舉所知以作貢獻而已參候

台安

弟　爾敬上　卅六年三月廿六日

再者吳君云部中選取三集團承辦賠償工廠之用意在於信任三集團能達成任務不為盟軍總部所指摘如是而已又及

中華民國　年　月　日

廠址江蘇六合縣卸甲甸　通信處南京頤和路廿三號　電話三三九九六　電報掛號四三五四

抄件

311

照抄范鸿畴先生三月廿七日覆傅先生函原文

永利化學工業公司錏廠用牋

第　號第　頁

冰兄賜鑒：廿六日手示敬悉。賠償工廠事，弟意能以得到燒碱廠爲好，因新廠計劃中有燒碱廠，如能分到此廠，則美借款亦可少用。兄謂如何？經部方面應否再去一談？乞酌。手此即請
大安

弟鴻疇敬上　三月廿七日

中華民國　年　月　日

廠址江蘇六合縣卸甲甸　通信處南京頤和路廿三號　電話三三九九六　電報掛號四三五四

范鸿畴、傅冰芝、赵如晏、谢为杰等关于赔偿问题的往来信函（一九四七年三月二十六日至四月十九日）

抄寄 川總碱廠

附件略

163

永利化學工業公司
YUNGLI CHEMICAL INDUSTRIES, LTD.

No. 1.

36年3月20日

永公賜鑒：

(一)由九州調查回團後，職等與盟總中管理還歸物資之負責人員商討後，同赴美軍商談。美軍方面注重數字，故請我方將調查情形，用表格式列出，作為報告。職等整理材料，並打字等，共編成26頁之詳細報告表，昨日始全部完成，由代表團用公函送美軍研究。職等閱計來日之第一項任務，已告結束。茲特將報告副本一份寄渝處，再寄我公，請查收為禱。

(二)調查結果。此次調查，知我硝酸設備，損失甚大。日人當年劫取時，並未全部運回，運回後，又不全部使用，彼等因採用日本陸軍省第一硝酸製造程序，選用我設備中之重要者，再配以日製之設備，成為一套，據云可日產15 Tons之硝酸。至於其他設備，棄置在旁，遺失生銹，在所不免。故在調查詳表中，所餘機件，實在甚少，(m) Missing 多於(s) found。而(s)項目下，有完全生銹破爛，不能作用者。

永利化學工業公司
YUNGLI CHEMICAL INDUSTRIES, LTD.

No. 2.　　　　年　月　日

甚为痛心。

(三)職等对于此次調查之结果，認为我方如能将日人全部設備取回接装，尚有出貨之望，不然则不成一套，在我方損失太大矣。根據以上情形，在美军管理歸还物资之部门，讨论及之。理由如下：

(1)硝酸全套设備，在製造程序上，各機件为不可分離者，我廠当日为一全套之设備，故现時亦需要全套，始能有用，如折散之後，在中國，在日本，均無完全之设備，兩皆無用。(2)中國現甚需要硝酸，硝酸进口運輸，皆为困難，非在本國製造不可。上面方面，製造 Sulfur black dye 需用硝酸甚急，而黑色染料，在中國一般人民衣服之習慣，最为普通。

彼等口頭答覆如下：彼等对以上情形，均甚同情，惟歸还物资之原则，在遠東委員会议决：(1)凡歸还物资，只限其原有物资。並只在日本海口交还。此原则如無改變，彼等無法另案辦理。故建议如下：

165

永利化學工業公司
YUNGLI CHEMICAL INDUSTRIES, LTD.

No. 3　　　　年　　月　　日

①凡永利原有之機件，作爲歸還物資，由該部門辦理。②其他日人配備之物資，因非永利物資，配成一套者，由中國代表團另向總部提供理由及意見，申請作爲賠償之一部份，同時歸於永利。但賠償係另一部門之工作，彼等無法辦理。

四）職等回團後（小組負責人員）研究以上各點，知賠償之原則，以消除日本作戰潛力之目的，並非以各盟國之需要爲目的，故在化工部門之賠償工廠，只限接觸法硫酸廠，及大部電解法之鹼廠，以消除製造發煙硫酸及綠氣之製造潛伏力。原則既已在遠東委員會決定好，硝酸設備，能否通融，甚成問題。現團中韓三組組長之意，謂爲一方面收集準備充分之材料及理由，待朱團長由中國回日後，再向最高總部，直接交涉。或有希望，現將部份負責人交涉，彼等不能對原則上，有權更改。無何結果也。職等即着手整理資料，以證明：①硝酸設備非全套取回，不

永利化學工業公司
YUNGLI CHEMICAL INDUSTRIES, LTD.

No. 4　　　　年　月　日

能公用。我廠以前為完全之一套。現時取回，如不成套，不能製造硝酸。（我方不能要求日方賠償金錢，以購買美國新設備，因此次大戰之賠償，以物資賠償為限，與上次大戰後金錢賠款不同），中國現時甚需在國內自製硝酸。②永利運到日本之硝酸設備，係在戰爭時代所增設者。日本和平工業所需之硝酸，可以設法查出，吾人設法証明此一套硝酸設備取去後，並不影響日本和平工業硝酸之需用量。則或亦為交涉之理由。以上資料，恐須若干日始能準備就緒，同時參觀工廠之資料，亦須整理，並加緊為之。

（三）德利君及李佐華君之信件，均已收到，亦有力証件之一。証明我廠當年為完全之設備。德利君出，中倘注意以下各點：①在日探訪關於硝酸廠用之釩接觸劑。②硫酸鍾之能否問題。③製衣鍾之觸媒劑問題。以上三問題，均我職等參觀時特別

167

永利化學工業公司
YUNGLI CHEMICAL INDUSTRIES, LTD.

No. 5　　　　年　　月　　日

留意之问题中，不得而知。就以上三问题，均有图样，及制造之方法。并得锰煤剂之样品数种，拟详作报告，以供我厂研究之参考。兹寄李德两君各一函，请代转为感。（本函由邮局寄，故两函均极简，请代为解释简单原因，并请将李呈我公三月十四函之章范情形，告知两君为感。）

（六）最近美国对华态度，赔偿事在报上又呈活跃。现美军已开始请中国方面，视察各指定作为赔偿工厂。先就工作机工厂，每次视察团中请专家两三人，详细查看，以备选择之用。据云，在赔偿各工厂中，有毫无损失者。机械方面，外国货，日本货，新旧均有。对于接收赔偿之国家，中国、菲律宾比较热心，澳洲次之，其他各国，均不甚注意也。

（七）我公司对于赔偿事项，未知最在国内进行如何？念念，如能申请硝酸、硫酸（重加），及工作机械若干，则将来湖南及塘沽，南京、四川各铁工厂，亦可充实。甲事如即请

公安

职 谢为杰
赵[illegible] 同启
三月廿四

再者，前次我公询及杰回国日期事，现硝酸厂详细调查机件事，已告结束，如先回国，一切以后事项，请赵如晏兄留东京办理，亦无不可，请示知尊意为祷。职杰又及。

永利化學工業公司錏廠駐京辦事處

鴻疇兄台鑒：昨來京偕本慈同之兩兄往訪經濟部工業司吴司長，吴君笑謂限五日内來決定辦法，然乎，則告以並非負責來作決定，不過願聞詳情，且盼保留至侯先生回方作決定而已。吴君表示允諾。據談，部擬以硫酸廠交永久集團辦，地點在大沽口，而以海洲燒鹼廠交天原集團，海南燒鹼廠交大柴廠集團，如表同意，可派人至日本親查各該廠何項機器須拆，將來即據所要機件估價，公家包運至上海設廠，地點可考慮變通，每一集團祇能擔任資金百分之三十乃至四十五，其餘未詳之點，可協商解決。燒鹼廠在日應附有動力設備云云。關於辦廠種類，愚意以燒鹼廠為上，硫酸廠次之，蓋戰前旭公即欲與民生公司在川合辦三十噸燒鹼廠，派同事兩位去犨縣兵工新廠實習，值戰事發而罷。侯先生去年出國前

字第　號第　頁　民國卅六年三月廿六日

154

永利化學工業公司錏廠駐京辦事處

字第　號第　頁　民國　年　月　日

曾有在塘沽或青島設立電解燒鹼廠之擬議，弟意侯先生回籌於燒鹼廠或仍有興趣，至於日本硫酸廠亦係釩觸媒法，與我廠相似，如歸我辦，自屬駕輕就熟，不過此時錏廠有百一二十噸硫酸之設備儘足敷出產百五十噸硫酸錏之用，單獨出售硫酸恐未必有如許市場，其獲利未必有燒鹼之厚，究竟電解燒鹼是否應較硫酸為更合乎需要，且更可獲利，弟在此未能臆斷，聊舉所知以作貢獻而已。匆候

台安

弟　爾敬上

171

中華民國駐日代表團用箋

永公賜鑒：三月廿四函中，附德利李佐華兩君各一短函，因係普通郵包，未能詳述各工廠情形，茲有團員赴滬，特託帶此函，請代轉交為禱。函中有德利君所問之Uhde Process catalyst及V_2O_5各問題，將另詳作報告，敬請

鈞安

職謝爲杰謹上

三月廿六日

抄傅先生卅六年四月六日致謝冰叔趙如晏兩先生函

冰叔
如晏兩兄台鑒：久未寄函，常覺歉然。今日爲星期日，得有餘暇清理積件，然當此柳媚花明之日，又不好終日伏案，仍復不能作事，奈何奈何。查卷二月廿六日之後，似即不曾寄書，惟於接三月十日來書，即曾囑盧鵬翔兄代筆寄郵票，頃聞實未曾寄，記憶有誤，遂致稽延，抱歉之至。

三月十日一信之外，並接二十、廿六日各書，欣悉一一。

侯先生上月廿二日到印度，約定滯印十日間即回國，現想不日抵滬。叔兄回國之期，愚意請俟侯先生抵京再定，因侯先生或有任務須兄在日辦理，回後再往自不方便，即使別無任務，亦不過使兄略誤歸期耳已。

迄今爲止，爲賠償事，總處於三月卅一日有文呈經濟部及行政院賠償委員會，是殆爲最後一次之總請求，以後再有呈文，當不過磋商細則而已。上項呈文總處或已抄底備查。關於部中批示吾公司之辦法，則有三月十七日經濟部批一件，並附民營工廠承辦日本賠償酸鹼工廠辦法十餘條，此件已由陳景兄抄底寄覽。接批文後，弟等曾訪吳澗東司長面談，其結果曾於三月廿六日函

報范鴻疇先生兹將抄底附覽兄等對此問題意見如何仍盼隨時見示以便由各方面折衷至當決定最後取捨

關於我硝酸廠設備情形誠如尊示所提非全套不能供我利用而欲得全套則事涉不同部門能通過於此不能通過於彼支離滅裂誠令人莫知適從仍望兩兄努力折衝必期於我有利

關於向部另請賠償電力工作機各節前數次晤及吳澗東氏亦曾提過吳似謂電力當儘公用機關如首都電廠之類優先取得且單位在萬啓羅以上無合我廠用者工作機則聞將由民營各工廠在滬組織聯合工廠經營未必能割裂分用所聞如此尚待向經部打聽好在侯先生即回吳氏尚待與侯先生詳談也

匆候

台安

弟 爾放 上

19存

永利化學工業公司錏廠

字第　　號第　　頁

汝叔
如晏兄同鑒：前由總處抄來經濟部京工字第三六七七一號批，暨其附件「民營工廠承辦日本賠償酸鹼工廠辦法」及賠償工廠名稱所在地產量等詳表各一份，曾已抄寄，諒荷 察收。兄等對於部批，有何 卓見，該項賠償各廠，兄等曾親見或知其詳情否？我公司以承辦何類何廠為合宜，便祈 惠示，以供參考，是感。順頌

旅祺

弟 傅爾攽 謹啟

卅六年四月十一日

據總處通知，致兄將於今日到滬，留一週來廠，併聞。

廠址：江蘇省六合縣卸甲甸　通訊處：南京頤和路二十三號　電話：三三九九六　電報掛號四三五四　南京

抄送192　附件未抄　第43次合佈

冰致
兩公鈞鑒：

(一)冰公四月六日手示及關於賠償工廠與鴻公往來討論兩函抄件，均已奉悉。郵票亦已收到，請勿念。

(二)函中詢及賠償工廠意見事，職等以為經濟部以前限定電解燒碱廠交天原及大崇集團，硫酸交永久集團承辦事。想因原定賠償只限30%，故化學工廠只願申請三數個，惟現時賠償百分數中國已增至45%，故此條件或可放寬。茲附寄報紙一份，請參閱。我廠最需電解碱廠，次及硫酸廠事，職等甚為贊同，並本此目的在此間特別留意之。

(三)關於設廠地點之事，職等愚意如下：(a)電解廠最好放南京，次為塘沽。(b)硫酸廠最好放南京，原因如下：

(1)南京接近市場需要，運輸、安裝、及管理之便利。燒碱在上海、漢口、廣州，均有相當大之用途，塘沽碱廠供給北方，南京燒碱供給中南兩方，再者所產氫氣可通入錏廠製錏，所產氯氣，可用龍潭石灰石製成漂白粉，供給在無錫上海一帶紗廠紡織之用。在南京之硫酸廠可與四川之錏廠配合以製硫酸錏，或有餘之酸尚可在上海一帶出售。

(2)電解燒碱廠在塘沽為第二適當之地，原因管理方便，惟氫氣出路，須另設法，如製成鹽酸，恐大量市場及運輸，在天津將成問題。酸廠在塘沽目前似不能独

193

立生存，市場及運輸均成問題。日本硫酸工廠之設立，均因先有肥料廠及其他化學工廠之需要，而後設之。並非先設立酸廠於某地，以等待其他工廠之設立。在海南島及海州各地，目前均有同樣困難，此事實向經濟部方面，需一一解說。

(二)硝酸廠歸還事，一方面已電外交部請電駐美F.E.C.代表力爭將整套交還永利外，另一方面，正與代表團內之法律顧問，及SCAP之法律顧問商討如何解釋F.E.C.之條文，使在可能範圍之內，設法將全套取回，因若只限定以前在中國之機件收回，則只有Burner及Tower，其餘均殘破不能再用，全部無用，如能全套收回，尚或有用，現正設法提出以下請求原因：(1)化學設置，非全套不可能生產。(2)中國現甚需要硝酸，非全套取回，不能立即作用。交涉結果，當再續報。

(三)最近公司計劃如何？生產如何？無日不懸念之中，關於職等在日工作之方針，請隨時指示，以便與國內連係，是所至禱！敬請

鈞安

職 趙如晏
謝為杰 謹啓
四月十四日

伯苓、鳳舉兩先生處已特致意

囑購植物圖書當留意尋購，請釋念

抄滬前總(36)字第四二號函　　卅六年四月十九日

逕啓者：頃由津轉到行政院賠償委員會卅六年四月七日京字第四五四號通知一件，以公司前呈被敵硝酸廠設備朽壞，請責令日本賠償一案，應以盟軍總部最近所訂表格填報，並須繳交物權及被敵證件，囑依式填報等因；茲將原文及表式照抄一份附上，即請察閱，查照前經填報各項文謝曹趙兩君帶台者，依式填明寄下，以便呈復爲盼。此致

鍾廠

附抄件

永利化學工業公司總管理處啓

永利化学工业公司关于赔偿问题的信函（一九四七年三月二十六日）

COPY　　　　172

Dear Mr. Dely:　　　　March 26, 1947.

I wrote a very brief note to you on March 24, because that letter was sent through the regular air mail. I am now writing you a detail letter which is a special delivery by one of our Chinese Mission members who will go to Shanghai to-day. We can not say much in an ordinary air mail.

Mr. Chao and I went to visit several chemical plants of synthetic NH_3, CH_3OH, urea, formalin, HNO_3, NH_4NO_3, $(NH_4)_2SO_4$, by-product coke oven, synthetic gasolin, electrolytic caustic soda, glass, cement, and solvay soda plants. We collected data, drawings, and discussed with technical men in charge of various plants about the problems we are interested. We shall start to arrange our data and drawings into reports for our company. Among the problems, we were particularly interested in the following topics:

1. Purification of H_2S from the water gas. There were three processes of wet method and one of dry box method. The Thylox process of the Kopper Co. (Germany) has been used by two plants. We got detailed instruction for the preparation of Thylox solution, and instructions of operation; and detailed drawings for the washers, oxidizer, sulfur autoclave, and report. Another plant used the Ammonium sulfite solution to absorb H_2S, the resulting solution is heated in an autoclave to form ammonium sulfate and free sulfur. The reactions are as follows:

$$4NH_3 + 3SO_2 + 3H_2O = (NH_4)_2SO_3 + 2NH_4HSO_3$$
$$2(NH_4)_2SO_3 + 2NH_4HSO_3 + 2H_2S = 3(NH_4)_2S_2O_3 + 3H_2O$$
$$2(NH_4)_2S_2O_3 + SO_2 = 2(NH_4)_2SO_4 + 3S$$

The NH_3 and SO_2 are the products of their ammonia and sulfuric acid plants. Another plant using the Siebelt Process of 7% soda ash solution in series with the Thylox process. We are trying to collect detailed informations for the Ammonium sulfite method too.

2. Catalyst is the second problem we are interested. We visited a V_2O_5 catalyst plant who made the Japanese V_2O_5 catalyst for our Nanking plant. They make the catalyst from the ore 'Vanadinite' produced from Peru, South America. We go through the whole process of the making and going to write detailed report. This process is called 'Osame' process which is really a modified 'Monsanto' process. Another plant using the ammonium vanadate to make catalyst which is a modified G.I. Process. We shall get this process in details too. The other catalysts like NH_3, CH_3OH, CO Oxidation (Both the pressure process and the atm. pressure process), and the synthetic formaldehyde, were also studied. The detailed process of du Pont's catalysts on NH_3 and CO Oxidation were obtained. Several samples of NH_3 catalyst of the Du Pont's Claude process, the I.G.Process, the N.E.C. process of the Sumitomo plant, and the Uhde process of East Asia Synthetic Co. were obtained, each in few grams. Talking about the Uhde catalyst in your last letter, it is blue color balls of 8 m/m dia. It is mainly $AlKFe(CN)_6$ and the likes;

$$3K_4(Fe(CN)_6) + 4AlCl_3 = Al_4Fe_3(CN)_{18} + 12KCl$$

The $Al_4Fe_3(CN)_{18}$ or the $KAlFe(CN)_6$ is mixed with the $(NH_4)_4Fe(CN)_6$ in or-ganic solvent to form paste. It is than dried, and pressed into balls. The catalyst is reduced in the converter of 95 atm. press. with N_2-H_2 gas containing more N_2 at 350° C. the $Fe(CN)_6$ is decomposed through Fe, C, FeC_2, Fe_3C_2, Fe_4N and N_2 as the temp. reached 360° C. to form active reduced iron which is the main body of catalyst for NH_3 synthesis. In the du Pont NH_3 catalyst, the artificial Fe_3O_4 is made by melting the steal scraps with pure O_2 gas in a magnesite lined crucible with addition of Al_2O_3. It is than crushed and used for By-product coke oven gas process of NH_3 synthesis. When water gas process is required, the catalyst is further melted in the electric furnace and 1% of K_2CO_3 is added. The addition of K into catalyst increases the activity at lower temp. but less stable at higher temp. In the pressure oxidation of CO, the catalyst is made by precipitation of nitrates of Cr., Cu, & Zn. the catalyst containing a mole ratio of CrO_3:ZnO:CuO = $1\frac{1}{2}$: 1 : $\frac{1}{2}$. In the atm. press. CO oxidation catalyst of I.G. process, oxides of iron and Cronmium are used but no MgO as we do in our case. The CH_3OH synthesis, ZnO:CrO_3 are used, while the mole ratio of Zn:Cr = 7 : 3. In the synthesis of formaldehyde form CH_3OH and Air, pure silver gause and copper gauze are used. We are sending you a picture we took for making the NH_3 catalyst in the magnesite crucible when O_2 gas is blown into the molten steel scrape. We watched the whole process that day when they made the du Pont catalyst. We shall write fully later.

3. Ammonium sulfate saturator's operation and design are the third problem which we are interested. We visited three sulfate plants making sulfate from ammonia and three plants from coke oven gas. It was found that in all the six plants, the saturators are installed on the ground floor (and none of them install their saturator at high elevation like we did). In one case, the saturator had been modified that lead vessel is crated with wood on the outside and lined with bricks in the inside. It saves the corrotion of the s teel outside shell of the saturator and prolong the life of lead a great deal by brick lining. I got a complete drawings of this saturator. Other operation details are also noted, such as using saturated ammoniated mother liquor for washing the crystalls, the mother liquor is not to be diluted with water, the concentrated H_2SO_4 is diluted with mother or water to form 50 to 70° Be' at the duriron pipe nozzle on the top of saturator, the airation of ammoniated mother liquor and using filter press to remove all the iron from it before sending back to saturator, etc. are those we thought in Nanking and going to try one by one gradually.

4. Other problems like the internal electric starting heater for the NH_3 converter, the recovery of CO_2 gas from the water scrubber, were also noted. In the Solvay process, we pay our attention to the various equipments used in three big plants in this country, their efficiency of operation, the compositions of mother liquors, and their tower conditions. By-products of caustic soda, $NaHCO_3$, $CaCl_2$, etc. were also interested. One plant owns a big glass plant, (the Asahi Glass Co.) and another owns a by-product cement plant of 1000 tons/day.

We are glad to learn that many improvements had been made in our Nanking plant and our production has been increased. I shall like to learn things from you when I go back to Nanking. We will bring all our informations back and discuss with all our engineers together.

With best wishes,

Very respectfully yours,

(S) W.C.Hsieh
J.Y.Chao

COPY

175

March 26, 1947.

Dear Mr. Lee:

We are glad to write letter in a more detailed way than we wrote to you day before yesterday, because this letter is delivered personally by one of our members of the Chinese Mission to Shanghai. We had lots of troubles with our ordinary mail air mails. Sometimes the letter may be kept a long time somewhere for some reason. All special letters are sent by our own members to the Shanghai post office when they carry the mail personally during their way back.

It was a very good chance for Mr. Chao and I to visit three Solvay soda plants in Japan. They are competitors to each other but welcome our Chinese Mission members to see them. One is the Asashi glass plant which you may know before. Another one is the Tokuyama plant who owns a by-product cement plant of 1000 tons per day. The third one is the Ube plant. They were built by separate capitals and claimed to be developed independently, but to us it seems one copied the other in some way. The Asashi glass soda plant may be considered the best among the three. The Ube plant is much the same with the Asashi. The Tokuyama plant was old and has much troubles. The neiboring plant, the Toyo soda plant, (assigned for reparation) is a modification of this plant. In all of these plants, sea salt from China and Korea are dissolved in a stationary tank and the brine is treated with milk of lime to remove Magnesium. The precipitate settled out by the Dorr thickener. The brine is then treated with CO_2 and some NH_3 in the tower washer to remove Calcium. It passes through the settlers, and absorbers, absorber coolers etc. to the carbonating towers. In one case, the CO_2 gas is fed in two places of the tower, conc. gas at bottom and lean gas at middle. All the brine coolers are in double tube forms. They use centrifuge for the filtration of bicarbonate and clained that it contains much less moisture and thus save the fuel in the calcination of soda ash. One of them using producer gas to heat the calcining rotary kiln. In making the caustic soda, they use the decomposer or the 'converter' is very much like a tower with steam inlet at the bottom. The $NaHCO_3$ is dissolved Na_2CO_3 solution. Another thing was noted that all the lime kiln are of concrete walls with fire brick lining. We got some data on the compositions of mother liquor at different points and materials balances of their plants. We shall try to arrange our data in reports for reference. Beside the main soda plant, we visited their by-products like the caustic soda, the bicarbonates, the calcium chloride, the glass plant and the cement plant. Their present trouble is in short of raw mateeials, coal and sea salt. Their production now are only a fraction of their designed capacities.

We also visited ammonia plant, coke ovens, sulfuric acid, nitric acid, urea, methyl alcohal, formalin, sulfate, nitrate, and went down to a coal mine of 10,000 tons/day capacity. They were quite interesting. We got some drawings and flowsheets of them. We shall like to discuss with you later.

With best regards,

Very respectfully yours,
W.C.Hsieh
J.Y.Chao

c/o Yungli Chemical Industries,Ltd.
No. 23, I-Ho Road
Nanking, China

Feb. 27, 1947.

Yungli Chem. Ind.,Ltd.
Nanking, China

Gentlemen:

I was engaged prior to the war in 1937 for a period of 5 or 6 years supervising the installation of your Ammonium Sulphate and Acid Works located at Hsieh-chia-tien. This work included a complete plant for the manufacture of Nitric Acid with a production of 10 metric tons per day of 24 hours continuous operation.

This plant was constructed entirely of new equipment according to designs supplied by the Nitrogen Engineering Corporation of New York, U.S.A.

Upon my return, for rehabilitation work, I find that this plant, for Nitric Acid, had been entirely removed and the building somewhat destroyed by bombing.

We are advised that this equipment was re-erected in Omuta, Japan, and operated there by them.

It has been our experience, in the operation of acid plants, that with reasonable care in maintenance and operation, these plants are subject to such corrosive conditions, that a period of 10 years would require the complete replacement of the equipment. And a period of idleness in an atmosphere of acid operation would be even more destructive.

Therefore, it is our considered opinion, that this equipment which had been dismantled and re-erected, and operated, probably, in adverse conditions for forced war production, would be in such condition that the entire recoverable value would not justify the costs of transportation and re-erection. We feel that the entire plant should be presented to reparations commission and the total original cost be claimed for compensation.

Even, under these conditions, the present costs of replacement would exceed the compensation awarded.

Therefore we would not recommend the return of this equipment as compensation, as we do not consider its value would justify the costs.

Yours truly,

G.T.Lee,
Engineer.

COPY

Feb. 12th, 1947.

177

Dear Mr. Dely:

We are here in Tokyo for little more than a month and everything is fine. We went to the American Headquarter and discussed with them about the nitric acid plant which had been looted by the Japanese and they just suggest us to make an inspection of the equipment in Omuta, and then make other discussions. We have seen some pictures which the Japanese sent to the Headquarter in which the equipments like high speed NO booster etc. were in very bad shape. We told the Headquarter that the equipments we had before in 1937 were perfectly new and good, and there were several American engineers who worked with us in 1937 before the war started in Shanghai, can be our witness. It would be very good for our negociation if you will kindly write a note to state that you were with the Chemical Construction people in our plant in 1937, and the situation of the plant at that time. Also express your opinion, as a chemical engineer sees it, about the looted nitric acid equipment. We appreciate it very much if you send us two copies with date and signiture of it.

We interview a German Engineer Mr. W.Braun who worked both in Japan and the Dairen, China for several years. I submitted a copy of our note on the interview for your reference.

We are very much interested in the sulfuric acid and alkali plants in Japan for reparation. These plants were comparatively new in process and equipment. The sulfuric acid plants were all of contact process with V205 catalyst. Because the Headquarter want to remove the contact plants away which produce fuming acid for war materials, and leave the lead chamber plants for the filtilizer works. The alkali plants were mostly electrolysis which produces Chlorine gas for war. Only one Salvey plant in the lot. Some of the references we sent to Mr. Foo may be interested to you.

I always remember to work with you in our plant and always learn things from your most kind instructions. How is everything going on there? I may go back to Nanking in the end of next month. Please send my best regards to Mrs. Dely. Hope to hear a few words from you. I thank you.

Very respectfully yours,

(S) W.C.Hsieh

P.S. Mr, Chao joins me to send you our best wishes.
We are leaving for Omuta tonight.

COPY

178

Feb. 12th, 1947.

Dear Mr. Lee:

I am glad to inform you that we are here in Tokyo for more than a month and going to make an inspection trip to Omuta plant for checking the looted equipment of the nitric acid plant. We negociated with the Headquarter some days ago and told them that our equipments in 1937 were all new and a few American engineers who worked with us in 1937 can be our witness. It would be very helpful to us if you would kindly write a note stating that what you know about the situation of our equipment before the war and your opinion about the looted equipment, as an engineer sees it, that had been used or laid down for ten years. Two copies of the statement with signiture and date will be very much appreciated.

We were also very much interested in acid and alkali plants for reparation. There are 23 contact sulfuric acid plants, 18 electrolytic caustic soda plants and only one Salvey soda plant of 560 tons/day capacity. We got some data about it and sent to Mr. Foo. They may be of some interest to you. The plant produces mostly caustic soda by caustizying with lime. The bicarbonate is dissolved in water and sent to converter in which CO_2 is driven out by steam to form mostly Na_2CO_3 in solution then treated with lime. This would save the energy of calcination. They use anthracite for lime kiln because coke is rather expensive. The calcination of bicarbonate is heated by producer gas, which I am not sure that are external heated or internal heated. From the weak CO_2 gas (only 55%) from the calciner, it seems to be internal heated like cement kiln use gas or powdered coal. Other things may be of interested to you, especially the material balance which is rather difficult to get. From an interview with their chief engineer, we learned that they sent CO_2 in to the tower at two entrances, the stronger gas at the bottom and the weaker gas at the middle. The sea salts are all obtained from China, and contain high $MgCl_2$ which is treated with lime in a settler before treated in the tower washer with CO_2 and NH_3 where Ca salts are removed. The ammoniated brine had less trouble of Mg ppt. and is further added with salt to bring to a higher Na content.

How are you these days? How are Mrs. Lee and kids at home in America. I always remember the days we stayed together in No.1 house and learn things from you. And also the nice bridge parties with Mr. Lu and my wife. Do you play some bridge once a while now? I play it in my sister's house. She told me to send you her best wishes.

Very respectfully yours,

(S) W.C .Hsieh

P.S. Mr. Chao joins me to send you our best wishes. We are leaving for Omuta tonight.

187

April 29, 1947.

Dr. W.C.Hsieh,
Tokyo, Japan.

Dear Dr. Hsieh:

Your letter No.1 dated the 14th. of April has been received. The three Japanese plants, one 30 tons of sulphuric acid pyrite burning plant and two small eletrolytic plants, represent a very small fraction that is to be allotted to private enterprises by the Government. Please let me know what are the plants which are reserved by the Government, and give me a list of these plants if possible.

Among the alkali plants, No.19 is the Ammonia Soda Plant under the name of Toyo Soda Co. which produces over 400 tons of soda ash a day. Please find out whether this Solvay Process soda ash plant is assigned to China or to other country, and if it is to be assigned to China, whether it is to be dismantled and removed now or in future.

I quite agree with you as to your idea of locating the sulphuric acid plant and the electrolytic caustic soda plants, but our first job is to find out what are the plants which are set aside for reparations to China and to Yungli before we can decide where these plants are to be located. In view of lack of information available to us in Shanghai, I am thinking to take a trip to Japan on behalf of the Ministry of Economic Affairs. I shall let you know my definite plan somewhat later.

Our production has been very fair. We are producing about 100 tons of ammonium sulphate in Nanking a day and about equal quantity of soda ash in Tangku. We are very badly in need of the nitric acid plant. It is absolutely necessary that we should get the complete plant back, because our nitric acid plant was complete when it was removed by the Japanese army and installed at the present site. The Japanese meanwhile may have modified some of the equipment or changed some parts of the machinery or added some little parts

--- 188

-2-

here and there, when they set up our equipment in Japan. This does not alter the fact that these parts belonged to the equipment which was stolen by the Japanese and which should be returned to us as a whole. The authorities in Japan must realize the fact that the Japanese had to make some changes in order to fit our equipment to their plant site, and in setting up our equipment in Japan, the Japanese had to supply some parts which they could not move from our Plant. So, by all means, we should have the complete plant back. Please emphasize this point in presenting our case to the authorities there.

Very sincerely yours,

T. P. Hou

TPH:PHL

傅冰芝、邢振有等有关日本赔偿及归还物资的往来函（一九四七年三月二十七日至五月十六日）

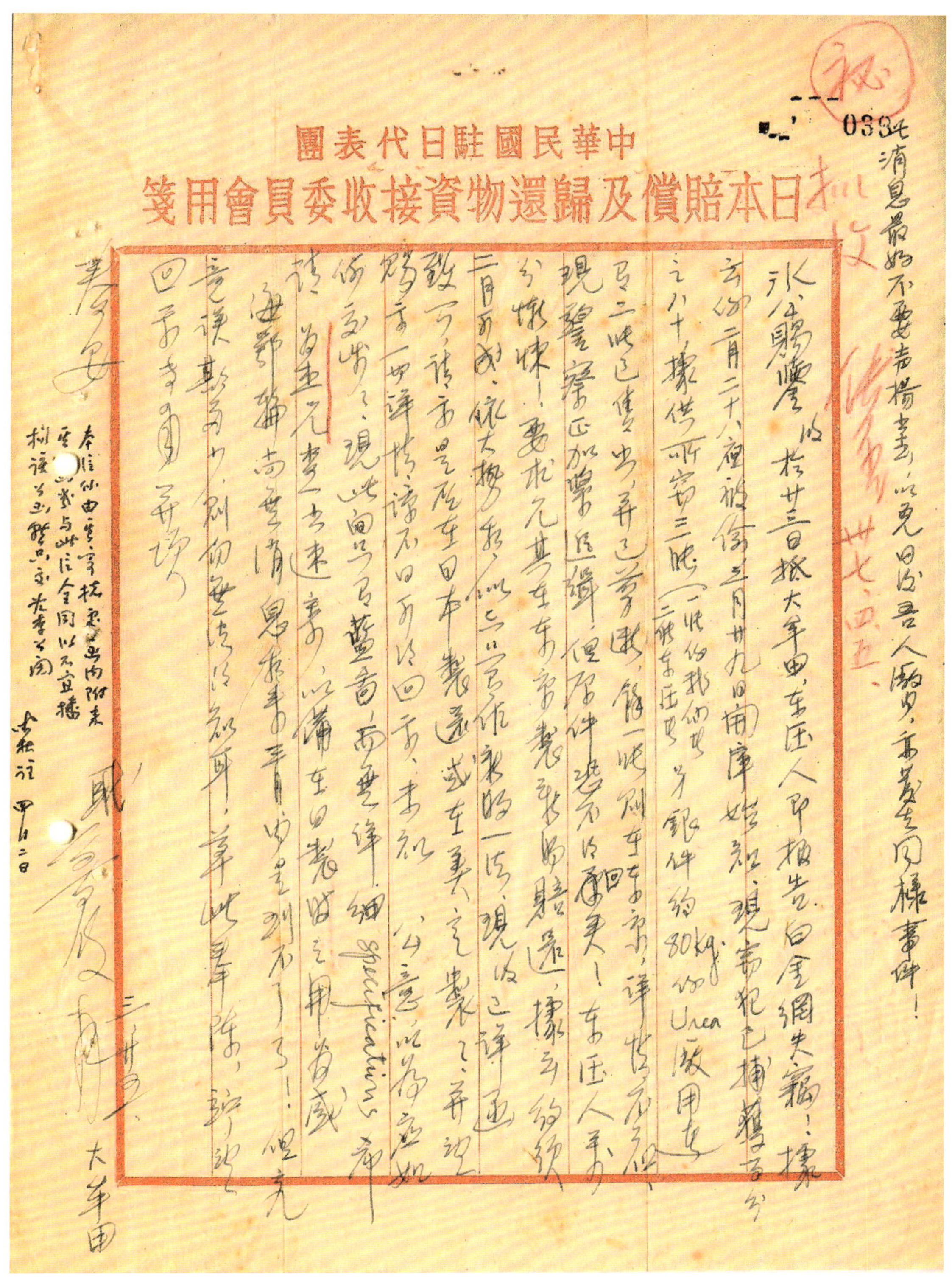

秘

033

中華民國駐日代表團
日本賠償及歸還物資接收委員會用箋

055

字第　　頁

總經理鈞鑒：遠教年餘，時為孺念。刻聆
鈞駕於美安返，不勝欣躍。振有自蒙錄用
迄已年餘，夙夜之心，未敢稍懈。茲有懇陳者：
振有前原為中華公司僱聘，歷廿餘年，自民念三
年承包永利工程起，念六年戰禍驟起，於秋向中
華即函電囑其停工，當由將該意奉陳
鈞前商洽，經
以員工挽留，並體念備至，或中華不添配傢具
及發給工資，永利決予負責給與，以此謹遵
公命，繼續工作，自七月起至十一月底，經付五月薪支

中華民國　　年　　月　　日

056

字第　　頁

永利支借國幣二千四百五十元正，計開預支全部工友工資
君壹萬壹千餘元，均錄有賬。以因時局緊急，即隨
永利西遷赴湘，為良心之累，致未追隨
鈞右，仍留滬摸看經過，於滬改組即稱中華公司
將賬據繳清並陳述
鈞意挽留情形，詎料主管外國人聲稱全部電
逕並催囑其將來返申，就料仍自動與永利商洽
繼了工作，致以將全部工具損失，雖將月包費
永利清給卿卿之數，不足償失十分之一，汝雖代
整一切暫難照發，振有仍在彼處工作，於月適歐戰

中華民國　　年　　月　　日

通訊處：南京[illegible]里二號　電報掛號：四三五四

057

字第　頁

暴帝外國人即整裝歸國，臨行曾給一函，嘱其候
中國重返，該物當予照給，或本人不克來華，可
將永利遺留工具全部給汝，以償此欵，亦不負汝
在中華二十餘年之誠樸。其後該函因日寇侵
犯租界時被搜出，當時受該威脅，種種已將此函
沒收。究竟根有入廠欵，詳陳
鈞前，未及二日
不即圖不赴義，以錢無從清進，而根有應在中華之
薪月支九十元，現日寧垂之八元九分，非敢填低，
實因一家七口生活高昂，不敷度日，並且長女

中華民國　年　月　日

通訊處：南京西華門三條巷六合里二號　電報掛號：四三五四

於本期高小畢業，欲昇學初中，為經濟無着，將擱於半途矣。振有個處文育，實不忍伊人仍蹈覆轍也。為此縷情具函，轉陳伏乞俯念苦情，設想待遇，並請給該孩以昭前約而援積苦。臨陳迫切，不勝翹企之至。肅此敬請

德安

晚 邢振有敬叩

卅六年四月 日

五真草浩書附

中華民國　年　月　日　字第　頁

通訊處：南京西華門三條巷文昌里二號　電報掛號：四三五四

南京國和路二十三號

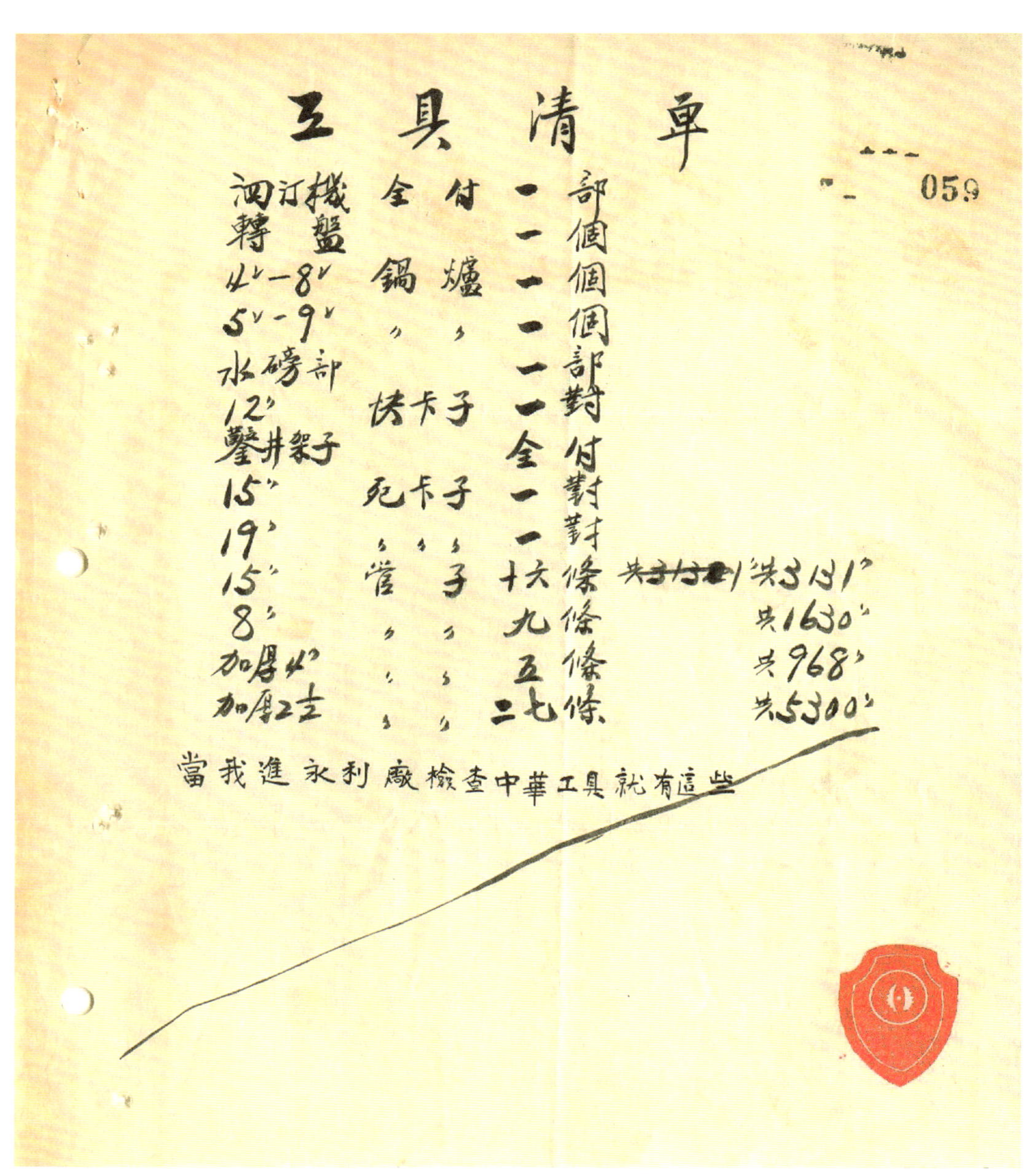

059

工具清單

洞汀機	全付	二部	
轉盤		一個	
4"—8"	鍋爐	一個	
5"—9"	〃 〃	二個	
水磅部		一部	
12"	活卡子	一對	
鑿井架子		全付	
15"	死卡子	一對	
19"	〃 〃 〃	一對	
15"	管子	十六條	共3131"
8"	〃 〃	九條	共1630"
加厚4"	〃 〃	五條	共968"
加厚2½	〃 〃	二七條	共5300"

當我進永利廠檢查中華工具就有這些

永利化學工業公司用牋

第　號第　頁

傳廠長鈞鑒：振有日前呈遞總經理一函，云已轉交鈞右。諒邀洞鑒。謹具之情悉戰前振有在中華公司服務與侯公面洽之事轍故歲餘未呈鈞覽。幸祈垂察。今得轉蒙鈞核，尚盼早日批示，俾解積困，而全季諾，不勝感戴翹企之至。謹此敬肅德安

邢振有謹叩

中華民國廿六年四月廿一日

廠址江蘇六合縣卸甲甸　通訊處南京南京頤和路廿三號　電話三三九九六　電報掛號四三五四　南京

061

永利化學工業公司用牋

第　號第　頁

廠長鈞鑒：為戰前中華鑿井公司廿六年七月至十一月振有未遵中華函電停工，經侯總經理挽留負責經費等內情，曾具日前呈侯公函內，業悉該件轉陳
鈞右，並於本（四）月二十一日振有備具一函呈達，諒邀
察閱。二十二日侯公離廠赴津，臨行面諭振有云：對此決不使之受損，業請
鈞座辦理等語。聆此，振有祇得靜待，至今已逾一週，尚未蒙
垂示，莫釋何意。今不揣冒昧，謹函重達，伏祈

中華民國　年　月　日

廠址江蘇六合縣卸甲甸　通訊處南京頤和路廿三號　電話三三九九六　電報掛號四三五四　南京

062

永利化學工業公司用牋

第　號第　頁

俯念困苦實情，早予頒發，以全前信而解懸困，不勝戴德之至。肅此敬請
公安

邢振有　謹叩

中華民國三十六年四月二十九日

刘[illegible]

063

字第　　頁

冰公廠長鈞鑒：日前暢聆

慈教，始成全之力，下懷銘感，匪言可宣。關於戰前包打深井工作用費及工資一節，業已面陳

侯總經理述明晚之一切痛苦矣，晚願在

侯公未出國之前得一結論，但迄今旬餘仍未解決，致感不安。今因債主索款更爲緊迫，實無法再予推延，故特懇祈

鈞座惠借國幣伍百萬元，以便償還，而免久累之苦。該款俟

侯公返廠時再行面請，俾得早日了結，是爲企禱。專此叩請

鈞安

晚邢振有謹上

中華民國三十六年五月七日

通訊處：南京西華門三條巷六合里二號 電話：四三五四

南京鐵礦路二十三號

字第 號第 頁

總經理鈞鑒上月謹呈一函蒙 批由廠長辦理屆茲一
月曾連呈三函未邀解決不勝憂疑民廿四年中華公
司派 晚來此至二十六年服務三年誠仰
鈞座德信致以戰時五月工作之 囑留謹遵
鈞命而戰後歸來荷蒙 錄用更感
厚澤誠信不負粗愚惟 晚半生之積蓄皆付此一空
一家七口自老子幼前途深感乏保障今幸
公重臨亟冀

中華民國 年 月 日

永利化學工業公司錏廠 065

字第　號第　頁

俯念愚情乞

予惠示合家戴

德沒齒不忘也肅此謹呈

敬請

德安

邢振有 謹呈

中華民國二十六年五月十六日

廠址：江蘇省六合縣卸甲甸　通訊處：南京西華門三條巷六合里二號　電報掛號：四三五四 南京

永利化学工业公司錏厂提供硝酸厂证明事项及文件一览表（一九四七年三月三十日）

永利化學工業公司錏廠提供硝酸廠證明事項及文件一覽表

證明事項	證明文件
(一)戰前完整	(1)外景照片一張 (2)敵據永禮化學工業株式會社史記一冊（該書第廿八—廿九頁所叙：……合成廠、硫酸錏廠及硝酸廠並無任何損毀） (3)前美駐華大使詹森氏參觀本廠留影一張（當時全廠開工情形為詹森氏所目覩）
(二)產權	(4)藍圖五張 YD-0-0-1至YD-0-0-5 (5)硝酸廠全套機器名稱、數量、承造廠名、本廠編號等一覽表一份 (6)謝、趙兩君携日之硝酸廠全部機器合約（副本及抄本）及發票（原副本）號碼清單抄本一份 (7)本廠現僅存之各種發票、裝箱單、運輸通知單原副本及抄本等四十七份
(三)參考資料	(8)謝、趙兩君卅五年十一月十五日出國前接洽經過報告一份 (9)謝、趙兩君在日以我國外交部代表名義於卅六年一月廿日交駐日盟軍總部節略抄本一份 (10)同前卅六年三月廿日節略抄本一份

行政院赔偿委员会关于检发查报须知及申请归还劫物表格依式填报送会以凭核办理事给永利化学工业公司的通知（抄件）（一九四七年四月七日）

195

抄行政院賠償委員會通知

發文京（卅六）字第〇〇四五四號

中華民國卅六年四月七日發出

事由：檢發查報須知及申請歸還劫物表格依式填報送會以憑核辦理由

案准外交部本年二月六日東孫字第2272號電轉經濟部函以據永利化學公司呈略以被劫硝酸設備拆壞請責令日本賠償一案查申請歸還劫物應以盟軍總部最近所訂表格填報并須繳交物權及被劫証件茲檢發上項表格一份即希依式填報并將所受損失依照前抗戰損失調查委員會所頒查報須知詳細填報送會以憑登記及核轉外交部飭駐日代表團辦理特此通知

右通知

永利化學公司

主任委員　翁文灝

永利化学工业公司总经理侯德榜关于请拆迁日本苏尔维法碱厂机器全套以充赔偿事呈经济部文（抄件）及经济部批复（一九四七年四月二十八日至六月二十八日）

313

中華民國三十六年四月二十八日

存根

弟江次令飭

抄送

總處

碱廠

京處

事由	擬辦	批示	備考
呈請拆遷日本蘇爾維法鹼廠機器全套以充賠償由			
附件			

字第　號　年　月　日　時到

收文　字第　號

呈為申請拆還日本蘇爾維法鹼廠機器全套以充賠償事：竊維公司自民國六年剏議建立蘇爾維法製鹼工廠於河北省塘沽，是時適值第一次世界大戰方殷，國內市場需要純鹼至切，誠為中國自營鹼業大好機會，顧大規模製鹼設計，不獨在中國尚無成功之先例，即在世界各先進國，亦莫不對此技術，緘秘不宣，令後起者無從借鏡。公司同人不避險阻艱難，不計成敗利鈍，暗中摸索，再接再厲，經過長久歲月始將中國製鹼事業之基礎奠定，畀舉世工業界一大震驚。不幸九一八事起，塘沽處於異族勢力壓迫之下，進展維艱。七七難作，公司權力遂唯有隨我國職撤退。九年以來，覆巢之下，自無完卵。自敵投降，公司塘沽鹼廠事業鈞部接收，並予發還。惟既橫遭敵偽蹂躪，機件窳敗不堪，識者視之直同廢鐵，謂非重新建設，不足以盡技術上之能事。今雖勉强復工，然產量遠不如前，維持消耗則倍增無算。此中苦情已於歷次呈報公司損失並申請賠償之呈文中縷悉陳明在案。竊思公司致力於製鹼事業垂三十年，以往貢獻誠愧無多，今後如有機會，自當竭盡棉薄，圖報稱於涓埃。獨以資金奇絀，有志未逮。海外後起工業國家，知公司於技術薄有成就，往往來求指導。所愧自身之廠，竟爾殘破簡陋，缺然無以示人，是不僅公司之恥，亦我國家之羞。竊查第一次日本賠償工廠名單之中，有東洋曹達工廠一所，設在山口縣德山富田地方，係屬蘇爾維式，與公司塘沽鹼廠之原則相似，假令該廠設備，尚合應用

，擬請拆遷運入國內，撥歸公司重建，充作應得賠償之用。公司深惟
鹼廠自遭敵佔，直接間接，損失無算，義應取得適當賠償，俾
昭公允。亦惟以公司多年經驗，得彼主要蘇爾維法鹼廠機器全套，
加以改良運用，方不負我 國家之委任。所有申請拆遷日本蘇
爾維法鹼廠全套機器以作賠償緣由，理合備文陳明，是否有當？
敬祈
批示祇遵，不勝迫切待 命之至。謹呈
經濟部

永利化學工業公司總經理侯德榜

通訊處：南京頤和路二十三號

抄件

京 312 處

永利化學工業公司錏廠用牋

抄件

經濟部批

發文京工36字第09398號
中華民國卅六年六月十八日發出

具呈人永利化學工業公司

卅六年四月廿八日呈一件為呈請拆遷日本蘇爾維法鹼廠機器全套以充賠償由

呈悉業予據情提交賠償委員會第四小組審核於第二批拆遷方案中提出俟確定後再行飭知此批

五人委员会、日本赔偿当局估计赔偿物资总吨数及标准工厂拆还演习经费估计表等（一九四七年五月七日至六月十八日）

297

47.5.17.

標準工廠拆遷演習經費估計表

日本商工省賠償實施局（作.2）

項目別 ＼ 工廠別		電力	燒碱	硫酸	鉄	鋼	工具機	鋼珠軸承	飛機
對象設備概要（公称能力）		178,500KW火力發電設備及其附屬設備	1,200 T/月隔膜式電解設備及其附屬設備.	1,500 T/A Lurgi式接觸硫酸設備及其附屬設備	350 T/A 鍊鉄炉兩座及其附屬設備	100T平炉1座 70T〃3座（約680Charge）及其附屬設備 3,000T Press1座 1,500T〃1〃及其附屬設備	工具機557部 其他機械 159部	工具機 ~~559~~ 360部 其他機械 36部	工具機 2,959部 其他機械 590部
拆卸總重量 T.		22,814		1,395	63,001		—	—	—
撤去重量 T		18,428	2,548	673	12,788	6,561	1,509	727	6,814
包裝重量 T		21,105	3,305	865	14,252	7,434	1,841	1,029	13,165
每噸拆遷所需經費 日圓 以撤去重量爲準	拆卸	3,020	2,530	5,090	10,670	5,160	170	780	445
	包裝	4,040	3,480	5,930	3,170	7,390	3,270	2,370	6,755
	運輸	1,990	3,220	3,450	830	20,460	4,820	3,420	5,940
	共計	9,050	9,230	14,470	13,670	33,010	8,070	6,570	13,140
以包裝重量爲準	拆卸包裝	6,170	4,620	8,600	11,500	11,080	2,830	2,220	3,730
	運輸	1,740	2,500	2,700	740	18,010	3,950	2,410	3,070
	共計	7,910	7,120	11,300	12,240	29,090	6,780	4,630	6,800

（琛）

抄送 總處 碱廠 總經理

密件

日本賠償當局最近切实估計賠償物資之總噸

Name of Industry	Net Wt.	Gross Wt.
1. Arsenal	1.229.769	1.660.189
2 Aircraft	366.218	512.704
3 Private Munition	200.704	280.997
4 Machine Tools	66.623	93.273
5 Ball Bearing	21.627	30.278
6 Thermal Power	178.740	254.592
7 Steel & Iron Works	900.298	1.125.373
8 Caustic Soda	43.062	53.820
9 Soda Ash	15.700	19.625
10 Sulphuric Acid	41.394	51.755
11 Synthetic Rubber	4.471	5.365
12 Private Ship Building	174.506	218.132
13 Laboratory	1.615	2.425
Total	3.244.727	4.308.528

附註；以上数字係六月十七日向商工省主管部分抄来者，惟賠償物資中，缺少輕金屬合成石油[illegible]二項。五月六日據商工省賠償主管人員談話，全部賠償物資總重量約為520万噸，每噸拆遷費用估計為12000日圓。又據去年十一月廿二日「第一新聞」所載估計拆遷所需包装運輸材料，係以賠償物資總重量550万噸為基數。總之，日本賠償物資總重量（連包装）恐不過500万噸左右。

五人委員会 36.6.18.

永利化学工业公司錏厂关于请力争将日方配件一并收回，在交涉期间公司同意暂租予日方继续使用事给经济部的报告（一九四七年五月十五日）

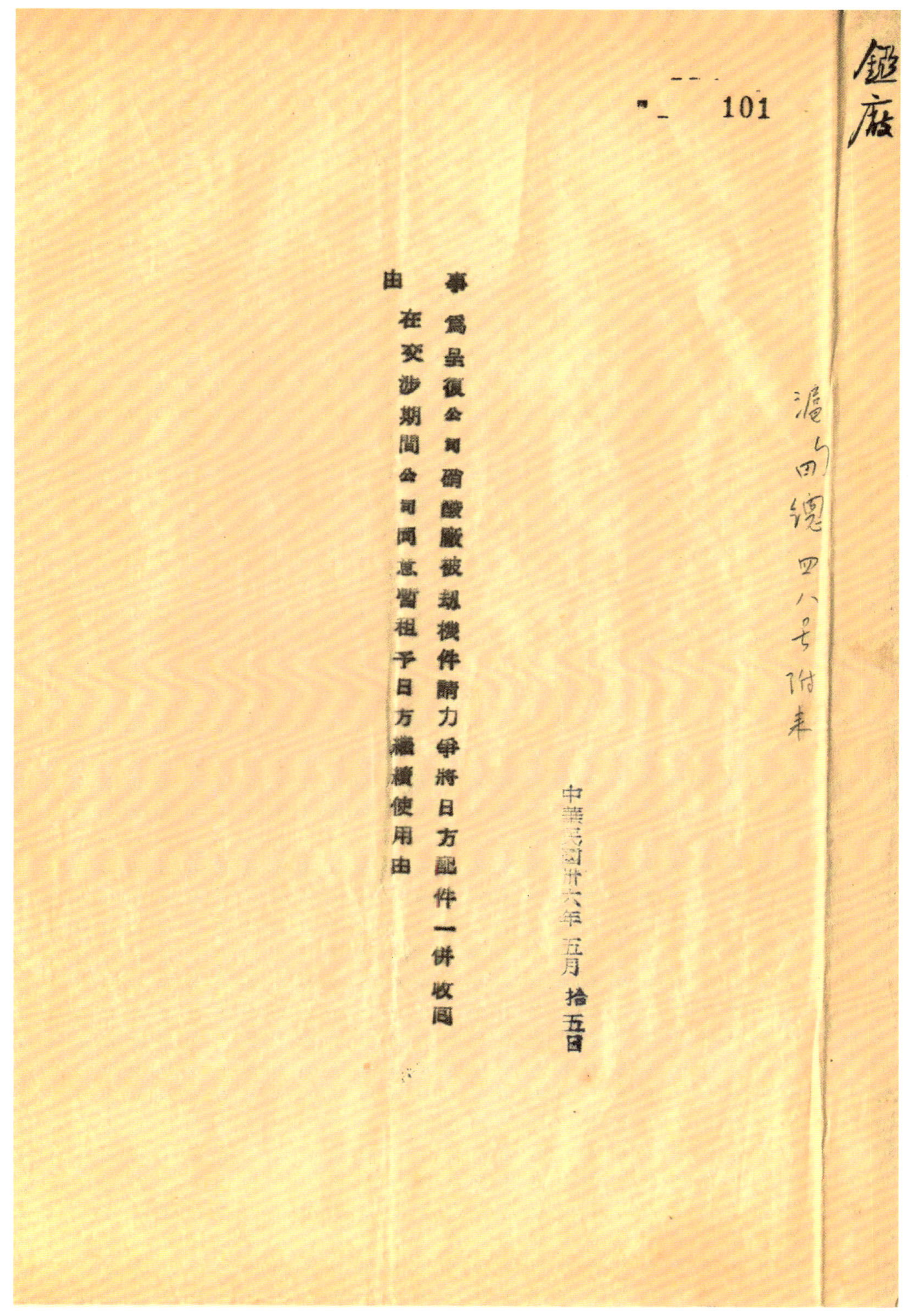

錏廠

101

滬向總四八号附來

事由 為呈復公司硝酸廠被劫機件請力爭將日方配件一併收回在交涉期間公司同意暫租予日方繼續使用由

中華民國卅六年五月拾五日

102

案奉

鈞部卅六年五月三日京工字第四二〇〇九號通知，內開：

「准外交部卅六年四月二十六日東字第八五五一號代電開：『據駐日代表團代電以被劫永利硝酸廠機器損壞甚多均由日方添配齊全此項配件若不一併歸還原機運回難以使用請速飭我方代表在遠東委員會力爭等情查遠東委員會規定被劫機器歸還限於現存原物茲欲將日方配件一併收回自須提請該會修改原議決案恐非短期所能實現在交涉期間為免我方負擔損失起見似可先由駐日代表團即洽盟軍總部由我方實行接管該項機器接收之後為免停工影響估價目的不妨於短期內暫租日方繼續使用關於租金之核收或用額定數目或照生產比例可

由駐日代表團查酌辦理並據前情除飭駐美顧大使在遠東委員會提請修改原議決案外相應抄同原代電請查照轉飭核復以憑核轉交涉

「等由並抄附駐日代表團代電一件合行抄發原件仰即核復為要」

等因；並抄發駐日代表團原代電奉此，查公司硝酸廠設備被劫運日使用多年，機器損壞，自可想見，若不連同配件一併歸還，不但難以使用，區區等廢鐵，應懇力爭修改原議決案，將日方配件一併收回，在交涉期間，為免負擔損失起見，公司同意遵照外交部擬議先由駐日代表團即洽盟軍總部由我方實行接管，暫租予日方繼續使用，一俟遠東委員會原議決案修改後，即行拆遷運回，奉令前因，理合呈復，敬祈

鑒核轉復，至為感禱。

104

謹呈
經濟部

永利化學工業公司謹呈
地址：上海四川路四一〇號

三十六年五月十五日

抄經濟部價配日本賠償工具機公告

查首批日本賠償我國之工具機經配交本部價配民營事業使用者共二千三百六十二部除約有三分之一因缺乏附件暫未接收外其餘均已裝箱將陸續運達上海凡在指定範圍內之國內民營事業均可遵照行政院所頒「民營事業申請價配日本賠償物資辦法」及附屬各辦法契約書表等之規定備具申請書及建廠或補充廠計劃書各三份逕向本部申請價配候彙核轉送行政院賠償委員會審定後再行訂立契約繳款提貨茲將價配範圍及機器種類數量價格地區限期等項公告於次：

一、價配範圍 首批日本賠償物資暫以下列各項民營事業為分配對象(1)製造或修理紡織機具之工廠(2)製造或修理造紙機具之工廠(3)製造或修理電器機具之工廠(4)增產煤斤需用工具機之礦廠

二、工具機種類及數量 計有鏜床二十部鑽床一百八十一部切齒機十三部磨床一百六十三部車床一千三百零七部銑床二百五十六部龍門刨床十九部牛頭刨床及其他一百八十三部彎摺機十二部水壓機二部機械壓機三十二部手壓機一百三十一部剪刀及衝眼機十七部鍛工機械二十四部線絲成形機二部共計二千三百六十二部各工具機另印有詳細清單

三、工具機價格 各項工具機之價格由經濟部財政部及全國性人民工商團體各派代表合組評價委員會依照行政院令頒評價辦法切實評議送由行政院賠償委員會審定

四、價配地區 (1)綏靖區暫行緩配(2)僻遠地區視交通情形酌配(3)未受戰事損失地區依需要情形酌配(4)其他地區依照「民營事業申請價配日本賠償物資辦法」所定標準儘先核配

五、申請限期 自登報公告之日起開始申請以三十七年三月十五日為截止收受申請書日期其在截止期後遲到之申請文件均留候第二批價配物資案內彙核審定各申請廠礦務須自行斟酌郵遞遲速趕於期前遞到

六、印刷品項目 (1)工具機詳細清單(2)民營事業申請價配日本賠償物資辦法(3)領價繳款辦法(4)申請書表格式(5)建廠計劃書格式以上各項印刷品共收工本費一十萬元各申請人可備價逕向本部或上海漢口天津重慶廣州各工商輔導處索取

中華民國三十七年一月二十八日公告

48　004

抄自三十七年一月廿九日大公報第二版

賠償物資價配民營

規定為工具機二千餘部

價配範圍以發展紡織工業為主

（本報南京廿八日專電）日本賠償我國首批工具機共9447部，其中以2362部，配交經濟部價配民營事業使用。該項工具機計有鏜床20部、鑽床181部、切齒机13部、磨床163部、車床1307部、銑床256部、龍門刨床19部、牛頭刨床及其他183部、彎摺机12部、水壓機2部、械壓机32部、手壓機131部、剪刀及衝眼機17部、鍛工机械24部、線絲成形机2部。各工具機聞已陸續自日本啓運，經濟部已令由上海工商輔導處接收保管，並依照院令，由經濟部、財政部及全國性人民工商團體各派代表合組評價委員會，切實評定，以便價配。這批工具机之價配範圍，是依照政府經建方針，適應當前需要，以發展紡織工業為主，其次為造紙工業、電器工業和煤鑛。凡製造或修理紡織造紙及電器等項机具之工業及增產煤斤之煤鑛，亦可請求價配。其餘各項工業目前暫從緩配，須俟第二次抽得工具机後再行價配。這批工具機以能迅速運用為

永利化學工業公司錏廠　　第 2 頁

最主要條件，凡交通不便之邊遠地方，或尚屬綏靖區域不易運往，難於短期內運用者，或未受戰爭損失而無急切需要之地區，均將暫從緩配。至申請價配之手續，須照院頒申請書及建廠計畫書格式填具同式三份，呈送經濟部，申請價配。經部彙核轉送行政院賠償委員會審定後，即可訂立契約，繳納價款，提取所購之工具機，裝置建設。該項申請日期為自公告之日起至本年三月十五日止。其工具機詳單及辦法等全份，可繳費一十萬元，逕向經濟部或上海、漢口、重慶、廣州、天津各工商輔導處索取。

赵如晏关于第一批赔偿机器问题致傅冰芝的函（抄件）（一九四八年一月三十一日）

附：第一批计件机器检验经过一览表、第一批计件机器先行接收数量分类统计表

116　166

永利化學工業公司錏廠

字第　號第　頁　年　月　日

抄趙如晏先生致傅冰芝先生三十七年元月卅一日函

冰公鈞鑒：茲寄上第一批賠償機器統計表、檢驗經過一覽表各一份，請查收參考。至國內分配辦法悉取決於南京賠委會，此地乃遵照國內辦理者，到該會一查自更清楚。專肅敬頌

崇安

晚趙如晏謹上

廠址：江蘇省六合縣卸甲甸　通訊處：南京（八）珠江路二十三號　電話：三三九九六　電報掛號四三五四　南京

第一批計件機器檢驗經過一覽表

三十六年十二月

廠編號	檢驗報告號	分配號數	廠名	廠址	檢驗人員	檢驗日期	我國分得機器總數	先行接收機器總數	先行接收之百分數
19-20	1	1-1	第一海軍技術廠釜利谷分廠	橫濱市磯子區	李待琛 王樹芳 周茂柏 唐崇禮 劉守愚 盧濟滄 方復鑾 張有穀 韓雲岑	10月14,20,23,24日	655	451	68.9
24-4	2	1-2	東京陸軍第一造兵廠仙台製作所	宮城縣仙台市原町	劉守愚 王經畯 方復鑾 韓雲岑	10月27,28日	744	473	63.6
24-5	3	1-3	多賀城海軍工廠	宮城縣多賀城市	仝上	10月29,30日	502	352	70.1
39-50	4	1-4	東京陸軍第一造兵廠瀧川分工廠	東京瀧川區瀧川町	仝上	11月6日	99	60	60.6
39-51C	5	1-5	東京陸軍第一造兵廠練馬陸軍倉庫	東京板橋區練馬	仝上	11月6日	119	74	62.2
19-18	6	1-6	東京陸軍第一造兵廠相模陸軍造兵廠	神奈川縣高座郡相模原町	李待琛 王樹芳 劉守愚 王經畯 方復鑾 韓雲岑	11月10,12,13日	1,120	967	86.3
19-32	7	1-7	橫須賀海軍工廠	神奈川縣橫須賀市	李待琛 唐崇禮 劉守愚 王經畯 方復鑾 韓雲岑	11月18,19,20日	1,513	610	40.3
01-60D	8	1-8	豐川海軍工廠	愛知縣豐川市	李待琛 劉守愚 王經畯 方復鑾 韓雲岑	11月24日	202	168	83.1
01-56	10	1-9	名古屋陸軍造兵廠千種製作所	名古屋千種區	仝上	11月26日	529	498	94.1
01-58	9	1-10	名古屋陸軍造兵廠鳥居松製造所	名古屋春日井市	仝上	11月25日	613	536	87.5
32-30	11	1-11	東京陸軍第二造兵廠香里製造所	大阪府北河內郡	仝上	12月1日	51	24	47.1
32-32	12	1-12	大阪陸軍造兵廠大阪製造所	大阪市東區杉山町	仝上	12月1,2,4日	1,253	744	59.5
13-53	13	1-13	大阪陸軍造兵廠白濱製造所	兵庫縣須磨郡白濱市	仝上	12月4日	162	101	62.3
11-5-5	14	1-14	吳海軍工廠播磨造船所	廣島縣吳市	唐崇禮 劉守愚 王經畯 方復鑾 韓雲岑	12月9日	243	163	67.3
11-5-7	15	1-15	吳海軍工廠水野造船所	廣島縣吳市	仝上	12月8日	341	170	49.8
27-1	16	1-16	川棚海軍工廠	長崎縣東彼杵郡川棚市	仝上	12月10日	639	594	92.9
27-4	17	1-17	第二十一海軍航空工廠	長崎縣大村市	仝上	12月11,12日	613	559	91.2
							9,398*	6,544	69.7

* 我國分得機器最初抽得總數為9,447部因平衡各盟國分得機器之價值及等級關係曾經調整後在賠償技術顧問委員會第十一次會議錄附件中最後修正為9,406部此次檢驗時盟總人員在32-32號廠內發現第2097,3427及3441號機器三部為木工機械又01-58號廠內第1570,1602及1606號機器三部經盟總研究係主體金屬成形機械(Primary Metal Working Equip.)均不應在此批分配之列業經決定保留故我國第一批計件機器分得實數為9398部

118

第一批計件機器先行接收數量分類統計表

三十六年十二月

廠編號	我國分得機器總數	先行接收機器總數	先行接收機器之類別及數量：工具機：鏜床	拉床	鑽床	切齒機	磨床	車床	銑床	龍門銑床	其他	合計	輔助金屬成形及切剪機械：彎摺機	水壓機	機械压機	冲剪眼刀及機	鍛工機械	線成形機械	手压機	其他	合計	先行接收機器之傳動及機件全缺情形：傳動情形：馬達全	馬達無或不全	皮帶軸傳動	人力工作	蒸汽水力或等	機件：相當齊全	不全
01-56	529	498	1	0	50	0	74	122	185	0	30	462	2	0	23	3	0	3	5	0	36	347	11	132	7	0	492	6
01-58	613	536	2	0	23	1	80	228	152	0	25	511	4	0	8	7	2	0	3	1	25	414	24	96	2	0	498	38
01-60D	202	168	0	0	8	1	14	71	45	0	24	163	0	0	2	0	0	0	3	0	5	151	10	4	3	0	163	5
11-5-5	243	163	12	0	11	4	18	65	11	3	14	140	2	5	0	6	10	2	0	0	25	90	47	12	2	12	147	16
11-5-7	341	170	7	0	16	5	5	94	24	4	7	162	1	0	1	3	0	1	2	0	8	63	78	24	5	0	153	17
13-53	162	101	1	0	13	1	18	32	11	3	12	91	2	0	1	3	4	0	0	0	10	72	13	13	2	1	98	3
19-18	1,120	967	38	2	68	15	95	471	146	20	53	908	3	1	32	6	13	2	1	1	59	683	141	137	2	4	908	59
19-20	655	451	2	0	33	8	28	240	48	4	44	407	7	6	10	13	5	1	1	1	44	209	224	5	7	6	(300)	(151)
19-32	1,513	610	31	1	53	19	49	227	52	15	72	519	15	9	5	22	35	2	3	0	91	132	352	81	10	35	523	87
24-4	744	473	2	0	1	0	18	221	16	1	43	302	0	11	148	0	0	0	12	0	171	90	316	50	17	0	409	64
24-5	502	352	1	1	26	1	36	135	112	0	29	341	0	1	8	0	0	0	2	0	11	254	35	58	1	0	306	46
27-1	639	594	7	2	54	12	54	285	97	0	67	578	0	0	4	4	6	0	2	0	16	491	46	50	2	5	518	76
27-4	613	559	6	1	73	19	93	208	89	0	32	522	4	3	12	11	3	0	0	4	37	365	147	45	0	2	527	32
32-30	51	24	0	0	0	0	1	1	0	0	2	4	0	0	0	0	0	0	20	0	20	2	1	1	24	0	24	0
32-32	1,253	744	43	0	49	4	49	285	104	41	96	671	0	3	12	7	49	2	0	0	73	312	293	95	0	44	688	56
39-50	99	60	0	0	8	0	1	26	8	1	0	44	0	3	2	0	0	0	11	0	16	1	1	44	14	0	53	7
39-51C	119	74	0	0	2	0	2	31	8	0	0	43	0	0	16	0	0	0	15	0	31	1	6	51	16	0	74	0
合計	9,398*	6,544	153	7	488	90	635	2,742	1,108	92	551	5,868	40	42	284	85	127	13	80	7	678	3,677	1,745	899	114	109	5,881	663
百分數	—	100	2.4	0.1	7.5	1.4	9.7	41.8	16.9	1.4	8.4	89.6	0.6	0.6	4.3	1.3	1.9	0.2	1.2	0.1	10.4	56.3	26.6	13.7	1.7	1.7	89.9	10.1
	100	69.7																										

* 我國分得機器最初抽得總數為9447部因平衡各盟國分得機器之價值及等級關係曾屢經調整後在賠償技術顧問委員會第十一次會議錄附件中最後修正為9406部此次檢驗時盟總人員在32-32號廠內發現第2097.3427及3441號機器三部為木工機械第11-5-5號廠第2172,2182號機器兩部為兵工機械又01-58號廠內第1570,1602及1606號機器三部經盟總研究係主要金屬成形機械（Primary metal working Equipment）均不應在此批分配之列業經决定保留故我國第一批計件機器分得實數為9398部　（）估計數字

永利化学工业公司关于将前准拨给补助费三百万元仍维持原案准予销案或比照政府规定之战前存款偿还办法交还事呈行政院文（一九四八年二月二十四日）

为再呈艰困恳将前准拨给补助费三百万元仍维持原案准予销案或比照政府规定之战前存款偿还办法缴还乞批示由

鈞會前以民廿六年八月鑒於當時抗戰情勢險惡，爲保存國家原氣計，經呈准在後方另建鹼廠，並蒙撥給補助費三百萬元，嗣又奉令改爲官股一案，經於去年十月十五日具呈縷陳辦理建廠及勝利後召開股東大會經過，懇請維持原案，仍准以補助費銷案，諒蒙鈞察，查公司戰時在川建設鹼廠，艱險備嘗，由國外內運器材，先後在香港，海防及滇緬路被敵封奪，損失慘重，嗣於萬分困難中得能產製純鹼，供應後方軍工需要，已盡最大努力，勝利以後，南北兩廠雖告收復，但經八年之佔領摧殘，已屬敗窳不堪，非復舊觀矣，修整裝配，耗費尤鉅，而產量仍難恢復戰前情形，處境之艱困，衆所週知，想亦早在洞[illegible]中央[illegible]現川省[illegible]廠仍在慘淡經營中，[illegible]本案又經上屆股東大會議決，

中華民國卅七年二月廿六日發出

075

061

請本維護民營工業之初衷，體恤商艱，維持原案仍以補助費銷案，而公司本屬純粹之民營國防化工重工業之一，其性質及創設經過，與其他行商　然不同，因不欲供敵利用，乃聲請　政府補助，俾在後方另建鹼廠，誓與國家共存亡，當時　政府暨　領袖嘉恤公司范總經理旭東之遠見及氣節與損失之慘重，第一次撥給之四十萬元亦係以補助令發下者，足見事無前例，後乏來者，其後中途令飭改為官股，戰時既無法召開股東大會，集議取捨，惶惑之情，實無已時，茲幸勝利復員，應懇體念公司戰時損失之慘重，勉力供獻於國於民者不無微勞，務乞一本愛護之初衷俯賜成全，仍請維持原案以補助費銷案，或比照政府規定之戰前存款償還辦法，以一千七百三十倍由公司備款一次繳付抵償之，基於公司之性

076

062

質不同及情形特殊，且原案本係密請予以補助，俾資遷建，應無顧慮其他行商效尤之必要，迫切陳辭，無任翹企待命之至，謹呈

行政院

院長張

副院長王

永利化學工業公司總經理侯德榜 謹呈

地址：上海四川中路四一〇號

永利化学工业公司铔厂与中华民国驻日代表团日本赔偿及归还物资接收委员会、行政院物资赔偿委员会督运委员会等关于日本劫夺永利化学工业公司硝酸厂全套机件设备督运回国往来函件

（一九四八年四月十二日至五月五日）

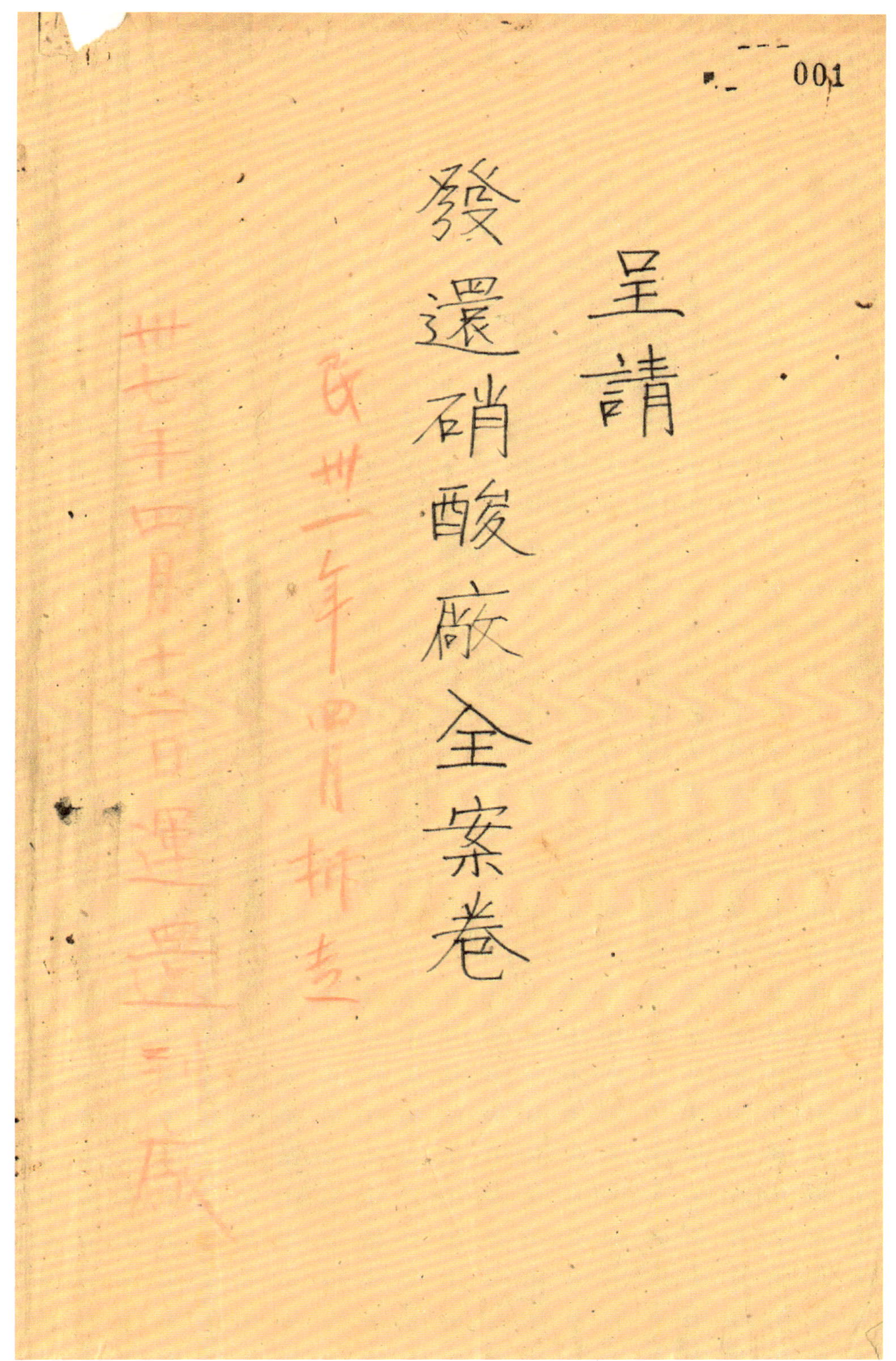

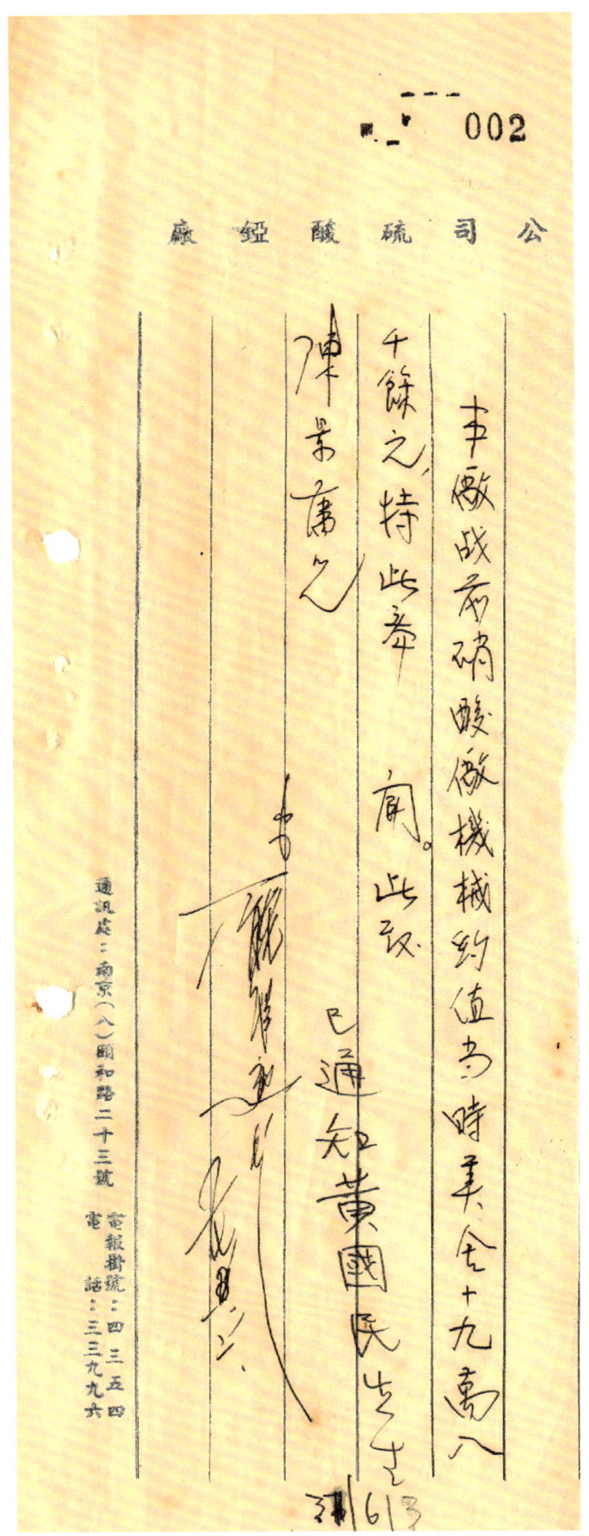

002

公司硫酸錏廠

本廠戰前硝酸廠機械約值為時美金十九萬八千餘元，特此奉
聞。此致
陳業廉兄

已通知黃國民先生

[illegible]

通訊處：南京（八）頤和路二十三號 電報掛號：四三五四 電話：三三九九六

613

永利化學工業公司錏廠

抄

總處

003

存根

錏總字第三五一號第全頁 卅七年五月三日

敬啟者：此次日本歸還封存敝廠物資硝酸廠全套機件設備，

荷蒙

鼎力交涉，關顧周至，得以順利接收。

隆情厚誼，無任感篆。查該項歸還機件計共一四八二件（據裝箱清冊），業由日本大牟田三池港裝海鄂輪於本年四月十一日安抵敝廠，刻正按照裝箱清冊清查點收中。除清冊中第四項在日本失竊之白金網壹張，以係主要並貴重機件之一，仍須瀆請

貴會惠予交涉追還原件或責令日本按照原件賠償外，特此奉聞，並致謝忱。敬祈

詧照，爲荷。

此致

中華民國駐日代表團

日本賠償及歸還物資接收委員會

永利化學工業公司錏廠 啟

廠址：江蘇省六合縣卸甲甸 通訊處：南京(八)頭和路二十三號 電話：三三九九六 電報掛號：四三五四 南京

駐京辦事處：同通信處

抄

005

永利化學工業公司錏廠

原件交京處黃樹人先生持往洽辦

日本賠償及歸還物資督運委員會代電

督(巴)儲字第二九〇號

中華民國卅七年五月五日

事由：電復歸還物資無專用許可證已請財政部轉飭金陵關知照由

永利化學工業公司錏廠鑒：錏總字第三四二號函悉。除將歸還物資之輸入並無專用許可證情由電請財政部轉飭金陵關知照外，特復。日本賠償及歸還物資督運委員會長微儲

通信處：南京(四)區行政院內

第　頁

006

永利化學工業公司硫酸錏廠

錏總(37)字第三四二號

卅七年四月卅日

敬啟者：前敝廠由日本大牟田三池港，装海鄂輪運回之日本歸還物資硝酸廠全套機件設備，諸荷鼎力協助，得於本年四月十一日順利抵廠，至深感紉。頃金陵關促敝廠補辦歸還物資輸入許可證，以完手續。查該項許可證之頒發，初僅限於賠償物資，嗣經鈞院通令，關於歸還物資，亦准援例辦理，相應函請惠予出具証明書，是感。

此致

行政院物資賠償委員會督運委員會

永利化學工業公司錏廠　啟

通訊處：南京(八)頤和路二十三號
電報掛號：四三五四
電話：三三九九六

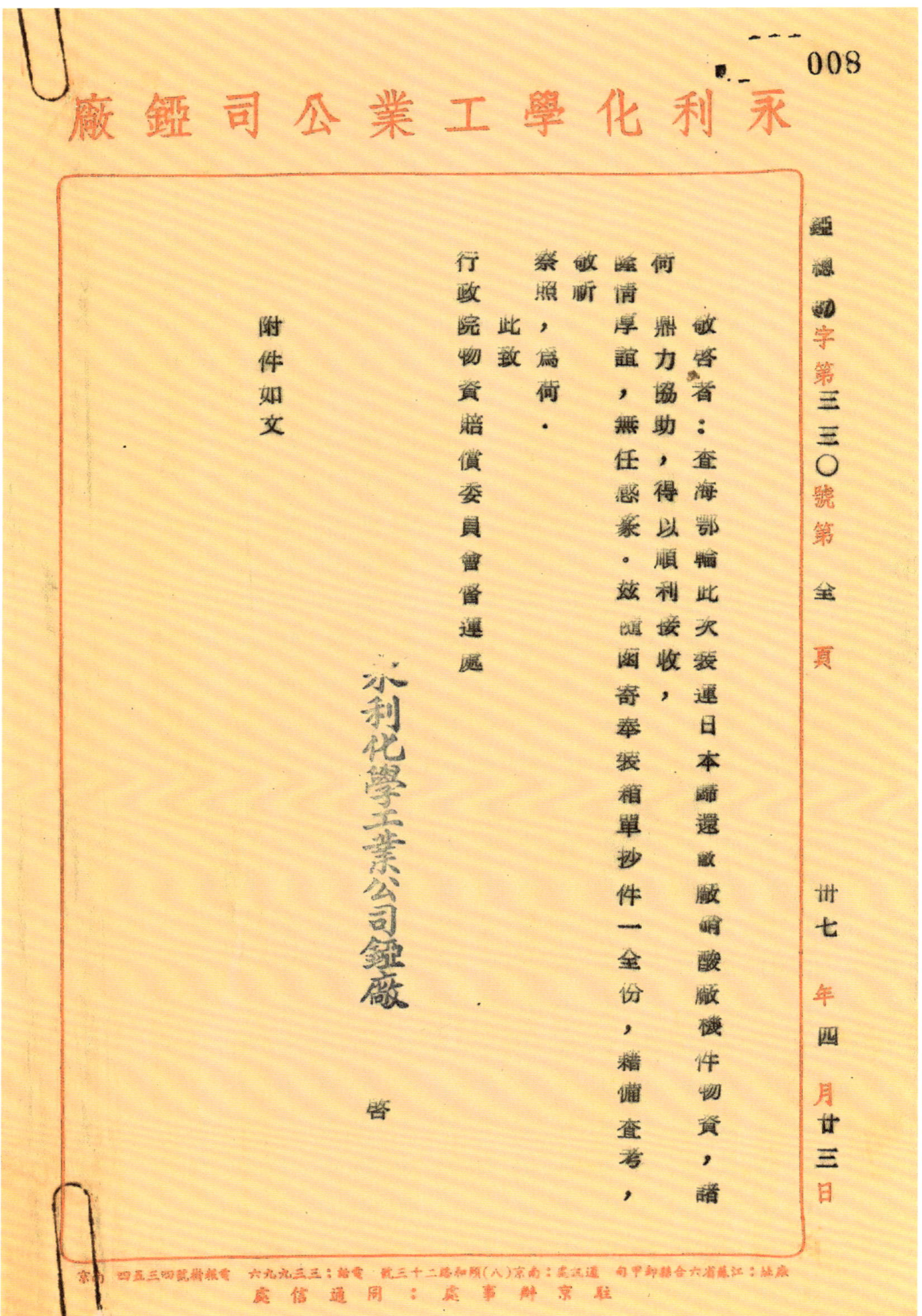

008

永利化學工業公司錏廠

錏總[illegible]字第三三〇號第　全　頁

卅七年四月廿三日

敬啓者：查海鄂輪此次裝運日本歸還敝廠硝酸廠機件物資，諸

荷

鼎力協助，得以順利接收，

隆情厚誼，無任感篆。茲隨函寄奉裝箱單抄件一全份，藉備查考，

敬祈

察照，爲荷。

此致

行政院物資賠償委員會督運處

附件如文

永利化學工業公司錏廠　啓

廠址：江蘇省六合縣卸甲甸　通訊處：南京(八)頤和路二十三號　電話：三三九九六　電報掛號四三五四南京

駐京辦事處：同通信處

永利化学工业公司铔厂申请价配日本赔偿物资补建厂计划书（一九四八年四月二十四日）

附：永利化学工业公司铔厂申请价配日本赔偿物资申请表

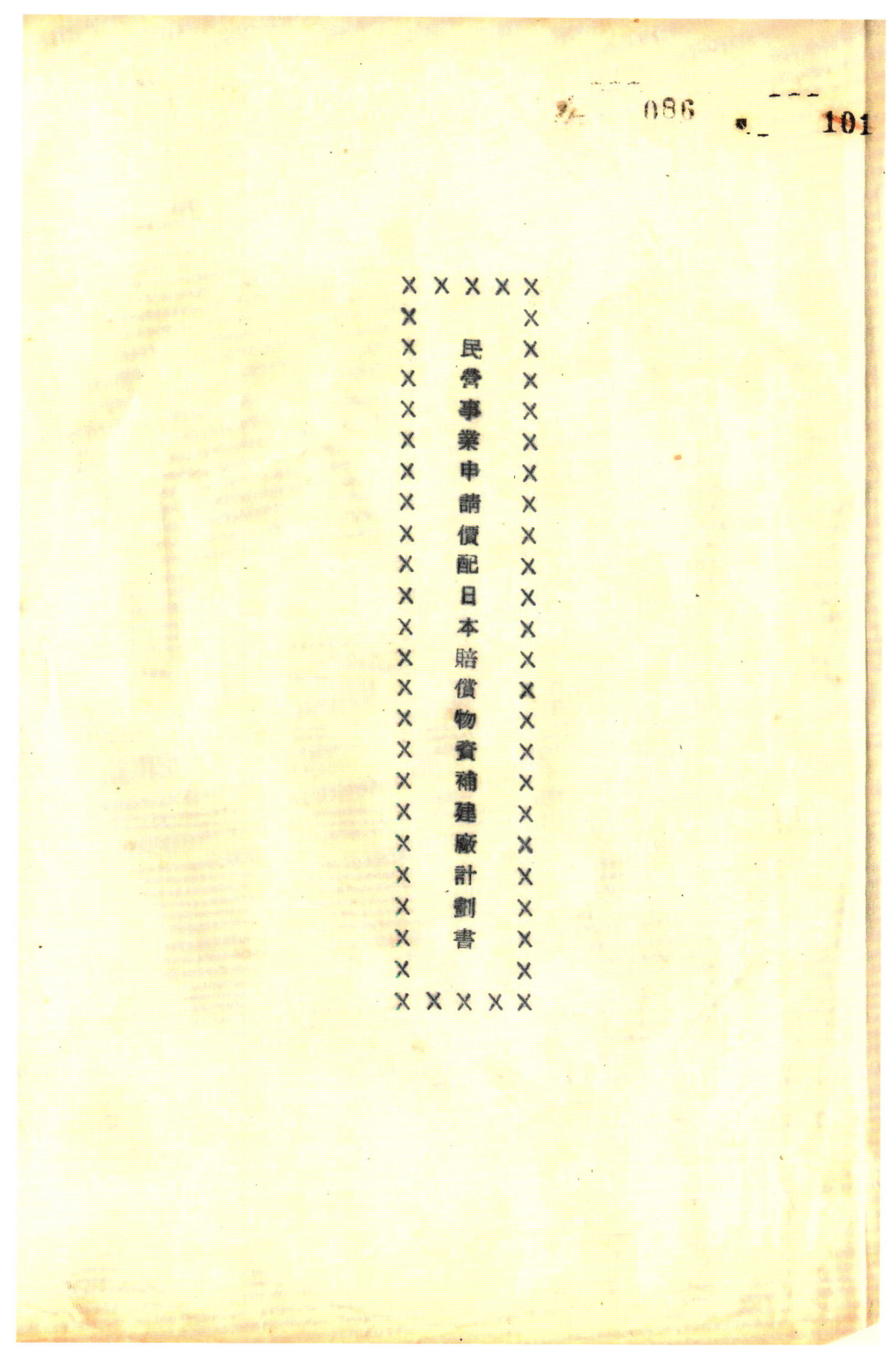

086　101

民營事業申請價配日本賠償物資補建廠計劃書

087

102

民營事業申請價配日本賠償物資補建廠計劃書

一、補充與新建廠名稱及地點：

1 廠名：江蘇省六合縣卸甲甸硫酸錏廠硝酸廠等。

2 地址：江蘇省六合縣卸甲甸。

3 廠基：廠基共約貳千畝，廠房約共陸百伍拾畝。

二、補充與建廠理由：

查公司戰前所建卸甲甸硫酸硝酸廠原有機電廠設備，因受日寇八年佔用，損壞至爲奇重，急需購置，方足以供應本廠各部機器添補製造及修繕之要求。

三、規模：

一、機器製造廠二、鍛煉場三、鉚工場四、鉛工場五、電機修配場六、模型場七、電焊場以上各場之設備除能從事普通機器之配件製造外，並擬能進而仿造國外定購之特種機器。預計全部設備計劃完成後，每月可出壹百伍拾噸之機器成品。

四、擬請價配日本賠償物資之種類及數量：

（詳見附表）

五、擬增添之設備：

（詳見二項補充與建廠理由欄）

六、工廠組織：

技師長一人，各場主任副主任各一人，技師副技師技術員各若干人。

七、集資總額：　國幣肆百柒拾伍億圓整。

一、價配賠償物資費　貳百億圓整

二、拆遷及運輸賠償物資費　柒拾伍億圓整

三、增添設備費　肆拾伍億圓整

四、購置廠基及建築房屋費　陸拾柒億伍千萬圓整

五、裝置設備費　叁拾億圓整

六、流動資金　伍拾柒億伍千萬圓整

八、內運計劃：

自行內運。

九、建廠時期：

本廠所屬機電廠均已具規模，補充較易，如大量價配機器運到本廠，預計半年內可以完成。

104

089

（一）開始建廠時期（詳上從略）

（二）完成建廠時期（詳上從略）

十、業務計劃：

（一）原料之供應

1.普通金屬及器材盡量在國內採購。

2.特種金屬及器材必要時在國外採購。

（二）製品之銷售及銷場

除盡量供給本公司各廠自用外，如有剩餘則以之供應國內市銷。

（三）收支概況　（從略）

（四）成本之預算　（從略）

（五）技術員之聘僱

除利用已有設備自行訓練外，並選派赴美實習與向國內各大學徵聘專門人才。

十一、除已派專門人員與各廠會同設計並實習外，且已着手從事國內各地所需各種鑛產之探勘，藉謀原料自給。

永利化學工業公司錏廠

民營事業申請價配日本賠償物資申請表

申請人永利化學工業公司錏廠茲依照行政院卅六年七月七日公佈之民營事業申請價配日本賠償物資辦法之規定申請配售表內所載各項賠償物資在江蘇六合縣卸甲甸本廠地方補充製造及修理電器機具工廠

謹填明本表所列各事項如左

申請廠鏞	永利化學工業公司錏廠					
廠長資歷	姓名	傅爾攽	年齡	六十三歲	籍貫	江西南昌
	性別	男				
	學歷	日本東京帝國大學工科大學造船工學士				
	曾任職務	曾任永利製鹼工廠工程技師工程部長暨本公司錏廠副廠長駐渝辦事處主任川廠副廠長等職現任永利化學工業公司協理錏廠廠長				
主任技師或總工程師資歷	姓名	章懷西 謝為杰	年齡	四十九 四十一	籍貫	江蘇江陰 福建林森
	性別	男 男				
	學歷	蘇州工業專門學校應化科 美國渥海渥省立大學化學工程哲學博士				
	曾任職務	曾任本公司塘沽鹼廠技師及川廠部長現任本廠技師長 曾任本公司川廠部長現任本廠技師長				
原有工廠設備及從戰時在後方工作成績與已否在經濟部備案或領有獎勵書狀	執有經濟部工廠登記證工字八二七四號一紙。本公司在川曾製造純鹼、並提煉人造汽油、供戰時後方工業及軍需之用。					
申請日本賠償物資之種類及數量（名目多者應另附表）	詳列附表					
擬舉辦之事業	補充製造及修理電器機具工廠					
集資總額及投資人姓名	本公司現資金額為國幣壹百億圓					
建廠地點	江蘇省六合縣卸甲甸					
希望物資運達沿海何港口	上海（或逕運至南京）					
預定建廠或補充完成時期	機件全部運到後，約半年內即可裝置完成					
建廠或補充完成後預計產品種類及每年產量	補充完成後，每天可增產約二分之一。					
附呈建廠計劃書	一份					

右表所列各項敬請

核轉審定准予配售謹呈

經濟部

申請人 永利化學工業公司錏廠

負責人 廠長 傅爾攽

中華民國 三十七年 四 月 二十四 日

工商部关于赔偿机械发现有遭故意破损事给永利化学工业公司的通知（抄件）（一九四八年八月二十八日）

006

抄送 物料部

抄工商部通知

卅七年八月廿八日
京賠37字七四一七二號

通知永利化學工業公司

案准行政院賠償委員會三十七年七月二十日京(賠)二字第六二〇九號代電開：

「據接收委員會寒申電稱日本賠償技術顧問委員會會議英代表謂該國運回之賠償機械發現有遭故意破損者請盟總賠償組注意當經決議各國如發現同樣情形應將損壞機器之詳情如(1)工廠編號(2)機器編號(3)裝箱號碼(4)損壞情形等列單送交盟總賠償組以憑核辦及懲處理合電請轉知有關單位如發現類似情形應迅即查明開具清單寄日以憑轉洽辦理再賠償機器缺少重要機件者如發現其有遭故意隱匿移去之可能亦可另行列單以便交涉等情查各機關接收日本賠償物資如發現有故意損壞者或缺少重要機件而有

故意隱匿移去之可能情事應即依照原電所列各點詳細列單送會以便轉飭洽辦嗣後接收機器如發現有同樣情事並希隨時列報本會核轉交涉據電前情除分電外相應電請查照辦理為荷」

等由到部查配售該公司之工具機如發現有同樣情事仰即依照附發之損壞情形報告表詳填二份送部以憑核轉特此通知

附承售第一批日本賠償工具機損壞情形報告表一份

承售第一批日本賠償工具機損壞情形報告表

工廠編號	機器編號	裝箱號碼	損壞情形	備考

某某（廠或礦公司）

永利化学工业公司铔厂关于高压机零件损坏无法修补续用拟向日本神户制钢所订制运回应用事呈工商部文及工商部批复（一九四八年九月十一日至十月二十日）

附：对日贸易计划

存根

抄送總處 復舊室 京處

趙魯 先生

143

097

永利化學工業公司鋲廠 呈 工商部

爲高壓機零件損壞，無法修補續用，擬向日本神戶製鋼所訂製，運回應用，謹編具零件名稱數量表等件，呈懇 示遵由。

如文

鋲呈(37)字第二四號

卅七年九月十一日

竊工廠在平時雖爲農肥製造機構，一入戰時，即可改製軍火原料，關係國防，至爲鉅大。故當民國廿六年抗戰發生後，最爲日敵嫉恨，迭派空軍前來襲炸。首都不守，工廠遂隨而陷入敵手，强佔使用，更極盡摧毁之能事。以是壽命足支十年而民國廿六年春方告成功之工廠，不幸在敵八年長期粗使暴用下，損壞至爲慘重。日敵投降後，公司奉令派員回廠辦理接收工作時，曾利用敵人原有技術人員，幾度試行開工，徒以軀殼僅存，機件碱腐，終告失敗。旋蒙 政府令由國行優予貸款，集中人力、物力，從事修葺，歷時十閱月，乃得補苴罅漏，勉强復工。然迄今兩載，以機器損壞過重，東滲西漏，修補工作無日中輟，耗費浩繁。而生產總額仍無法恢復戰前工廠設計時預定每日產量之目標。揆之恆情，任何工廠，在此種產量不能達到相當設計數字，而所耗電力、動力以及人員、材料等費絕難減少之現狀下，決不能繼續存在。然工廠尚能支持以迄今玆者：賴有　政府不斷實際援助；而工廠同仁亦均能遵守范故總經理旭東先生之指示，事業目的在期爲社會大衆謀福利之原旨下，咸能黽勉將事，力求報稱；以待日本賠償物資之運回配給，俾將無法應用之機件一一更換，藉使生產量早能恢復舊觀。詎意有關工廠戰時損失報告暨附表自從卅六年一月廿七日由公司以總普字第八號呈遞送鈞部，懇於首批撤卸日本國內性質相同工廠機件時撥給工廠，以彌損失以來，時逾一年，賠償機件猶稽輸入；而工廠前項戰時損失報告表內所列之高壓機零件 Liners & Piston Rings for Gas Cylinders 及 Liners

& Piston Rings for Steam Cylinders 等，已陷無法再行修補，繼續使用絕境。查工廠採用之高壓機，原係德國 Rheinmetall-Borsig 製造，現該廠業被解散，致工廠急待補充之高壓機零件，無法向其訂購，僅日本神戶製鋼所保存德國原圖樣，可以仿造；爲濟急計，爰擬懇祈

鈞部，准由工廠直接向日本神戶製鋼所洽訂趕製上項零件，運廠應用，以維生存。至所需全部工料費用如何支付？以事關對外貿易，自當遵待

指示辦理。爲此理合編具擬購高壓機零件名稱及數量表一紙，暨節抄工廠戰時損失報告表內所列有關此項損失原文一份，備文呈乞

鑒核，並懇

批示祗遵，不勝迫切待命之至。

101 147

謹呈

工商部部長陳

附呈：擬向日本神戶製鋼所訂購之高壓機零件名稱數量表一份

戰時損失報告表內所列有關高壓機損失原文節抄一份

具呈人 永利化學工業公司錏廠

通訊處：南京（八一）頤和路廿三號

抄工商部批

菱文京國37字第七九七五四号
中華民國卅七年十月廿日發出

原具呈人永利化學工業公司錏廠

三十七年九月十一日呈一件為擬向日本訂購高壓机各種零件懇示遵由

呈件均悉查所請擬向日本訂購高压机各種零件尚屬需要按照現行對日貿易規章對日貿易以易貨為原則該廠應備具履歷表六份相片二張貿易計劃三份公司登記执照影片一張經由上海市商会轉呈本部再予核办如該廠不擬易貨自備外滙訂購所需器材可按照現行「中央銀行外幣外滙存款支付办法」办理並逕向輸出入管理委員会洽办茲檢發履歷表及貿易計劃表式各一份仰即知照此批。

抄發履歷表及貿易計劃表式各一份

對日貿易計劃（表式）

民國三十　年　月　日製

（一）輸出部份

品名	擬輸出數量	單位	單位價格	合計價格	備註
總計					

（二）輸入部份

品名	擬輸入數量	單位	單位價格	合計價格	備註
總計					

填表說明：

（一）品名應用最通行之名稱並須附註英文

（二）單位欄應與「一九四八年對日輸出入貨品計劃表」內各貨品所列之單位相同

（三）單位價格欄進口貨以美金計算出口貨以法幣計算

日本归还物资处理委员会关于硝酸铔厂设备中之被盗白金网筛一案给永利化学工业公司的通知（抄件）

（一九四八年十月十五日）

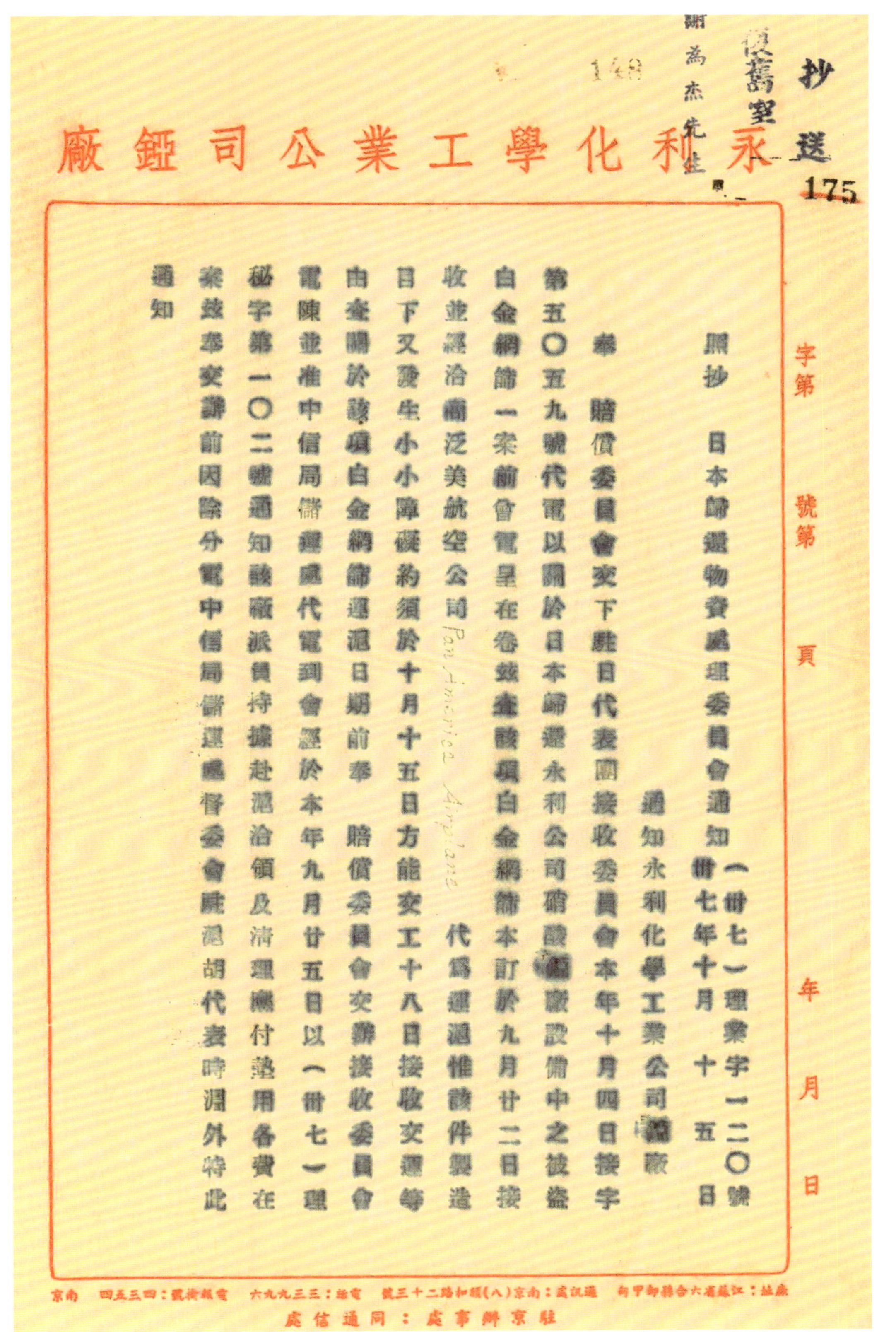
抄送

侯德榜室

謝為杰先生

148

175

永利化學工業公司錏廠

照抄 日本歸還物資處理委員會通知 （卅七）理業字一二〇號

卅七年十月十五日

通知永利化學工業公司錏廠

奉 賠償委員會交下駐日代表團接收委員會本年十月四日接字第五〇五九號代電以關於日本歸還永利公司硝酸錏廠設備中之被盜白金網篩一案前曾電呈在卷茲查該項白金網篩本訂於九月廿二日接收並經洽商泛美航空公司代爲運滬惟該件製造日下又發生小小障礙約須於十月十五日方能交工十八日接收交運等由奉此關於該項白金網篩運滬日期前奉 賠償委員會交辦接收委員會電陳並准中信局儲運處代電到會經於本年九月廿五日以（卅七）理秘字第一〇二號通知該廠派員持據赴滬洽領及清理應付墊用各費在案茲奉交辦前因除分電中信局儲運處督委會駐滬胡代表時潤外特此通知

Pan America Airplane

廠址：江蘇省六合縣卸甲甸 通訊處：南京（八）頤和路二十三號 電話：三三九九六 電報掛號：四三五四 南京

駐京辦事處：同通信處

工商部与永利化学工业公司订立的民营事业价购日本赔偿物资契约及契约价购等（一九四八年十月二十五日）

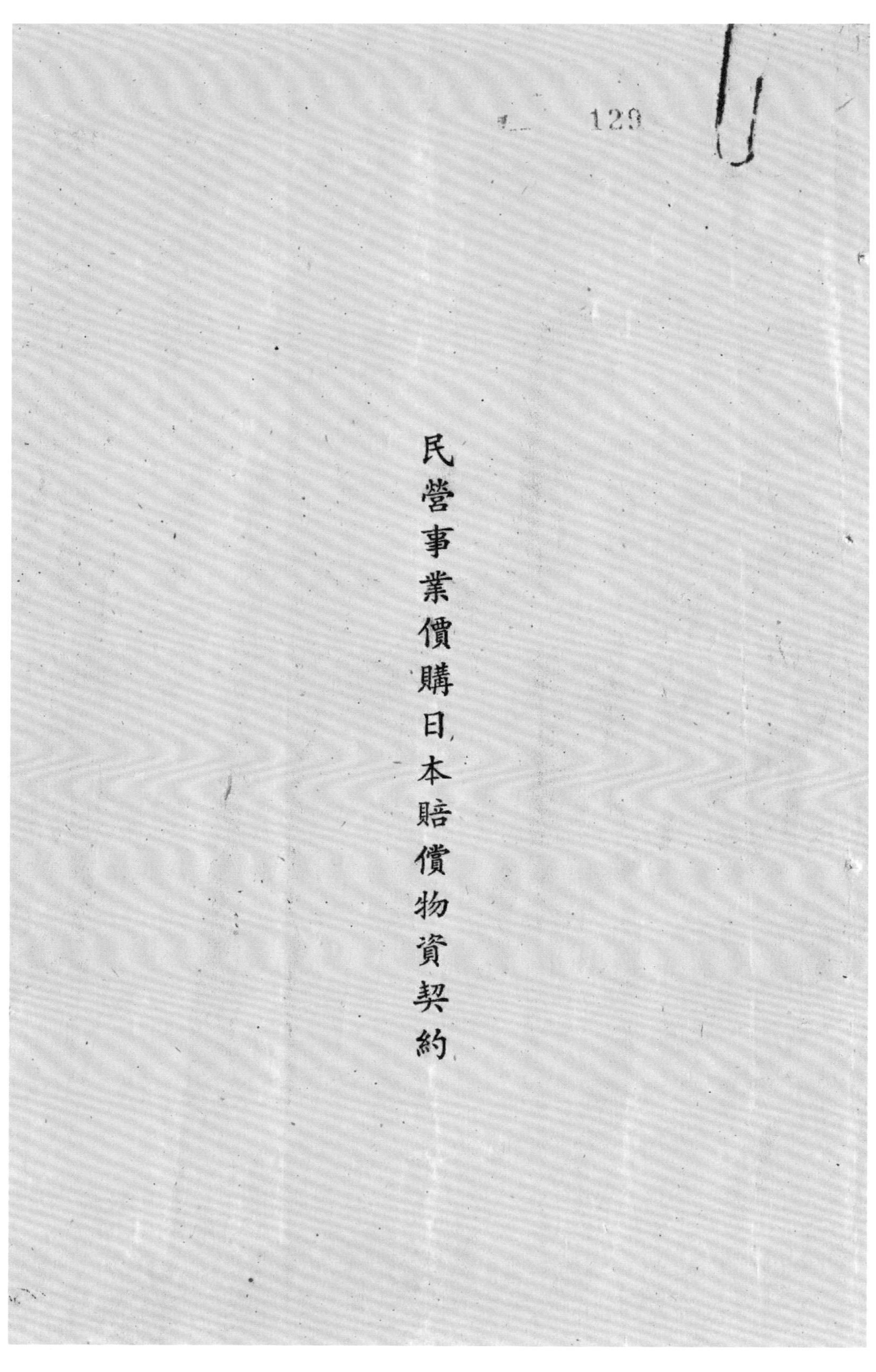
129

民營事業價購日本賠償物資契約

民營事業價購日本賠償物資契約

（以下簡稱甲方）

並契約人 永利化學工業公司錏廠 部（以下簡稱乙方） 茲因甲方奉准價購

日本賠償物資承辦工廠除依照（民營事業申請價配日本賠償物資辦法）規定辦理外關於所購該項物資之接受驗收及繳付價款等項訂明條款如次：

（一）本契約所價購之物資承購人（即甲方）應悉依民營事業申請價配日本賠償物資辦法之規定繳納全部價款甲方即或在戰時受有損失不得藉口請求將其未來應得之賠償費在價款內扣抵

（二）甲方價購之物資其詳細清單以在東京盟軍總部發表拆遷工廠設備中所列各項機器設備之品名種類式樣規格能力大小及數量為準

（三）甲方價購之物資於物資運抵我國港口時即在船邊點收甲方並應設有負責接收單位準備存放該項物資之倉庫

（四）自我國港口起貨所需費用由甲方自行負擔

（五）如甲方對第三第四兩項未經準備存放該物資之倉庫其起卸存儲保險保管等項事務得由乙方代為辦理但所有各該項費用概由甲方按照乙方已代付之數額於提取物資時一次繳交乙方歸墊

（六）自日本港口運抵我國港口之該項物資所需費用如交收完畢後由甲方於三日內備款一次逕向乙方繳納轉交歸墊

（七）甲方點收物資時應分批出具收據以為接收該項物資之憑證俟全部物資收到後再行換掣總收據

（八）甲方所購物資如在拆遷途中遇有遺失損壞情事時得在全部價款內減繳該損失部份之價款惟對交貨與繳款之規定不生任何影响

（九）甲方所購物資之價值以照評價委員會評定數額經審定者為準並以美金為計算單位

026

（十）甲方繳納價款依左列之規定辦理

甲、本契約所列價購物資價款全部計美金壹萬玖仟玖佰叁拾柒元捌角伍分叁厘正

乙、核定可價購時繳納初估評定價款百分之五之保證金計美金玖佰玖拾柒元正 元

丙、物資在日本起運尚未全部運達我國港口期內繳納初估全部價款百分之十五計美金貳仟玖佰玖拾元正 元（其物資已運達我國港口者本項價款與保證金同時繳納）

丁、點交物資前繳納全部初估評定價款百分之二十計美金（因係內遷工廠得分五六兩期繳納）元憑收據點交物資

戊、評定價與初估價如有出入其差額於下次繳付價款時補足或扣除之

己、其餘未繳價款計全部評定價格百分之八十五共美金壹萬陸仟玖佰肆拾柒元捌角伍分叁厘正自乙方正式通知甲方接收單發出之日起算分六期繳納每六個月繳納一次其繳納期限及數目如次表

期別	到期 年 月 日	金額	約估全數百分比
第一期	三十八年四月廿六日	計美金叁仟玖佰捌拾柒元陸角正（約估數）	初估評價20%
第二期	三十八年十月廿六日	計美金叁仟玖佰捌拾柒元陸角正（約估數）	初估評價20%
第三期	三十九年四月廿六日	計美金貳仟玖佰玖拾元正（約估數）	初估評價15%
第四期	三十九年十月廿六日	計美金壹仟玖佰玖拾肆元（約估數）	初估評價10%
第五期	四十年四月廿六日	計美金壹仟玖佰玖拾肆元（約估數）	初估評價10%
第六期	四十年十月廿六日	計美金壹仟玖佰玖拾肆元捌角伍分叁厘（約估數）	初估評價10%

應繳價款內扣除之

（十一）前項價款繳付時得按當時中央銀行掛牌美金市價比率折合法幣繳付

（十二）甲方對於應繳價款不得拖延如過期未繳時其應繳未繳之款應由甲方及其保證人連帶負責清償乙方認為必要時亦得依民營事業申請價配日本賠償物資辦法第九條之規定處理之甲方放棄先

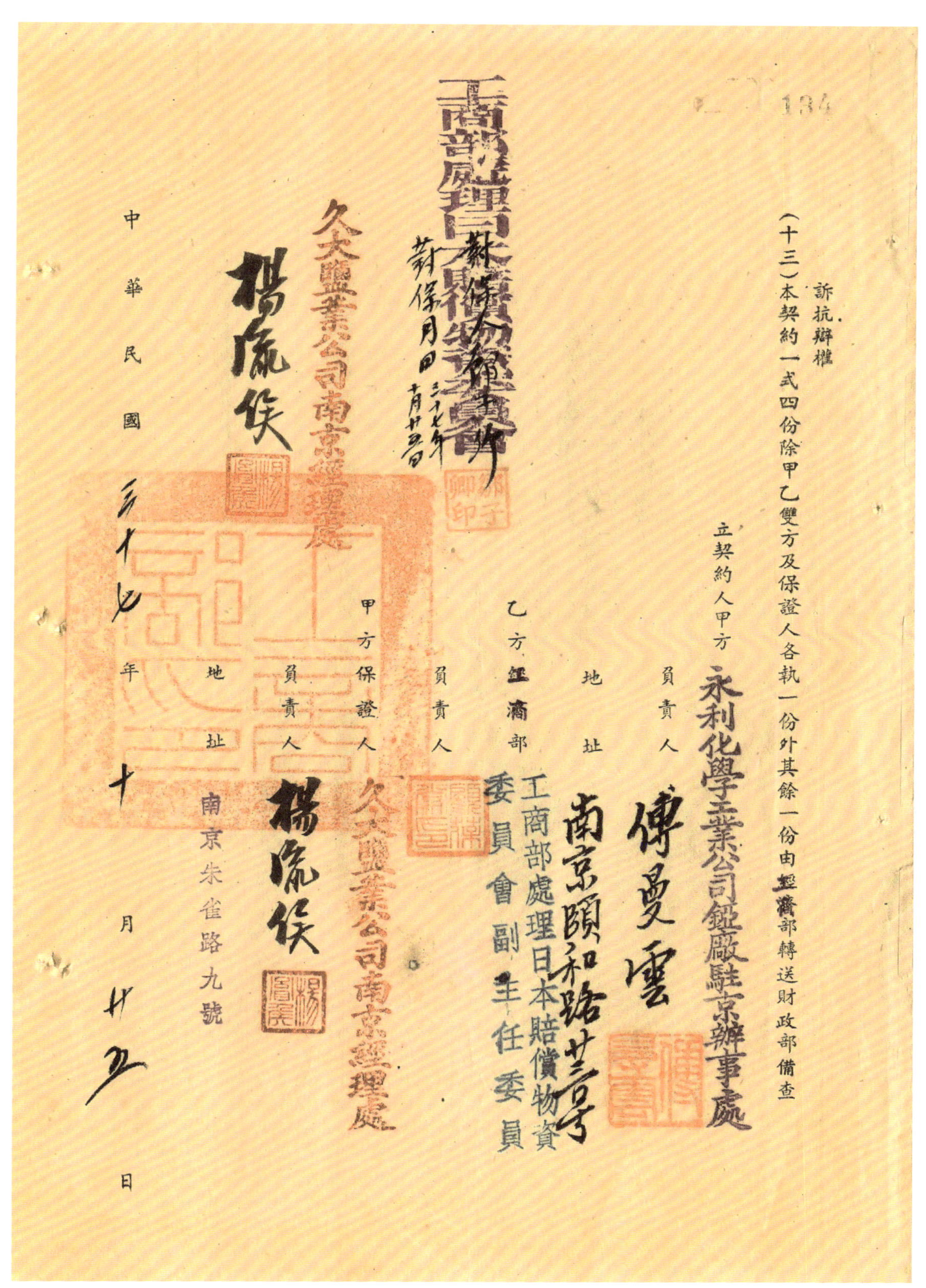

134

訴抗辯權

（十三）本契約一式四份除甲乙雙方及保證人各執一份外其餘一份由經濟部轉送財政部備查

立契約人甲方 永利化學工業公司錏廠駐京辦事處

負責人 傅曼雲

地址 南京頤和路廿三號

乙方經濟部 工商部處理日本賠償物資委員會副主任委員

負責人

甲方保證人 久大鹽業公司南京經理處

負責人 楊勵侯

地址 南京朱雀路九號

久大鹽業公司南京經理處

楊勵侯

中華民國三十七年十月廿五日

163

198

编號 83

本契约價購各工具機清單

機器名稱	分類號碼 S.C.C. Code No.	部數	每部機器號碼 position Code No.	機器暫定價值	海運費
Drilling Machine	34-13-592	1	2464	1394.305	33,586
Grinding Machine	34-15-190	1	4172	2665.544	79.818
Lathe	34-16-1121	1	9576	251.074	21.949
"	34-16-1131	1	10682	854.171	另行通知
"	34-16-1151	2	13354	1326.137	另行通知
			13362	1326.137	另行通知
"	34-16-1161	1	14264	591.649	70.119
"	34-16-1918	1	16624	731.626	69.778
"	34-16-9006	1	20396	905.687	715.221
"	34-16-9007	1	20402	1302.981	233.807
Shaper	34-19-124	1	27442	707.690	50.661
Mechanical Press	34-43-174	1	29824	7880.852	328.104
Total		12		19937.853	

工商部配售本公司日本賠償工具機清單

總號	分類號碼	機器名稱	機器號碼	機件情形	共裝幾箱	箱號	存倉號碼	附註
2464	34-13-592	Drilling Machine	1751	Complete	1	394	1401	
4172	34-15-190	Grinding Machine	447	Without Motor		618	1111	
9576	34-16-1121	Lathe	691	Complete	2	108	1318	
						109	1319	
10682	34-16-1131	"	974	Complete	1	397	1708	
13354	34-16-1151	"	680	Complete	1	287	1705	
13362	34-16-1151	"	569	Complete	1	241	1756	
14264	34-16-1161	"	3211	Complete	1	255	110	
16624	34-16-1918	"	3919	Complete	1	357	1017	
20396	34-16-9006	"	303	Complete	3	208	E636	
						209	E628	
						210		
20402	34-16-9007	"	2697	Without Motor		1141	638	
27442	34-19-124	Shaper	91	Without Motor		154	1367	
29824	34-43-174	Mechanical Press	3131	Complete	6	1143	658	
						1144	1214	
						1145	1215	
						1146	1216	
						1147	1218	
						1149	1217	
29824	34-43-174	Mechanical Press	3131	Complete	2	1148	E685	
						1142	E684	

167

第一聯

繳款通知單

繳款人	繳款性質	限期			金額	國庫
		年	月	日		
永利化學工業公司錏廠	補繳海運費(29824号續到兩箱)				U.S.$324 282	向上海南京東路119号二樓5B室交通部日本賠償及歸還物資運輸處上海辦事處換取送款簿赴央行業務局繳款

以上通知

永利化學工業公司錏廠

(繳款人)

工商部

(此處顧係常蓋章)

37年10月26日

此聯送繳款人

編號·第 56 號　Page 1

提取日本賠償工具機通知單　正本

通知：永利化學公司

查下開日本賠償工具机經由本部核轉行政院賠償委員會審定配售該廠（公司）使用業經訂立價購契約其應繳之款亦經該廠（公司）付清茲以該項工具机業已運抵上海招商局第　碼頭倉庫仰即派員於本年　月　日以前持同正式收據及繳款收據前往該地倉庫提取逾期如未提取即應按月另收儲倉費用特此通知

本單副本第三四聯兩份寄交上海工商輔導處

工商部　37 年 10 月 29 日

總號	分類號碼	機器名稱	規範	機器號碼	機件情形	共裝箱數	箱號	存倉號碼	附註
2464	34-13-592	Drilling Machine		1751	Complete	1	394	1401	
4172	34-15-190	Grinding Machine		447	Without Motor		618	1111	
9576	34-16-1121	Lathe		691	Complete	2	108	1318	
							109	1319	
10682	34-16-1131	"		974	Complete	1	397	1708	
13354	34-16-1151	"		680	Complete	1	287	1705	
13362	34-16-1151	"		569	Complete	1	241	1756	
14264	34-16-1161	"		3211	Complete	1	255	110	
16624	34-16-1918	"		3919	Complete	1	357	1017	

主管	顧條常（章）	記帳人	陳可權（章）	覆核人	譚哲（章）	核對人	陳可權（章）	製單人	昌利（章）

契約號碼 83

說明 (1)上開之總号，分类号碼，机器名称，規範，机器号碼及機件情形係根據盟總所發之清單及我國駐日代表團之檢驗報告填寫。
(2)提貨人於提貨時應當面開箱点驗（其開箱費用由提貨人自理）如有缺損，應在正式收據上註明，事後申請，本部概不受理。

第一聯：由價購廠商存查。通知單正本，寄交價購廠商以憑前往倉庫提貨，提貨之後，本聯

~~165~~ 168 206

169 ~~166~~

通知單第56號　Page 1　提取日本賠償工具機正式收據　收據正本　編號：

承購廠商　永利化學公司　提貨日期：　年　月　日

下開日本賠償工具機業經本　提訖並經開箱點驗確與下開各節符合

此據

（廠商圖記必須與印鑑片字樣相符）　（負責人簽名蓋章）　（點驗人簽章）　（提取人簽章）

契約號碼 83

總號	分類號碼	機器名稱	規範	機器號碼	機件情形	共裝幾箱	箱號	存倉號碼	附註
2464	34-13-592	Drilling Machine		1751	Complete	1	394	1401	
4172	34-15-190	Grinding Machine		447	Without Motor		618	1111	
9576	34-16-1121	Lathe		691	Complete	2	108	1318	
							109	1319	
10682	34-16-1131	"		974	Complete	1	397	1708	
13354	34-16-1151	"		680	Complete	1	287	1705	
13362	34-16-1151	"		569	Complete	1	241	1756	
14264	34-16-1161	"		3211	Complete	1	255	110	
16624	34-16-1918	"		3919	Complete	1	357	1017	

最後核對		主管		發貨人		覆核人	譚哲(章)	核對人	陳可權(章)	製單人	昌利(章)

註：憑據提貨，如有遺失，須先掛號。

第二聯：收據正本，提貨之後，由倉庫負責人加蓋「提訖」字樣，送由上海工商輔導處轉呈工商部核對存查。

207

通知單第56號 Page 1　提取日本賠償工具機正式收據 收據副本　編號：

承購廠商　永利化學公司　提貨日期：　年　月　日

下開日本賠償工具機業經本　提訖並經開箱點驗確與下開各節符合

此據

（廠商圖記必須與印鑑片字樣相符）　（負責人簽名蓋章）　（點驗人簽章）　（提取人簽章）

契約號碼 83

總號	分類號碼	機器名稱	規範	機器號碼	機件情形	共裝總箱	箱號	存倉號碼	附註
2464	34-13-592	Drilling Machine		1751	Complete	1	394	1401	
4172	34-15-190	Grinding Machine		447	Without Motor		618	1111	
9576	34-16-1121	Lathe		691	Complete	2	108	1318	
							109	1319	
10682	34-16-1131	"		974	Complete	1	397	1708	
13354	34-16-1151	"		680	Complete	1	287	1705	
13362	34-16-1151	"		569	Complete	1	241	1756	
14264	34-16-1161	"		3211	Complete	1	255	110	
16624	34-16-1918	"		3919	Complete	1	357	1017	

主管		發貨人		覆核人	譚哲(章)	核對人	陳可權(章)	製單人	昌利(章)

註：收據正本已於　年　月　日送由上海工商輔導處轉呈工商部

第三聯：收據副本，提貨之後，由發貨人存查。

~~167~~ 170

208

~~169~~ 171 209

編號：第56號 Page 2 提取日本賠償工具機通知單 正本

通知：永利化學公司

查下開日本賠償工具机經由本部核轉行政院賠償委員會審定配售該廠（公司）使用，業經訂立價購契約，其應繳之款亦經該廠（公司）付清，茲以該項工具机業已運抵上海招商局第 碼頭倉庫，仰即派員於本年 月 日以前持同正式收據及繳款收據前往該地倉庫提取，逾期如未提取，即應按月另收儲倉費用，特此通知。

本單副本第三、四聯兩份寄交上海工商輔導處

工商部 37年10月29日

契約號碼 83

總號	分類號碼	機器名稱	規範	機器號碼	機件情形	共裝幾箱	箱號	存倉號碼	附註
20396	34-16-9006	Lathe		303	Complete	3	208	E636	
							209	E628	
							210		
20402	34-16-9007	〃		2697	Without Motor				
							1141	638	
27442	34-19-124	Shaper		91	Without Motor		154	1367	
29824	34-43-174	Mechanical Press		3131	Complete	6	1143	658	
							1144	1214	
							1145	1215	
							1146	1216	
							1147	1218	
							1149	1217	
		-----Total-12-----							

主管	顧祿常(章)	記帳人	陳可權(章)	覆核人	譚哲(章)	核對人	陳可權(章)	製單人	昌利(章)

第一聯：通知單正本寄交價購廠商以憑前往倉庫提貨，提貨之後，本聯由價購廠商存查。

說明 (1)上開之總号、分类号碼、机器名称、規範、机器号碼及機件情形係根據盟總所發之清單及我國駐日代表團之檢驗報告填寫。

(2)提貨人於提貨時應當面開箱点驗（其開箱費用由提貨人自理），如有缺損，應在正式收據上註明，事後申請，本部概不受理。

通知單第56號 Page 2 提取日本賠償工具機正式收據 收據正本 編號：

承購廠商 永利化學公司 提貨日期： 年 月 日

下開日本賠償工具機業經本 提訖並經開箱點驗確與下開各節符合

此據

(廠商圖記必須與印鑑片字樣相符) (負責人簽名蓋章) (點驗人簽章) (提取人簽章)

總號	分類號碼	機器名稱	規範	機器號碼	機件情形	共裝幾箱	箱號	存倉號碼	附註
20396	34-16-9006	Lathe		303	Complete	3	208 209 210	E636 E628	
20402	34-16-9007	"		2697	Without Motor		1141	638	
27442	34-19-124	Shaper		91	Without Motor		154	1367	
29824	34-43-174	Mechanical Press		3131	Complete	6	1143 1144 1145 1146 1147 1149	658 1214 1215 1216 1218 1217	
		Total-12							

最後核對		主管		發貨人		覆核人	譚哲(章)	核對人	陳可權(章)	裝單人	昌利(章)

註：憑據提貨，如有遺失，須先掛號。

第二聯：收據正本，提貨之後，由倉庫負責人加蓋「提訖」字樣，送由上海工商輔導處轉呈工商部核對存查。

契約號碼 83

172 169 210

173

170

211

通知單第56號 Page 2 提取日本賠償工具機正式收據 收據副本 編號：

承購廠商 永利化學公司 提貨日期： 年 月 日

下開日本賠償工具機業經本 提訖並經開箱點驗確與下開各節符合

此據

(廠商圖記必須與印鑑片字樣相符) (負責人簽名蓋章) (點驗人簽章) (提取人簽章)

第三聯：收據副本，提貨之後，由發貨人存查。

契約號碼 83

總號	分類號碼	機器名稱	規範	機器號碼	機件情形	共裝幾箱	箱號	存倉號碼	附註
20396	34-16-9006	Lathe		303	Complete 3		208 209 210	E636 E628	
20402	34-16-9007	"		2697	Without Motor		1141	638	
27442	34-19-124	Shaper		91	Without Motor		1154	1367	
29824	34-43-174	Mechanical Press		3131	Complete 6		1143 1144 1145 1146 1147 1149	658 1214 1215 1216 1218 1217	
		Total-12							

主管		發貨人		覆核人	譚哲(章)	核對人	陳可權(章)	製單人	昌利(章)

註：收據正本已於 年 月 日送由上海工商輔導處轉呈工商部

編號：第 56A 號 Page

提取日本賠償工具機通知單　正本

通知：永利化學公司

查下開日本賠償工具機經由本部核轉行政院賠償委員會審定配售該廠（公司）使用業經訂立價購契約其應繳之款亦經該廠（公司）付清茲以該項工具机業已運抵上海招商局第　碼頭倉庫仰即派員於本年　月　日以前持同正式收據及繳款收據前往該地倉庫提取逾期如未提取即應按月另收儲倉費用特此通知

本單副本第三四聯兩份寄交上海工商輔導處

工商部　37 年　10 月　29 日

總號	分類號碼	機器名稱	規範	機器號碼	機件情形	共裝幾箱	箱號	存倉號碼	附註
29824	34-43-174	Mechanical Press		3131	Complete	2	1148 1142	E685 E684	
	------------Total-2-Cases------------								

主管	顧葆常（章）	記帳人	陳可權（章）	覆核人	譚哲（章）	核對人	陳可權（章）	製單人	昌利（章）

說明（1）上開之總号，分类号碼，机器名称，規範，机器号碼及機件情形係根據盟總所發之清單及我國駐日代表團之檢驗報告填寫。
（2）提貨人於提貨時應當面開箱点驗（其開箱費用由提貨人自理）如有缺損，應在正式收據上註明，事後申請，本部概不受理。

第一聯：通知單正本寄交價購廠商以憑前往倉庫提貨，提貨之後，本聯由價購廠商存查。

契約號碼 83

171　172　212

通知單第5(A)號 page　　提取日本賠償工具機正式收據　收據正本　　編號：

承購廠商　永利化學公司　　提貨日期：　年　月　日

下開日本賠償工具機業經本　　提訖並經開箱點驗確與下開各節符合

此據

（廠商圖記必須與印鑑片字樣相符）　（負責人簽名蓋章）　（點驗人簽章）　（提取人簽章）

總號	分類號碼	機器名稱	規範	機器號碼	機件情形	共裝幾箱	箱號	存倉號碼	附註
29824	34-43-174	Mechanical Press		3131	Complete	2	1148 1142	E685 E684	
		--------------------Total-2-Cases--------------------							

最後核對		主管		發貨人		覆核人	譚哲(章)	核對人	陳可權(章)	製單人	昌利(章)

註：憑據提貨，如有遺失，須先掛號。

第二联：收據正本，提貨之後由倉庫負責人加蓋「提訖」字樣，送由上海工商輔導處轉呈工商部核對存查。

契約號碼 83

172 173 213

通知單第56A號　Page　提取日本賠償工具機正式收據　收據副本　編號：

承購廠商　永利化學公司　提貨日期：　年　月　日

下開日本賠償工具機業經本　提訖並經開箱點驗確與下開各節符合

此據

（廠商圖記必須與印鑑片字樣相符）　（負責人簽名蓋章）　（點驗人簽章）　（提取人簽章）

總號	分類號碼	機器名稱	規範	機器號碼	機件情形	共裝幾箱	箱號	存倉號碼	附註
29824	34-43-174	Mechanical Press		3131	Complete	2	1148 1142	E685 E684	
		----------Total-2-Cases----------							

主管		發貨人		覆核人	譚哲(章)	核對人	陳可權(章)	製單人	昌利(章)

註：收據正本已於　年　月　日送由上海工商輔導處轉呈工商部

第三聯：收據副本，提貨之後，由發貨人存查。

契約號碼 83

~~173~~

214

工商部处理日本赔偿物资委员会为缴纳保证金及机器价款等事事给永利化学工业公司的公函（抄件）（一九四八年十月二十六日）

附：缴款通知单

存档

原件寄

總廠

照抄工商部處理日本賠償物資委員會公函

抄件

453

188

永利化學工業公司錏廠

民 字第五十六號　第一頁　卅七年十月廿六日

查該廠申請配售日本賠償工具機一案業經行政院賠償委員會審定並經本部檢發空白契約與須知等通知遵照辦理及由該廠派員來部正式訂立契約各在案茲檢發繳納保証金及機器價款繳款通知單及繳納海運費繳款通知書等之第一聯第三聯各一份又繳納本部代墊之起卸存儲保管等款繳款通知書第一聯第三聯各一份希即分別向上海外灘中央銀行及繳款通知單上所註機關接洽繳款又附發提取所承購已運到上海各工具機提貨通知單及提貨正副收據各一份每份計〇紙希即逕向上海江西路一百一十五號工商部處理日本賠償物資委員會上海辦事處接洽提取工具機各手續為荷此致

永利化學工業公司錏廠

附發繳納價款繳款通知一份

繳納海運費繳款通知單一份

通訊處：南京（八）頤和路二十三號　電報掛號：四三五四　電話：三三九九六

抄件

154

189

永利化學工業公司錏廠

字第　號　第二頁　年　月　日

繳納代墊之起卸等費繳款通知單一份

提貨通知單一份計　紙　另寄

提貨正副收據各一份每份計　紙　另寄

工商部處理日本賠償物資委員會

（長　戳）

啟

（此處顧徐帝蓋章）

廿七年十月廿六日

通訊處：南京（八）頤和路二十三號
電報掛號：四三五四
電　話：三三九九六

155　190

抄件

繳款通知單

第一聯

繳款人	繳款性質	限期			金額	國庫
		年	月	日		
永利化學工業公司錏廠	保證金×$\frac{1}{2}$				U.S.$498500	上海外灘中央銀行轉國庫
	工具機總值$\frac{15}{100}$×$\frac{1}{2}$				U.S.$1495000	仝上

以上通知

永利化學工業公司錏廠

（繳款人）

工商部

（此處顧倸常蓋章）

37年10月26日

此聯送繳款人

抄件

156 — 191

繳款通知單

第一聯

繳款人	繳款性質	限期			金額	國庫
		年	月	日		
永利化學工業公司錏廠	海運費				U.S.$1730 672	向上海南京東路117号二樓58室交通部日本賠償及歸還物資運輸處上海辦事處換取繳款
						簿赴央行業務局繳款

此聯送繳款人

以上通知

永利化學工業公司錏廠

（繳款人）

工商部

（此處顧葆常蓋章）

37年10月26日

抄件

157　192

第一聯

繳款通知單

繳款人	繳款性質	限期			金額	國庫
		年	月	日		
永利化學工業公司錏廠	起卸存儲保管費				U.S.$797 000	向上海江西中路115號二樓工商部處理日本賠償物資委員會上海辦事處接洽繳款

此聯送繳款人

以上通知

永利化學工業公司錏廠

（繳款人）

工商部

（此處須條常蓋章）

37年10月26日

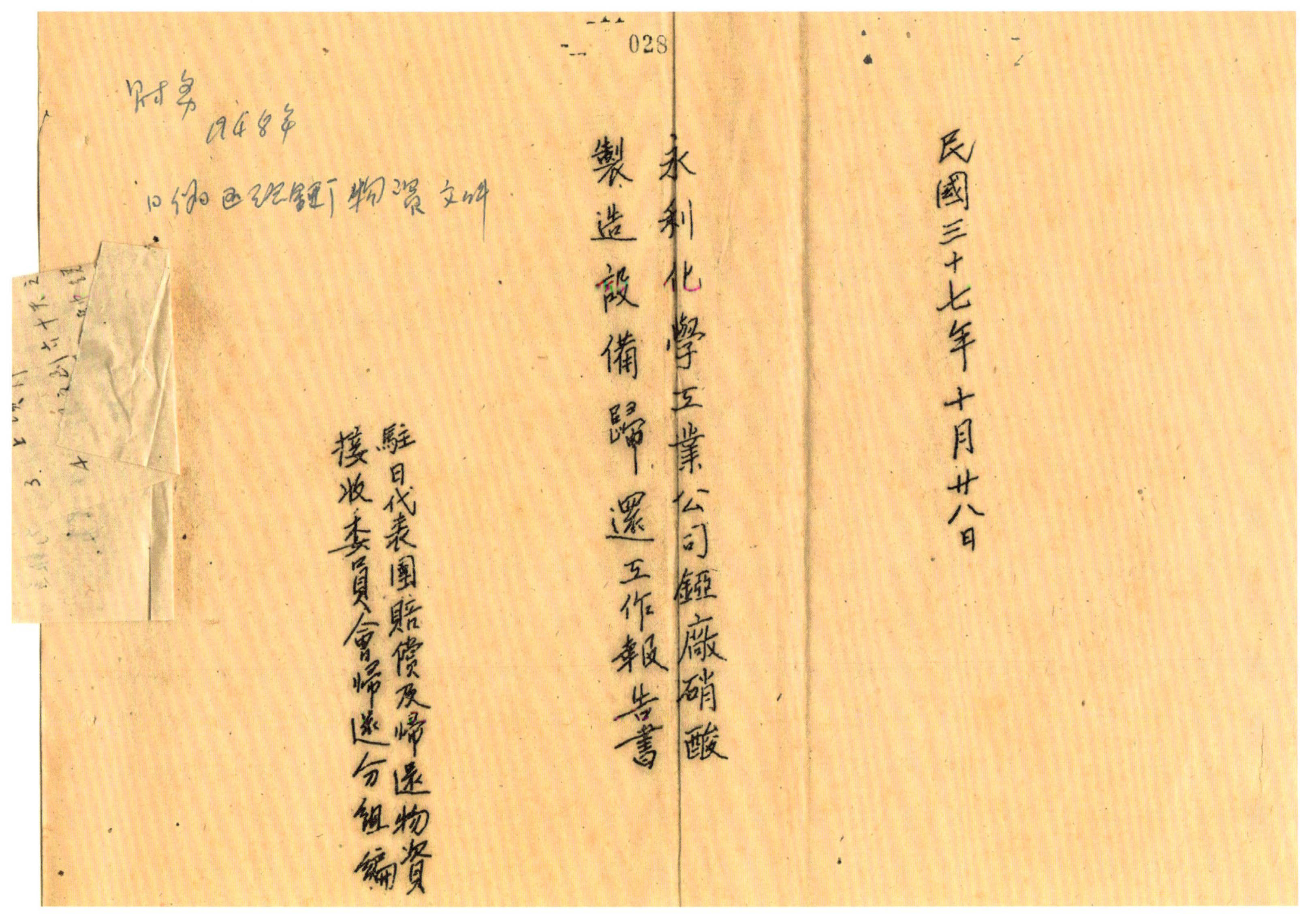

永利化學工業公司錏廠硝酸製造設備歸還工作報告書

駐日代表團賠償及歸還物資接收委員會歸還分組編

民國三十七年十月廿八日

*錏 誤
氨 正

永利化學工業公司錏廠硝酸製造設備歸還工作報告

(一)永利錏廠設立經過及硝酸製造設備被劫情形

硫酸錏工業，平時製造化學肥料及化工原料，戰時則可以供應軍需，為化學工業之柱石，關係國計民生至深且巨。於九一八事變後，政府積極提倡建設各種重要工業，永利公司在政府督導之下，負責創辦硫酸錏廠，技術方面獲得美國 CHEMICAL CONSTRUCTION CO.（簡稱 C.C.C.）之協助，廠址設江蘇省六合縣卸甲甸，濱長江北岸，在浦口下游約十公里，與南京燕子磯隔江相對。該廠內容包括錏*（錏）、硫酸、硫酸錏、硝酸等四種主要製造部分，以生產量計每日可產錏*四〇公噸，濃硫酸一一五公噸，硫酸錏一五〇公噸，濃硝酸一〇公噸，建廠工程自民國廿四年春開始，至民國廿六年五月，先後順利完成，全部開工出貨，為我國之最早硫酸錏廠，當時頗引起中外之注意。不久七七事變爆發，情勢轉緊，該廠更努力硫酸錏生產外，并趕製硝酸及硝酸錏，供應國防需求。至廿六年十月，該廠因前後三次遭敵機轟炸，機器損毀甚重，被迫停工，但硝酸製造設備則幸告無恙。及至首都告急，工廠人員乃於不得已中，隨國軍撤遷四川，當時因時間倉促，限於交通工具，以致主要生產設備，均不及內徙。

首都淪陷後，永利錏廠被敵海軍陸戰隊佔領，民國廿七年一月，三井物產會社派員調查後，三月間即由三井系東洋高壓會社派遣技術人員四十餘人，從事修理工作，七月間繼續增派至百名，約費時十個月，大體修復。民國廿八年五月，以敵偽合作方式成立偽永禮化學工業株式會社，設總店於上海，支店於東京，將硫酸錏廠改名為浦口工業所，資本金定為一千萬日元，股東為三井物產、東洋高壓及偽南京政府實業部，實際上主權完全操於三井財閥之手，蓋三井財閥蓄意侵略此項事業已久，在我創設硫酸錏廠之初，即蓄心調查，密探消息，一切舉動均預定有計劃。硫酸部分復工出貨之後，更計劃將硝酸部復工，製造無烟火藥。

(1)

之原則關係重大，乃將詳情報部，請向遠東委員會力爭修改此項辦法。

至於如何接收，乃技術問題。日政府所報被劫機器設備清單，既與我不符，應先就實際情形調查清楚，再作決定。本團以實地查認，應派遣熟習該項機器情形者前往，且歸還問題須從詳討議，如監督拆卸裝運，亦需派人督視，因此乃決定由永利公司派專人來團，負責辦理。並通知其攜帶有關文書及證件，以利進行。因盟總處理被劫物資案件，極重視法律上之根據，辦理交涉時必須提供證件，方為有力。

永利公司接到通知後，派定錏廠技師長謝為杰、化工研究部副部長趙如晏來日，經由部令任命為本團專門委員，以臨時人員資格來團辦理此案。謝趙兩員於民國卅六年一月十日到團，攜帶文件計有左記十一種：

1.國民政府工商部給予永利公司錏廠註冊執照照片。
2.購買機器設備之合同及發票。
3.永利公司錏廠帳冊內關於硝酸部之細目。
4.硝酸部設備照片。
5.美駐華大使詹森氏參觀永利錏廠時紀念照片。
（詹森氏現任遠東委員會秘書長）
6.永利公司美籍顧問工程師李佐華、德利兩氏對錏廠硝酸部情形之證明書。
7.永利錏廠硝酸部建廠及開工記錄。
8.硝酸部製造設備全套圖樣。
9.偽永禮化學工業株式會社史誌。
10.偽永禮會社與日本東洋高壓間移送之硝酸設備賣買契約。
11.勝利後永利公司錏廠接收清冊。

以上文件，內容相當完備，足資佐證。為求易於明瞭真象起見，特為草成："A brief history on the looted equipments of Ammonia

(3)

025

"Oxidation plant of Yung-li Chemical Industries Co. Ltd."一文，送備盟總方面參考。一月廿四日，由顧專委毓麟先生陪同謝適爾貝，特柔經日本專家介紹，前盟總民間物資供應組賠償物資股，作初次之接洽，盟總方面由Miss Falkenstein代表洽議。Falkenstein為視察專家，曾一度赴大牟田，我方即將準備文件及有關資料等提出，詳細說明，並出示各種證明文件。Falkenstein亦將渠所攝照片，及日方呈報之調查表，擬定設備既置賠償等各之份，交我方參考，經與我方所有既定資料對照之下，遂即發現若干部份已經改動，非實地視察無從辨識。雙方交換意見後，商定由本團派謝適爾貝赴九州大牟田實地視察，以再做進一步之商討。

謝適爾貝於二月十四日首途赴大牟田，計留兩週，就東洋高壓大牟田工業所樣適工廠內保留之硫酸硝酸設備，對照原來圖樣及表冊，逐一查對，製成詳表。凡關於設備之現狀，何者存在，何者遷失，何者曾經修改，何者業經修配，何者損毀殘缺，所有詳細情形，均據實記錄。此外並攝照片證明。謝適爾貝提出之報告書，對日方報來內容，均有對照說明，因此前此發生之疑問，悉告明瞭。

經此次調查後，發現原有設備損毀甚多。據日人報稱，係由我國拆遷時途中不注意所致。失去部分，亦復不少，現有設備齊全之一套，許多部份曾經修改，已非舊觀。其中主要重要部份，如下表所示：

024

(4)

Name of Equipment	原件 No. of sets in China (1937)	在日情况 No. of sets & Conditions in Omuta (1947) Damaged & Replaced	Lost & Replaced	附記（損壞及遺失原因） Remarks	
	原件	損壞經換新	遺失而換新		
Motor Driven Air Blower 電動吹風機（空氣）	2		2		
Motor Driven Blower for NO 電动NO送氣機	1	2		Original set was damaged by air raid 2 smaller sets in series are replaced	原件在空襲中炸壞，換二套小号
Nitric Acid pumps 稀硝酸泵（搪瓷）	7		6	1 set is omitted	1套被取消
Motor Driven Gravity Feed Acid pumps 給硝酸泵	2		2		
Variable Stroke water pumps 可调節衝程水泵	2		3	3 cooling water pumps are replaced（可调節水量）	换三件水泵
Motor Driven self Priming Pumps 電动自注酸泵	2		2		
Sulfuric Acid Pumps (93%) 93%硫酸泵	2		2		
Nitric Acid Concentrator 硝酸濃縮器	1	1		Original set parts are missing	原件遺失
Absorption Towers and one Oxidation Tower 吸收塔及一個氧化塔	9			1 Alkali Scrubbing Tower is added	加一件

其他部份多少均有變動，惟程度則深淺不一。

現有之整套硝酸設備，雖較破舊，但收回全套尚堪使用，在我國急需建設情形之下，實有其特殊之價值。經本團仔細研究之後，乃決定改變方針，要求歸還現有之全套設備，所據理由如次：

1.永利公司原有者乃整套全新設備，且至被拆時尚未開[illegible]，關於此點可以永禮會社史誌之記載為證。

2.化學製造設備全體構成一部機器，缺少任何一部份均將使整

（5）

套設備未來作用，且設備中之各部份對於全體而言不可分性，倘如拆卸之一部份回華，則將失其效用。故須將全套設備視為一體，方可以請歸還。

3.遠東委員會希望被劫物資之歸還，亦在補救被害國之損失，此類化學工業設備，必需整套歸還，否則等於廢鐵，徒為糟塌。

本廠先將上述三項之調查報告提供盟總C.P.C.參考，然後繼以口頭交涉。盟總民間物資保管組（C.P.C.）當時對於原有設備之歸還，毫無異議，對於日方修配之代替品歸還，則以符於遠東委員會規定，不予同意。（根遠東委員會規定被劫物資歸還辦法內關於工業被劫僅限於歸還原物）雖經本廠前述理由一再說明，C.P.C.當局均未肯表示贊允，堅守對字句之解釋，殊嫌過於固執，而忽視事理。如堅持只能歸還原物，則凡經日本修理處所，均應一一取去，如是并非歸還原物，實乃歸還廢鐵，殊不合情理，殊屬不平。最後C.P.C.稱該物資組主任 Le Lavaseur 表示，此為遠東委員會所決定，盟總不便有所更動，如本廠認為非全套歸還不可時，最好要求遠東委員會改定原則，或另以要求賠償方式將日本配件列為賠償品。

交涉至此已成為爭取原則問題，蓋與本案同一性質者尚有其他各處被劫物資之被改裝者，今後更可能有同性質案件發生。本廠以爭取所[illegible]歸還之原則，關係重大，殊有必爭，乃呈請向遠東委員會力爭修改歸還原則，業求根本解決。同時在東京方面，則與盟總關係人員多方接洽，求其明瞭實情，協助解決。因盟總處理歸還案件重視法律上之根據，關於法律上應注意之點，曾經法律顧問[illegible]詳加研究，並承遠東國際軍事法庭中國檢察官向哲濬、倪顧問徵燠參加意見，倪顧問并特為向盟總C.P.C.法律顧問Judge McMahon數度接洽，頗能得其同情。同年四月廿一日本廠特送函盟總C.P.C.政策顧問及法律顧問請予考慮辦法，不久得其口頭答覆，謂此案情形盟總內部業已明瞭，可能同意我方要求，惟手續改變，仍須預先徵

(6)

022

得遠東委員會諒解，才能辦理，盟總已向遠東委員會請示。

遠東委員會方面除由本團三部請顧大使外，同年五月初遠東委員會我代表團楊顧問雲竹返日赴任，乃面陳經過，并將有關資料請帶華盛頓參考。七月間得遠東委員會我代表團通知，謂此案經向遠東委員會提出後，即交小組會議討論，美國代表向我建議，永利公司及廣東敏縣兩案，為求迅速解決起見，可由中美雙方會同辦法，不必力爭修改既定原則，以免拖延。美國代表對我要求表示可予支持，囑在東京與美國駐盟總代表團聯絡，就此與盟總洽辦。又經本團再商洽，始獲得盟總同意。適於七月底永利公司總經理侯德榜博士來日考察，非賴會同催辦，八月廿八日C.P.C中之Mr. StepleTone已親通知本團，謂盟總方面已決定准將日方既往達同意承辦該案一并歸還。九月八日由謝專委為求赴CPC與盟總方面直接商量人員面將應歸還該項設備各事項決定，凡屬該硝酸設備關連部分，即為日方修配者，亦一體歸還我國，其為日方從新添製，則除陵封製造設備之便利，不生影響者，不包括在內。如日方添設之第十號吸收塔，予以剔除，即其一例。其他設備統在歸還之內。九月十八日盟總以第十三號令，亦正式答復本團，准以整套設備歸還我國，并飭日政府於兩月內拆卸包裝完畢，以備接收。我方要求至此得以圓滿，交涉遂告一段落。

(三) 拆卸及包裝

硝酸設備之拆卸包裝及運輸等不比一般工具機器，應特別注意，發生之損失破壞情形，本團認為有派員監督之必要。謝專委因事回國，由外部任命永利公司錏廠副技師長[illegible]為本團專門委員來日繼續辦理。十一月十六日至福岡，即奉派赴大牟田監督拆卸工作，并視察其拆卸包裝情形。至工廠由日本貿易廳負責監督，將來關於拆卸不久，因公文輾轉費時，并以日本內部，對此方面(?)

付鑿運後如何處理，曾發生疑問。經CPC明白解釋後方正式動工。故較預定日期遲延月餘。當趙雨亭與德國馬爾錫公司CPC之負責人Dr. Lehrer接洽後將大部田正奇工作，應由彼承包，惟當時所余內部之填土尚碼頭應立取出，運輸已裝，經詳根據我在部設備情形加以研究，乃決定不必取出，既可省工，又可避免損失，其他臨時發生之技術問題，均就地一一予以解決。關於運輸問題，該大倉因工場往部設備倉庫容積均甚微小，故德方設有五十噸之大起重機，及六噸重之活動小起重機等設備，頗為方便，且一噸之大機可以直接裝船，將來回此港之轉運接收，應無問題。迨貨物運倉到港後先期回國，運事委託留大倉因臨時到試。拆卸中國工作不慎，打撈之兩設備及起重機吊圓塞即決定由日方負責補償。拆裝工作原定十二月中旬可以完工，後以日本東洋高壓株式會社移運之泥港碼頭，因吸水搬運設備等大批運至倉庫，整齊運費，直至民國卅七年一月中旬始告完畢。

（四）拆卸及運輸

020

永利錏廠設備經拆卸後共計一四八二件，毛重五三〇公噸，體積約二〇〇〇尺噸，最大件也限收發每件約重十七公噸，大小為2600mm×2600mm×16020mm，計有十一大件，裝運頗費周章。

關於歸運辦法，我國雖向遠東委員會力爭，應歸日政府負責運送并賠償損失，但迄今尚無結果。現行歸運辦法，可以利用歸運船隻及日本至該國搬運日僑船隻之空餘噸位，但實際上我國日僑已遣送完畢，僅有歸運船可以利用。當時有永源輪約二五〇〇噸，預計可於卅七年五月間修復歸運，但該船僅能承載小件，至大件則無法裝載。海南號油船雖適當，因該輪本身機器尚未修復。乃利用招商局　錄回者，為防范危險計，未便承裝。嗣以永利公司急於運回安裝復工，乃由該公司與招商局商議，派專輪接運，所有費用歸該公司自理。本團派員赴吳港，派定周勤識於三月廿七日抵大阪裝運三六件。

(8)

被盜報告，東洋高壓會社負有保管責任，表示願以所存其他白金網改製新品賠償，當時情形均經函福岡縣軍政府CPC方面證明在案。

海鄂輪於三月廿九日駛抵大牟田三池港，四月三日裝載完畢正式簽字接收，本團代表為舒宗鎏專員，日政府代表為外務省第二課大谷課長，美軍方面在場者有福岡縣軍政府CPC人員Mr. Miller。除白金網一件留後另行歸還外，此次共計接收一四八二件，交由海鄂運回。海鄂輪於四月四日開出，四月十一日駛抵南京對岸永利錏廠碼頭，四月十三日卸載完畢，統由永利公司錏廠分別接收。

（五）白金網被盜及其賠償新品之歸還

白金網用於錏之氧化觸媒，乃硝酸設備中最重要部分。永利公司原有白金網合錢二卷，網之直徑為1800mm，雙層，計重229t.o.。自歷經日政府保管以來，即由東洋高壓保存於該會社彥島工廠硝酸部倉庫中。此次被盜，據日方報告，完全由於保管人之疏忽，三月十九日始行發覺，當時并有東壓同樣大小白金網若干同時被盜。但其他小型白金網亦保存同一倉內則未被盜，由此推察可知事出有因，至少盜竊者必洞悉其中情形。東洋高壓理應負賠償責任，準備改製新網應用。但因日本之白金全部在盟總嚴格統制之下，非經盟總許可不克動用。本團據東壓報告，以責任全在日方，即函盟總請其責令日政府照我原有規格製新品賠償。事經月餘，未獲答復，後經CPC負責主管人Mr. Meyer面告，知CPC對於全案對於挪用其他白金提供賠償尚有反對意見，因此CPC內部意見尚不一致，須待主管參謀長核定後方能決定施行。本團以白金網在硝酸設備中最為重要，其他部分既已歸還，此件不宜久懸，乃於五月十二日由團長及張委員會主任委員分別致函盟總參謀長Gen. Miller及CPC主管人Gen. Janey請予協助。五月廿一日盟總參謀長復函可以照辦。日本現存白金網僅田中貴金屬會社一家，因此網尺寸較大，必須先精製白金，重新抽線，約需時三個月，預計九月十五日完工。關於白金應加銠（Rhodium）問題，因含銠與否對白金網壽命關係甚大，永利侯總經理自美來信敘述甚詳，乃請盟總CPC方面予以考慮。後經CPC召集關係方面開會討論，盟總經濟科學組代表稱日本現有銠總量不過數百公分，全部由盟總押收，不能動用，即作罷。白金網本身於九月十五日如期完成，惟張緊白金網之Nichrome合金圈係日本係初次試做，一再失敗，直至十月十八日始全部製就，正式驗收。

關於白金網之運輸，本已洽妥汎美航空公司PAN AMERICAN AIRWAY及World Line，臨時以該公司無直接飛行，乃改交美軍空運隊Military Air Transport Service於十月廿七日運滬，交由中信局儲運處收轉永利公司。所有運輸及保險費用統由永利公司担負。近據永利公司報告，四月間運回之硝酸設備，大致已安裝就緒，約可於明年春季復工。

018

（六）總論

查本案自民國卅五年二月轉至東京以來，首由我軍事聯絡組向盟軍總部洽辦，本團成立後，先由張組長鳳舉偕專門委員乞村經辦，旋移交本團賠償委員會接辦，卅六年四月本會成立，乃改移本會歸還分組承辦，自開始至完結全部交涉計時兩年又八個月。本案為交涉歸還之第一件，在盟軍總部處理案件中屬於此類性質者亦以本案為嚆矢。辦理此案既無先例可循，而遠東委員會所定歸還原則對於工業設施之歸還復欠週到，盟總初亦不肯予以同情之考慮，若是乃不得不爭取修改原則。因此大費周折，交涉中以此段最為吃力。決定歸還後關於派員監督拆裝、雖屬小節，亦難即予同意，干關多處已盡全交涉斡旋之力、而盟總雖不願其他盟國對日本直接

（2）

前前节题、但实际上亦有此必要、因此亦增加不少阻碍也。本案之
从此之久、本案圆满解决、其中经过艰苦复杂、兹摘记本节于上。（完）
「附录」

List of Ammonia Oxidation Equipment of Yungli Chemical Ind. Ltd., Nanking, China
at
Toyo-koatsu Co., Omuta, Fukuoka, Kyushu, Japan

Name of Equipment	No. of sets in China 原件数量 件	No. of sets & conditions in Japan 在日本情况 (1) used 件	(2) damaged & not used 件	(3) changed & repaired	(4) lost & replaced	(5) lost & not replaced	Remarks 1. 在用(日方) 2. 损坏,未用 3. 换,修复 4. 遗失,新配 5. 遗失,未配
废热锅炉 Waste heat boiler	1		1				Some parts lost
滤空气器 Air filter	1			1			Original set badly damaged, One equivalent set is used
电动空气吹风机 Motor driven air blowers	2				2		Original sets not found, equivalent sets replaced
运NO气机 Motor driven blowers for NO	1			2			Original was damaged by air raid, 2 smaller sets in series were replaced
冷凝器 Condensers	2	2					Some parts are changed & some missing
氨水泵 Aqua ammonia pumps	2					2	No aqua NH_3-pumps are used
硝酸泵 Nitric acid pumps	7				6		One set is omitted
电动压酸泵 Motor driven, gravity fed acid pumps	2				2		
可调节行程水泵 Variable stroke water pumps	2				3		3 cooling water pumps were replaced
氨饱和器 Ammonia saturator	1	1					Some parts missing
氨燃烧器 Ammonia burner	1	3					Parts missing, 2 small sets were added
酸冷器 Acid cooler	1	1					
硝酸储罐 Nitric acid storage tanks	2	2					One tank was corroded and patched
液位桶 贮水桶 Level tank & water storage tank	1 each		1 each				Some parts missing
吸收塔(8) 氧化塔(1) Absorption towers(8) oxidation tower(1)	9	10					one alkali scrubbing tower was added
预热器 Preheater	1		1				Some parts missing
硝酸浓缩器 Nitric acid concentrator	1			1			Parts are missing
铂网 Platinum gauze	1	5					4 small pieces are used for the 2 small sets of ammonia burners
铂网洗涤器 Platinum gauze washing pan	1	1					Slightly damaged
铂网支圈 Platinum gauze holding ring	1		1				Some parts missing
铅制杂件 Misc. Lead parts for various equipments	1		only small parts				Most parts are missing

→ CONTINUED —

(11)

日本运中国硝酸厂设备装箱单（即实运中国者）

List of Equipment at Omuta Works of the Toyo High Pressure Industries K. K. to be Packed for Restitution to China

	Item No.	Name of Parts of Equipment	Quantity	Method of packing required	Remarks
饱和器	1.	Saturater	1 unit	B & C	Rings B
氨燃烧器	2.	Ammonia burner	1 unit	B & C	Small parts B, large casting C
铂网洗涤器	3	Washing pan for platinum screen	1 unit	B	
铂网	4	Platinum screen	1 sheet	B	Suspended, anchored and boxed
铂网托圈	4A	Platinum screen handling ring	1 unit	C	
气体初步冷凝器	5	Primary gas condenser	2 "	C	
吸收及氧化塔	6	Absorption and oxidation towers	9 "	B	
吸收塔填充瓷圈	7	Porcelain rings for absorption towers	228 M^3	B	
漂白塔	8	Bleaching tower	1 unit	C	
硝酸冷却器、管、支架	9	Nitric acid cooler, pipe and support	2units	C	
吸收塔之平台、楼梯	10	Platform & ladder of absorption towers	2 "	S	
硝酸储存器	11	Nitric acid reseroir	2 "	S	
废热锅炉	12	Waste heat boiler	1 "	S & C	Head C
预热器	13	Preheater	1 "	S & C	Head C
空气过滤器	14	Air filter	1 "	B	
气体增压机	15	Gas booster（压气机）	2 sets	B	
热酸器	16	Acid heater	1 unit	C	
冷酸器	17	Acid cooler	1 "	C	
液面控制槽	18	Level control tank	1 "	C	
蒸馏水槽	19	Distilled water tank	1 "	C	
加硫酸槽	20	Sulfuric acid feed tank	1 "	C	
加硝〃〃	21	Nitric acid feed tank	1 "	C	
除水塔	22	Dehydration tower	2 units	B	Very brittle
除水塔滴水盘	23	Drip pan for dehydration tower	2 "	C	
除氮气塔	24	Dinitrating tower	2 "	B	Very brittle
冷凝器	25	Condenser	2 U	B	" "
收集器	26	Reservoir	1 "	C	
浓缩器（塔）	27	Concentrator	2 "	B	" "
冷凝器与浓缩器之法兰	28	Flanges for condenser and concentrator	150 sheets	B	
硝酸冷却槽	29	Nitric acid cooling tank	2 units	C	
硫酸冷却器之蛇形管	30	Snake fihured pipe for sulfuric acid & cooler	7 pieces	C	
〃〃〃〃之铅板	31	Lead plate for sulfuric acid cooler	1 roll	C	
18-8不锈钢凡而及考克	32	18-8 stailess valves abd cocks	19 pieces	B	
各种铁凡而	33	Iron valves, various	10	B	
各种法兰	34	Various flanges	205 "	B	
控制板	35	Control board	1 sheet	C	
电动空气吹风机	36	Motor driven air blowers	2 units	B	
硝酸泵	37	Nitric acid pumps	6 "	B	
电动重力加酸泵	38	Motor driven gravity feed acid pumps	2 "	B	
水泵	39	Water pumps	2 "	B	
浓缩硝酸单元	40	Nitric acid concentration unit	1 "	B	
控制板上之表计	41	Meters for control board	1 "	B	
自动温度纪录设备	42	Pyrometer system	1 "	B	
合金凡而及考克	43	Alloy steel valves and cocks	1 set	B	
酸泵	44	Acid pumps ——保修科有一个	2 units	B	
硫酸泵	45	Sulfuric acid pumps	2 "	B	
亚硝酸气体抽风机	46	Nitrous acid gas exhausting fan	1 unit	B	
管子附件如凡而管等	47	Pipings & auxiliaries like valves, fittings, etc.	1 set	B	
电器零件	48	Electrical parts	1 set	B	
塔内之耐酸砖	49	Acid proof bricks in towers	1 set	B	
流量计	35A	Flow meters	1 unit	B	

√ 原件运回

× 日本赔偿

(13)

侵取及　在戰時在中國時所

盟國遣回日人掠奪物資手續

Abstract of SCAP directive for the "Restitution of Leoted Property"

"1. Immediate steps should be taken to restore to Allied countries objects in the 4 categories listed below which are found in Japan and which are identified as having been located in an Allied country at the time of occupation of that country, and which were removed fraud, or duress by the Japanese or their agents. The fact that payment was made should be disregarded unless there is conclusive evidence that fraud or duress did not take place. Restitution of any object included in category a which follows should be deferred, however, so long as its retention is required for the safety of the occupation forces. In such cases the Supreme Commander for the Allied Powers should provide an explanation of reasons for retention and an estimated date of restoration.

a. Industrial and transportation machinery and equipment.

b. Gold, other precious metals, precious gems, foreign securities, foreign currencies, and other foreign exchange assets.

c. Cultural objects.

d. Agricultural products and industrial raw materials.

"2. Steps should be taken to restore to Allied countries ships of all types and sizes found in Japanese waters which are identified as having been registered in an Allied country at the time of seizure or sinking by the Japanese or their agents, or at the time of acquisition by the Japanese or their agents by fraud or duress. The fact that payment was made should be disregarded unless there is conclusive evidence that fraud or duress did not take place. Restitution of such Allied vessels should be accomplished as rapidly as conditions permit and should be completed not later than 31 December 1946.

"3. With the limits of feasibility, ships damaged or sunk and found in Japanese waters, on the request of the claimant country should as a matter of priority be salvaged, repaired, refitted, as may be necessary to permit their return in a condition substantially similar to that at the time they came in to Japanese hands. The cost of necessary salvage, repair and refitting in Japan should be borne by the Japanese Government but should be applied against the reparations apportionment.

"5 The claimant government should take delivery at a point in Japan, designated by the SCAP except that in the case of Allied vessels subject to restitution, SCAP may at his discretion make delivery at Western Pacific points outside Japan whenever delivery will thereby be facilitate. Expenses incurred after delivery to the claimant government should be borne by that government, except that in the case of delivery within Japan, relevent transportation expenses within Japan and any dismantling, packing and repair necessary for proper transpotation, including the necessary manpower, materials and organisation, should be borne by Japan and be included in restitution. The recipient government should indemnify the SCAP a against all claims made in respect of the property received.

Abstract of Memorandum from SCAP to Japanese Government, (AG 386.6 13 Sep. 47, CPC/FP. (SCAPIN 4541-A)

"2 The Japanese Government is directed to pack the ammonia oxidation equipment looted from the Yungli Chemical Works, Nanking, China, now installed at the Omuta Works of the Toyo High Pressure Industry K. K., Shinkai-Machi, Omuta City, Fukuoka Prefecture, Kyushu, preparatory to the restitution of this equipment to the Government of the Republic of China. Inclosed are a list of the items to be packed and instructions as to the method to be used in packing this equipment.

"3 A memorandum directing the restitution of subject equipment will be issued at a later date.

"4 Report of the action taken in compliance with paragraph 2 above will be submitted to General Headquarters, Supreme Commander for the Allied Powers, Civil Property Custodian, within sixty days of date of this memorandum.

014

(14)

永利化学工业公司为办理工商部配售铔厂日本赔偿工具机十二部事致该公司总管理处的函（一九四八年十一月十五日）

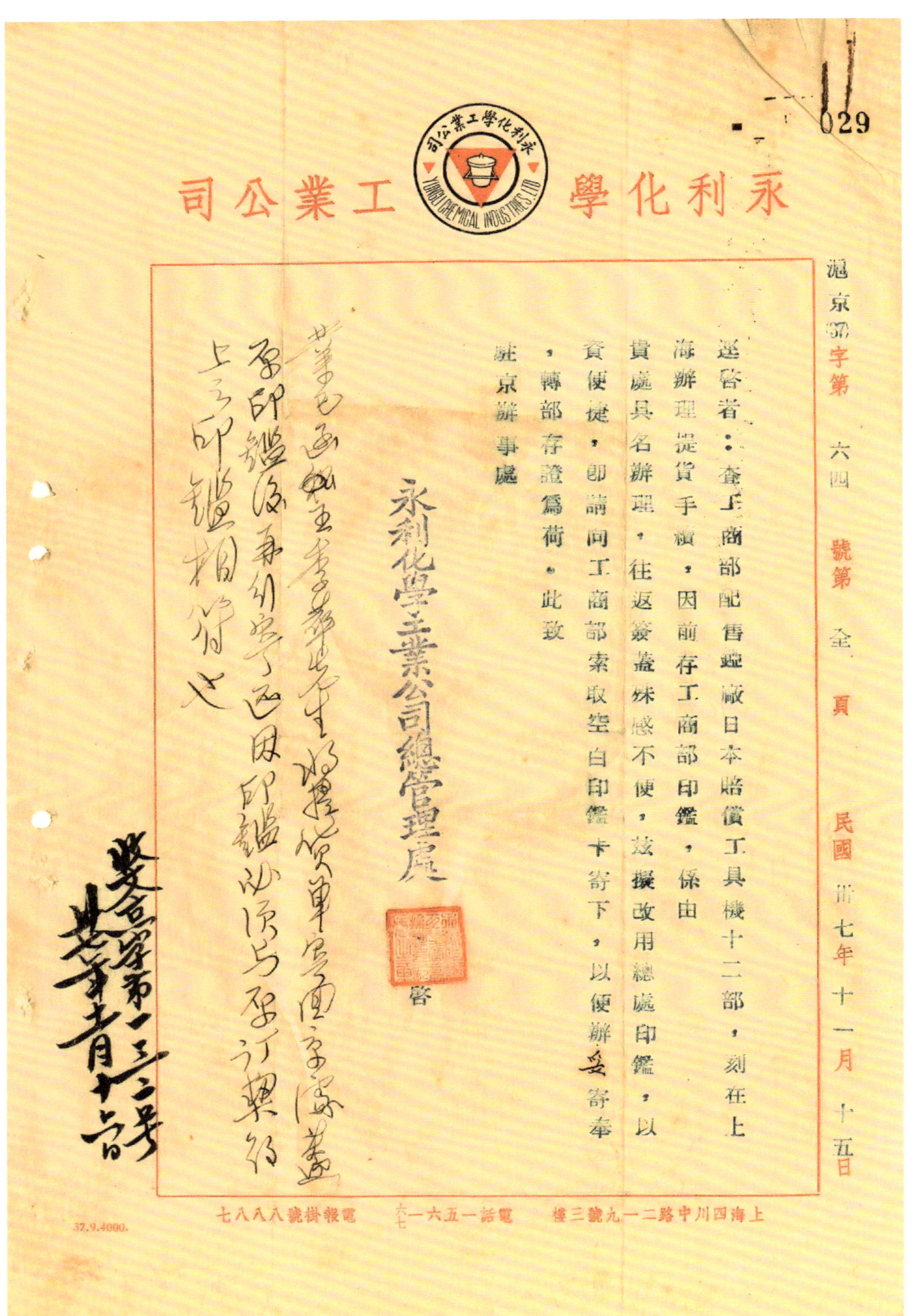

029

永利化學工業公司

滬京(37)字第六四號　第全頁　民國卅七年十一月十五日

逕啓者：查工商部配售錏廠日本賠償工具機十二部，刻在上海辦理提貨手續，因前存工商部印鑑，係由貴處具名辦理，往返簽蓋殊感不便，茲擬改用總處印鑑，以資便捷，即請向工商部索取空白印鑑卡寄下，以便辦妥寄奉，轉部存證爲荷。此致

駐京辦事處

永利化學工業公司總管理處　啓

此事已函知在京辦理出售提貨單處蓋用印鑑後再行寄還，因印鑑必須与原訂契約上之印鑑相符也

發京字第一三二號　卅七年十一月十六日

上海四川中路二一九號三樓　電話一五一六六 一七　電報掛號八八八七

37.9.4000.

工商部为价配民营事业之日本赔偿机器价款暂照盟军总部原核定价百分之五十计缴事给永利化学工业公司的通知（一九四八年十二月七日）

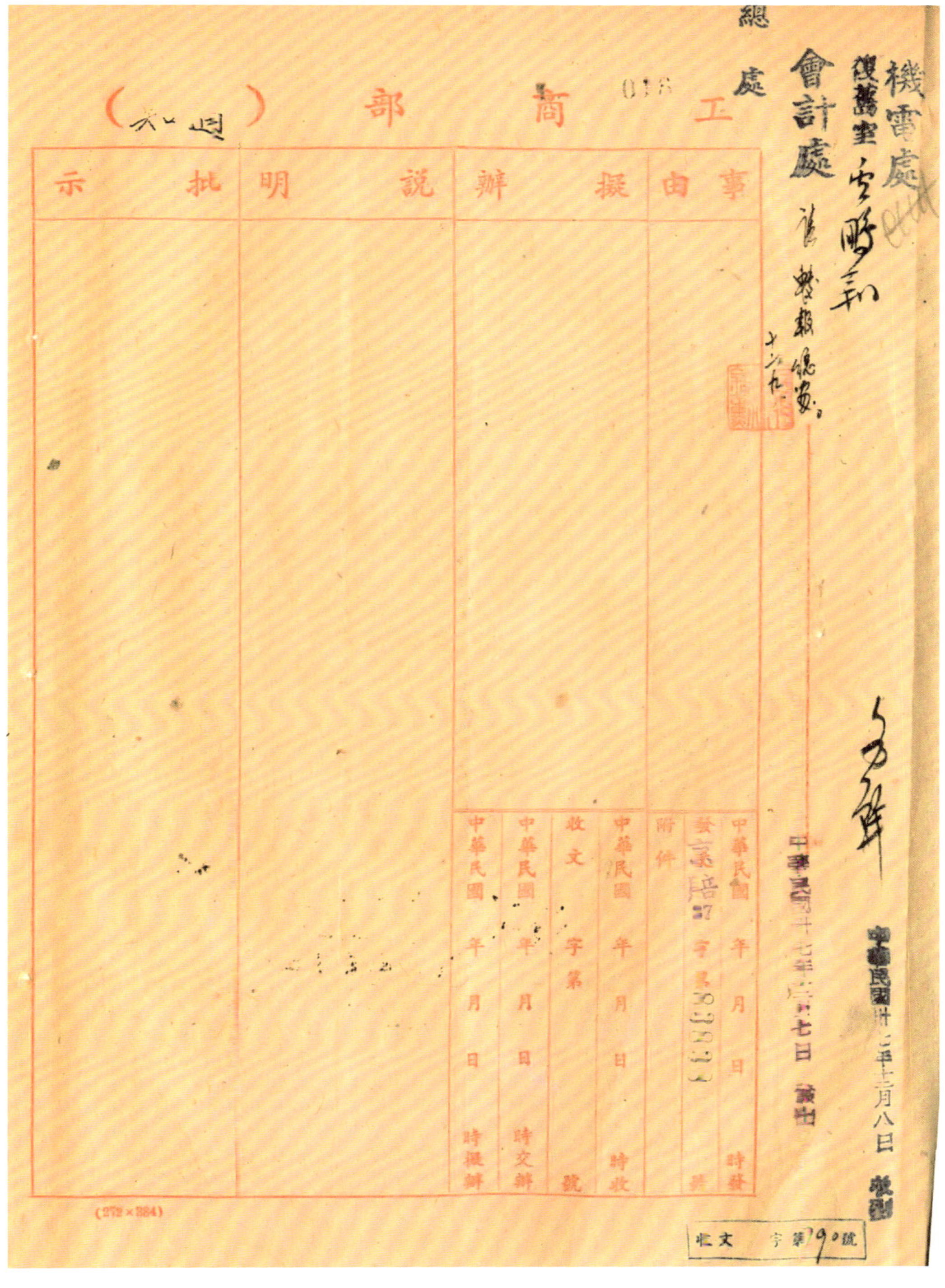
工商部（知通）
事由 | 拟办 | 说明 | 批示

007

通知永利化学工业公司

案奉

行政院三十七年十一月十八日卅七法字第五一三一一号训令开：「查赔偿民营事业之日本赔偿机器价款暂照盟军总部原核定价百分之五十计缴，计价单位仍以美金计算，前经本院第十八次会议决议通过。兹该项机器价款并依照规定美金价款一元折合金圆券四元缴纳，经先后分令该部及赔偿委员会遵照办理在案。兹据财政部本年十一月十三日财库一字11916号代电称：『金圆券发行办法业经修正公布，美汇改为金圆二十元，所有赔偿民营事业之日本赔偿物资价款应自公布之日起改按上项比率折计缴库，除电国行并分电查照外，请饬遵』等情，应准照办。除指复并分行赔偿委员会知照外，合行令仰遵照办理」等因。奉此，特此通知。

018

中華民國三十七年十二月　日

校對陳希浩

監印曹用章

永利化学工业公司关于日本赔偿机器经过情形给中国人民解放军上海市军事管制委员会、驻经济部处理日本赔偿委员会上海办事处接收专员的函（抄件）（一九四九年七月二日）

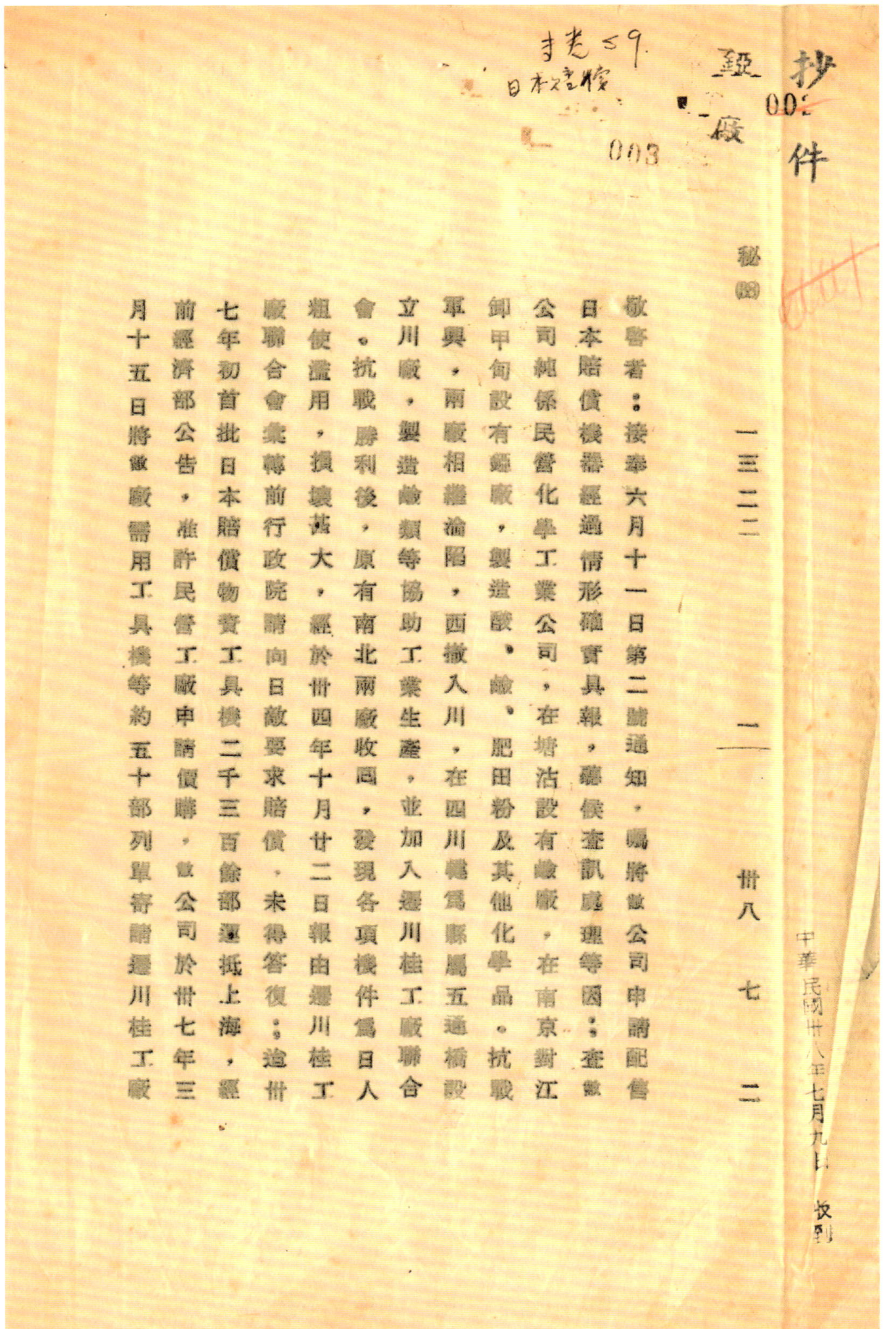

抄件

經廠

秘(略)　一三二二　一　卅八　七　二

中華民國卅八年七月九日收到

敬啓者：接奉六月十一日第二號通知，囑將敝公司申請配售日本賠償機器經過情形確實具報，藉候查訊處理等因；查敝公司純係民營化學工業公司，在塘沽設有鹼廠，在南京對江卸甲甸設有錏廠，製造酸、鹼、肥田粉及其他化學品。抗戰軍興，兩廠相繼淪陷，西撤入川，在四川犍為縣屬五通橋設立川廠，製造鹼類等協助工業生產，並加入遷川桂工廠聯合會。抗戰勝利後，原有南北兩廠收回，發現各項機件為日人租使濫用，損壞甚大，經於卅四年十月廿二日報由遷川桂工廠聯合會彙轉前行政院請向日敵要求賠償，未得答復；迨卅七年初首批日本賠償物資工具機二千三百餘部運抵上海，經前經濟部公告，准許民營工廠申請價購，敝公司於卅七年三月十五日將敝廠需用工具機等約五十部列單寄請遷川桂工廠

秘函　一三二二　二　卅八　七　二

聯合會彙集申請辦理，幾經週折，始接前工商部卅七年八月十二日京賠閩字第七二九二二號通知，（原文抄附）核准配售工具機十二部，經經部訂立契約。（原約抄附）後以該批機器所訂價格遠較當時市價或在國外訂購價格為高，如工廠均覺無力負擔，復請由遷川桂工廠聯合會據理向前行政院申請核減，後得該院卅七年十月一日七法字第四三七二一號批文，（原文抄附）准予核減百分之五十，分期繳納。敝公司所得價配工具機十二部，共計美金九，九六八，九二元。敝公司於卅七年十一月四日繳付價款及運費計：（一）保證金及總價百分之十五，（契約第十條乙、丙兩項）計美金一，九九三．五〇元，折合金圓七，九七四．〇〇元。（二）起卸存儲保管費美金七九七．〇〇元，折合金圓三，一八八．〇〇元。（三）

秘(四)　一三二二　三　卅八　七　二

海運費美金一，七三〇·六七元，折合金圓六，九二二·六九元。四、補繳海運費美金三二四·二八元，折合金圓一，二九七·一三元。以上各項，均執有收據可查。其餘未繳部分，計美金，四七三·九三元。分爲六期繳納，每六個月爲一期，已於契約內載明。（契約第十條所列各美金價格係未經核減半數者，請注意）。第一期原應於本年四月廿六日到期，因戰事關係，未接前工商部通知繳款，尚未繳納。敝公司所購工具機十二部，共裝廿二箱，（名稱及箱號詳列契約所附清單）業經於首批繳納各款後提出。除總號二〇三九六內有一箱，因重量體積均大，運輸不便，尚存滬待運外，其餘均已運抵敝廠。奉令前因，謹將敝公司價購日本賠償工具機經過情形，陳明如上，並附各項有關文件抄奉　份。敬請

006 005

秘(卅) 一三二二 四 卅八 七 二

鑒核是幸。此上

中國人民解放軍上海市軍事管制委員會

駐經濟部處理日本賠償委員會上海辦事處 接收專員 孫 鍾 啓

附件如文

永利化学工业公司拟购日本赔偿工具机六部种类、数量、售价清单及价购日本赔偿工具机清单（一九四九年十月二十一日）

永利化學工業公司擬購日本賠償工具機六部種類數量售價清單　026

機器名稱	分類號碼 S.C.C. Code No.	部數	每部機器之編號 Position Code No.	機器暫定價值	照全值以50%計算之現值	起卸存儲保管各費（以現總價8%計算）	海運費
Drilling Machine	34-13-592	1	2464	1394.305	697.153	55.772	33.586
Grinding Machine	34-15-190	1	4172	2665.544	1332.772	106.622	79.818
Lathe	34-16-1151	2	13354	1326.137	663.069	53.046	另行通知
			13362	1326.137	663.069	53.046	另行通知
〃	34-16-9007	1	20402	1302.981	651.491	52.119	233.807
Shaper	34-19-124	1	27442	707.690	353.845	28.308	50.661
total		6			4361.397	343.913	397.872

永利化學工業公司價購日本賠償工具機清單

機器名稱	分類號碼 S.C.C. Code No.	部數	每部機器之總號 Position Code No.	原價 機器當時價值	原價 起卸存倉保管各費（以原價6%計算）	原價 海運費	現價 院令以50%計算之價值	現價 起卸存倉保管各費（以現價6%計算）	現價 海運費
Drilling Machine	34-13-592	1	2464	1394.305	83.658	33.586	697.153	55.772	33.586
Grinding machine	34-15-190	1	4172	2665.544	159.933	79.818	1332.772	106.622	79.818
Lathe	34-16-1121	1	9576	251.074	15.064	21.949	125.537	10.043	21.949
〃	34-16-1131	1	10682	854.171	51.250	另行通知	427.086	34.167	另行通知
〃	34-16-1151	2	13354	1326.137	79.568	另行通知	663.069	53.046	另行通知
			13362	1326.137	79.568	另行通知	663.069	53.046	另行通知
〃	34-16-1161	1	14264	591.649	35.499	70.119	295.825	23.666	70.119
〃	34-16-1918	1	16624	731.626	43.878	69.778	365.813	29.265	69.778
〃	34-16-9006	1	20396	905.687	54.341	715.221	452.844	36.228	715.221
〃	34-16-9007	1	20402	1302.981	78.179	233.807	651.491	52.119	233.807
Shaper	34-19-124	1	27442	707.690	42.461	50.661	353.845	28.308	50.661
Mechanical Press	34-43-174	1	29824	7880.852	472.851	328.104	3940.426	315.234	328.104
Total		12		19937.853	1196.271	1603.043	9968.927	797.514	1603.043

美金22737.167

美金12369.484

約合金圓券二 49,477

較廉 22737.167－12369.484 ＝美金10,367.683

按照#78775通知

原價及現價已算出如左。是否購買，請

謝侯敬思、冰叔先生

永利化学工业公司呈盟军最高统帅部申请归还劫物表格（时间不详）

139

永利化學工業公司錏廠稿紙

發文　字　號
中華民國　年　月　日
文別
發往機關
擬稿人
事由
時：
地：

申請賠还劫物表格

呈：盟軍最高统帥

(一)按照联合国遠東委員會共同簽訂、并由駐華盛頓之联合參謀首腦部於一九四六年七月廿五日指令盟軍最高統帥遵行之條文，謹提呈賠還下述產業之申請。其由於日本帝國政府，日本軍隊，有關之代理機構或個人、或日本國民之行為，致申請人遭受損失之法益、物權或管轄權為：

甲，產業詳情（陳述為保証符合鑑定所必要之事實，包括順序之數目、企業名牌、日期、照片，及類似之適當事項）、

複閱人：

永利化學工業公司錏廠稿紙

發文　字　號　中華民國　年　月　日　文別　發往機關　事由　擬稿人

乙、產權証明（陳報全部事實及境況，并附全部証明文件之副本，該項文件為說明申請人獲得產權之經過者，包括地址、及國籍，如申請人不屬於所在地之政府）：

內，隨同產業之移動而損及其法益，物權或管轄權之各種情況、環境、以及期限（包括或有之有關事件）之簡報，包括地點，日期，及其他確當資料：

(二)申請人得由駐在日本某地之本國政府官方代表處，或由日本國外太平洋西部某地（僅限於船舶一項）、於本件所申請之產業交付時，據當時實情，領取之。

(三)所請產業核准歸還後，倘有其他國家或其人民對同一產業

複閱人：

141

永利化學工業公司錏廠稿紙

發文　字　號
中華民國　年　月　日
文別
發往機關
擬稿人
事由

作衝突之申請時，原申請人所屬國政府得採取適宜及公允之調措，并遵從盟國间之内部決議。

(四)此項申請之審核，將不損及申請人所屬國政府对日本帝國政府，就本件所述主体之產業所有之任何其他權利或要求。

(四)此項申請之審核，將不影响申請人所屬國政府对日本帝國政府所擬得之任何其他權利或要求中，與產業有关本件所述主体之產業之事实

(四)申請人所屬國政府对日本帝國政府所提之任何其他權利或要求中有关於即為本件所请物之產業時，此項申请，應作無效。

複閱人：

七、重建

復舊及擴充工作之現在及將來

本廠建廠工作開始於民國廿四年，完成於廿六年春季。當時原設計產量為年產硫酸錏44,170噸，茲將各種產量詳列如下：

(1) 液體錏（銨）　　日產 40 公噸

(2) 硫酸（100%）　　日產 112 公噸

將以上(1)及(2)兩種產品化合製成硫酸錏如下(3)

(3) 硫酸錏（銨）　　日產 150 公噸

(4) 硝酸（98%）　　日產 12 公噸

試工結果，產量恰如原來設計。廿六年秋季，對日抗戰開始，於八、九、十三個月中，曾受敵機轟炸三次，多數部份被毀，十二月隨首都淪於敵手。抗戰八年中，日人曾修復開工，但以限於修理材料，產量始終未能恢復原定產量，最高每日僅產液錏30公噸；戰爭後半期，日敵更將硝酸廠設備全部拆運至日本，裝設於九州福岡縣大牟田市東洋高壓會社之橫須廠內（三井系統）。勝利後，全廠經九個月之修復工作，始將硫酸錏各部復工，出產量僅及戰前四分之三。硝酸廠亦經過三年餘之努力交涉，於卅七年冬始自日本運回，現安裝工程已完成90%。

為求恢復戰前產量，須將現有機件大部加以修換及添配補充，甚至需予增加，如發電設備等是也。蓋以戰前首都電廠發電機器當時為新裝置者，供給南京以外，餘量甚大，故可供給本廠綽有餘裕，且工業用電，定價特別低廉，惟該廠戰時以受日人損壞，迄未能恢復戰前之發電量，加以南京至浦口之江底電纜，於戰後三年中，竟斷絕三次之多，每次修繕，動輒數月，致本廠全部因而停工，損失不貲，故亟需增添自己發電設備，以為一勞永逸之計。

又肥料之有利於農作物，漸為農民所認識，尤以江南及沿海諸省如蘇、浙、閩、台、粵、冀等省為甚，本廠所產硫酸錏每年僅達四萬噸之譜，實屬杯水車薪，供不應求，第一步擴充計劃，擬先將此廠增產三倍餘，即年產硫酸錏165,000公噸（即日產450公噸），俾利全國農產物之增加，茲將擬定擴充計劃及理由約述如下：

1. 本廠因技術上之進步，可將原有設備之各主要部份（如錏合成器）及各補助機件加以改良或補充，即可達擴充之目的，其法將原來日產40公噸液錏者，可增至日產70公噸（即我廠原有之一套），原來日產30公噸液錏者，可增至日產50公噸（即原為四川廠所購置之一套）。目前四川一套業已於卅七年改造竣就開用，工作成績曾達每日40公噸之數。至南京原有之一套，則正待改良，以增產量。

2. 電力部份，為應付將來擴充後之新計劃，須添加7500K.W.之發電設備，但原為四川廠購置之發電設備為4500K.W.，故除將四川廠者移用於本廠外，僅需再增3000K.W.即足。此項機器，正由美國出進口銀行協助購買中。

3. 硫酸廠設備，原為每日出產硫酸錏112公噸，現經添加設備，已達日產130公噸之譜，為應市面需要，及日產450噸硫酸錏（360噸98%硫酸）計，擬擴充至日產硫酸500噸之量。

3

0012 ~~018~~ - 039

為實現上述復舊及擴充計劃，除已獲有聯合國救濟總署中國分署協助之1,834,000美元外，尚需如下之設備資金（僅指美元部份，國内部份尚不在内）：

1. 為完成擴充設備----------美金 877,967元

2. 為修換及補充現有設備--------美金 374,325元

3. 為購置建築材料及自己製造之一部份設備之五金材料--------美金 1,176,336元

4. 運輸保險雜費及意外費--------美金 572,800元

共計美金 3,001,428元

上述3,000,000美元，前曾向經濟援華會請求協助，以時局關係，未能成功。故此後如欲完成此項擴充工程，對於此款必須設法新籌措。至時間方面，如機件陸續到達後，則預計仍須二年方可完成。

茲再將本廠目前各部擴充工作已達之程度開列如下：

部份	工程	目前已完成進度
煤氣部	機件	70%
〃	廠房建築	地基挖土完畢
氫化部	機件	40%
〃	廠房建築	設計完成，尚未動工
高壓精煉合成三部	機件	50%
〃	廠房建築	90%

0013　　019　　046

硫酸部	機件	20%
〃	廠房建築	地基土方完畢
硫酸錏部	機件	20%
〃	廠房建築	地基挖土完畢
動力室	機件	80%（已裝完1500KW發電機一部）
〃	廠房建築	40%
給水設備	機件	20%
〃	廠房建築	尚未動工
冷水塔及水泵房	機件	30%
〃	廠房建築	地基75%

4. 原料情況：

本廠原有設計，以採用山東中興煤礦之焦炭、安徽淮南煤礦之煙煤，及安徽馬鞍山或廣東英德之硫鐵礦為主。抗戰勝利後，因中興煤礦於戰爭中屢被破毀，且交通阻隔，焦炭無法南運。本廠不得已而向各處零星收購，北至開灤、井陘，南達台灣，西及川湘贛，且曾一度用澳洲及加拿大焦炭，（係由國民黨偽經濟部配給者，忍痛用之，得免於停工！）因路既遙遠，又限於運輸工具，中途失事損失屢聞，其艱苦之情形難以言宣。硫鐵礦以在近區衹無匱乏。此後政局大定，交通即將恢復，中興煤礦之復工，不但關係華東區之民生、工業，本廠之擴充前途，實待之若大旱之望雲霓也。

希政府加以扶助，俾早期復工為幸。

又本廠至花旗營一段之鐵道支路，以連於津浦路，在抗戰前早經測量就緒，未及開築。此項原定計劃，應請政府協助，俾早完成，以期減輕本廠煤焦運費，間接可減低本廠產品成本也。

永利化学工业公司錏厂胜利后的第一次厂务会议记录（一九四六年三月十九日）

No. I

011

字第　號　年　月　日

永利化學工業公司錏廠勝利後第一次廠務會議紀錄

日　期　卅五年三月十九日下午二時

地　點　本廠第一村

出席人　傅冰芝、章懷西、吳駿侯、趙文珉、陶壽康、楊運珊、姜聖階、江國棟、嚴振常、李滋敏、王道盛、劉本慈、侯敬思、于錫泰、潘祖栽、孫洪恩

主　席　傅冰芝　　紀錄　陶壽康

甲、主席報告事項：

（一）今日開廠務會議，為本人八年餘回廠第一次，我們經过了八年長期抗戰，得能舊地重逢，共聚一堂，非常愉快，所引為遺憾者，范總經理在勝利以後，不多幾天不幸逝世了，現在本團

體艱鉅嘗的復員工作，再不能得到他的領導。侯先生以原任首席協理，代行總經理職權，秉承範先生苦幹精神，必能發揚光大，希望各位齊心合德格外努力，向前猛進，燃源問題，不但秦皇島方面，正在積極設法，還在台灣方面，探索來源，想來不久，可有辦法，目前唯一目標，即為完成下月開工出貨任務。

(二)關於同人待遇，本人在渝時，曾屢次參與侯先生與各位協理之會議，已定有調整辦法，在幣制未改革之前，底薪暫時不動，所有津貼自二月份起，實行調整，即以生活指數作標準，隨物價漲落為轉移，似較公允。

(三)本廠工程各部組織，早具雛型，現事務部、工訓部亦相繼成立，工訓部在茅仲英先生未到廠前，即請[illegible]映思先生以副

字第　　號　　年　　月　　日

部長資格主持辦理

（四）各部添用職員，必須依照已往慣例辦理，即不妨先由各方保荐或介紹，經本廠審查，認為適合需要，然後約請試用，試用合格再行呈請總處發表。未得本廠同意，不得逕行派人來廠，假令不合需要，碍難峻拒。

（五）本月份同人伙食費，陡漲甚鉅，物價高漲，影響果大，但管理不嚴，亦是原因之一。茲指派章懷西、趙文珉、劉本慈、陶壽康、孫洪恩等五人，組織膳食委員會，共籌整理辦法，並指定章先生為主任委員，至工廠補助截止時期，應以留川同仁家屬三分之二抵達錏廠時截止。（只限由川廠、渝處或本公司其他機關調錏廠者為限）慈註

（六）廠中現有傢具，皆屬公司財產，凡戰前有家眷住廠之同人，其自備傢具，悉已散失，自得享有借用之權，此項

借用傢具，須先由主管部辦理調查登記，再作合理分配。

(七)川京字第七號公函通知，YA-81-下-10，YA-81-乙-乙-2，YA-81-乙-乙-4，YA-81-乙-乙-9，YA-81-乙-乙-14，各種藍圖已經寄出。

(八)壽樂先生三月六日自上海來函報告，本廠開工用煤甚多，曾迭向農林部次長、農業司司長、行總聯總各方面接洽輸航裝運秦皇島之煤，結果尚稱滿意，現此事已由協理李倜夫先生繼續折衝云。

(九)警衛隊現有漆仲權、曾權二君，擔任正副隊長，漆曾兩君均係中央陸軍軍官學校畢業，經驗豐富，定能勝任裕如。惟組織伊始，彼輩或不明公司歷史，仍須由主管之事務部隨時訓導，並灌輸本廠固有之苦幹精神。

(十)總處發表南京辦事處，直屬於本廠，定名為永利化學工業公司鋏廠南京辦事處。

005 5

字第 號 年 月 日

(十)規定工人加工辦法，每加工六小時作一工，通告周知。

討論事項：

1.主席提議：

現在留廠日籍員工，是否繼續留用案。

決議：暫留至開工兩個月後再定。

2.主席提議：

據楊慨候先生函告，擬將永利輪出租與招商局應如何審理案。

決議：俟楊慨候先生還滬後再定。

3.主席提議：

團部請求本廠，每逢星期日鳴放汽笛一次，以寓紀念七七之意，應否照辦案。

決議：照辦並通告周知。

4. 主席提議：

向贊辰先生二月八日函稱，鉄廠剪刀機，運渝費用，約需壹百伍拾萬元，渝漢及漢宜間，運輸更感困難云云，應如何處理案。

決議：改用本廠卡車隨同給水泵馬達等共重三噸餘，一併裝載啓運。

5. 章懷西先生提議：

廠房屋頂漏水，必用白鉄皮修理，材料費需千萬元，以上應如何辦理案。

決議：儘量少購材料，以修理維持不漏為原則。

6. 章懷西先生提議：

魯波先生寄來技工名單一份，應如何處理案。

決議：由各部圈選，送工訓部彙辦，僱用手續並規定之以

007

字第　號　年　月　日

遇舊技工（戰前各部門開工之識字技工）進廠，經主管部審查確屬技術優良者，可照職員待遇。

7. 楊運珊先生提議：

去年請購黃砂，至今運々不到，以後是否應加強採購案：

決議：俟陳同之先生到廠磋商辦理。

8. 江國棟先生提議

本廠開工，各部職員缺額尚多，應如何辦理案：

決議：由各部開具應添職員職别人數，送技師長統籌辦理。

9. 劉本慈先生提議：

開工作單，應如何規定簽字案：

決議：歸各部主管人簽字，但各部應將工作單兩聯，送機電部，隨由機電部送技師長，或廠長，聯簽字，同時開始工作。

10. 侯蔭恩先生提議：

本廠修理房屋，需用磚瓦甚多，是否應將磚窑恢復工作案

決議：招僱窑工進行（李滋敏先生報告，廠内江边舊有磚窑二座，現已与種地人郭興工作，公司收時利益，値百抽五，究竟要与否，請公決，又王道盛君云：燒磚非須俟煤到後，不能開办）

11. 侯蔭恩先生提議：

廠中用水設備，有給水、凉水、井水、家庭用水四種，應歸何部管理案：

決議：統歸機電部主管。

中国工业之花——复兴中的永利錏厂（刊载于一九四六年八月六日《申报》）

（九） 星期二 申報 中華民國三十五年八月六日

接收後的塘沽新港

我國艦隊在哈城

中國工業之花 復興中的永利錏廠

社會服務

答復讀者

金星皮鞋公司謝啓

台灣氧氣廉價出售

永利化學工業公司錏廠稿紙　039

發文　字　號

中華民國　年　月　日

文別

發往機關

擬稿人

事由：本公司事業之展望　⑫

本公司事業之目的，在於為中國建立重化學工業。依普通見解，所謂重化學工業，不外酸類、碱類、化學肥料、煉焦等數種。茲即就此四種範圍，將本公司業務分別加以述之如下：

（1）製酸工業——無機酸以硫酸、鹽酸、硝酸三种為代表，俗稱三酸。三酸外，磷酸亦為無機化工中不能缺少者。此四种酸，其有硝、鹽與磷三種，均可用硫酸處理而得，故普通稱硫酸為工業之母。本公司在六合之錏廠，與將由在株洲創設之湘廠，均產硫酸，並均利用合成氨氧化以製硝酸。鹽酸亦將採用電解食鹽法，從事製造，計劃已定，廠設塘沽。

（2）製碱工業——碱業有純碱、燒碱（或稱苛性碱）、潔碱之分。本公司以純碱為主。而純碱廠

複閱人：

040 永利化學工業公司錏廠稿紙

發文 字 號
中華民國 年 月 日
文別
發往機關
擬稿人
事由

設在塘沽，採用蘇爾維法。創辦之初，因全世界碱業之嚴守秘密，孤軍無援，奮鬥十年，始告成功，在國際上爭得莫大之榮誉。該廠战時淪入敵手，產量低落，勝利收復，經修理開工，已漸入正軌，但以機器受損過烈，終難恢復舊日盛况矣。本公司現正向政府交涉，拆運日本碱廠以充賠償。該廠附設燒碱及潔碱廠，規模亦甚大，其燒碱係採用石灰苛化純碱法製造之。又本公司在塘沽即擬設立電解食盐廠，其主要產品亦為燒碱。本公司總經理侯德榜氏更於戰時再發明永利侯氏製碱法，使碱廠與錏廠相需為用，對化工界貢獻甚大，亦即擬於六合錏廠廠址內設廠開製。

(3)肥料工業——化學肥料可分為三大類：一為氮素肥料，二為磷質肥料，

複閱人：

041

046

永利化學工業公司錏廠稿紙

發文　字　號

中華民國　年　月　日

文別

發往機關

擬稿人

事由

三為鉀質肥料。三類肥料，性能各異，普通施用時，多參合之
种兼用之。本公司六合錏廠之主要出品為硫酸錏，即為氮肥之
一种，目下年產約三萬五千噸，但以農村需要過殷，供不應求，現
已決定擴充產量至十萬噸，同時並計劃在株州另設一廠，日產額
定四百噸。六合錏廠又利用氨氣氧化而得硝酸，與純碱化合成硝酸鈉，即人造硝石，與石灰石中和得
硝酸鈣，與氨氣中和，可得硝酸錏，均為氮肥。又
氯化錏，亦為近代新肥料之一，功用與硫酸錏相等，本公司侯氏製
碱法副產品中即有此物。此外氨氣與炭酸氣在相當壓力與溫度
中可製尿素，為優等氮肥，本公司亦注意此物，貢獻中國新農
各廠，均擬儘量生產。至於磷肥與鉀肥，本公司亦在注意調

複閱人：

047

042 永利化學工業公司錏廠稿紙

發文 字 號 | 事由 | 中華民國 年 月 日 | 文別 | 發往機關 | 擬稿人

原料，並已在安徽無為縣領得礬石礦權。蓋此礬石礦中蘊藏鉀質甚富也。

(四)煉焦工業——煤為煉焦之原料，焦炭用途甚大，錏廠須焦炭以製石灰氮，鹼廠須焦炭以製炭酸氣，故酸、鹼、煉焦三种工業，互相關切。煉焦工業不獨其所出產之焦炭，非常重要，其一切副產，亦均極有價值。

本公司擬在湘廠，即將創設日產三百噸之煉焦廠一處，設計業已完成。其所出副產（如煤氣、氫氣、輕油、煤膏、甲酚等），均將加以利用。

由上述四節，乃本公司事業之目的，倘能成功，則中國重化學工業之基礎，可以奠定矣。茲更將本公司現有及擬設各廠，表列如下：

(甲)塘沽河北塘沽 純鹼廠 日產 噸。（附設）燒鹼廠 日產 噸。

複閱人：

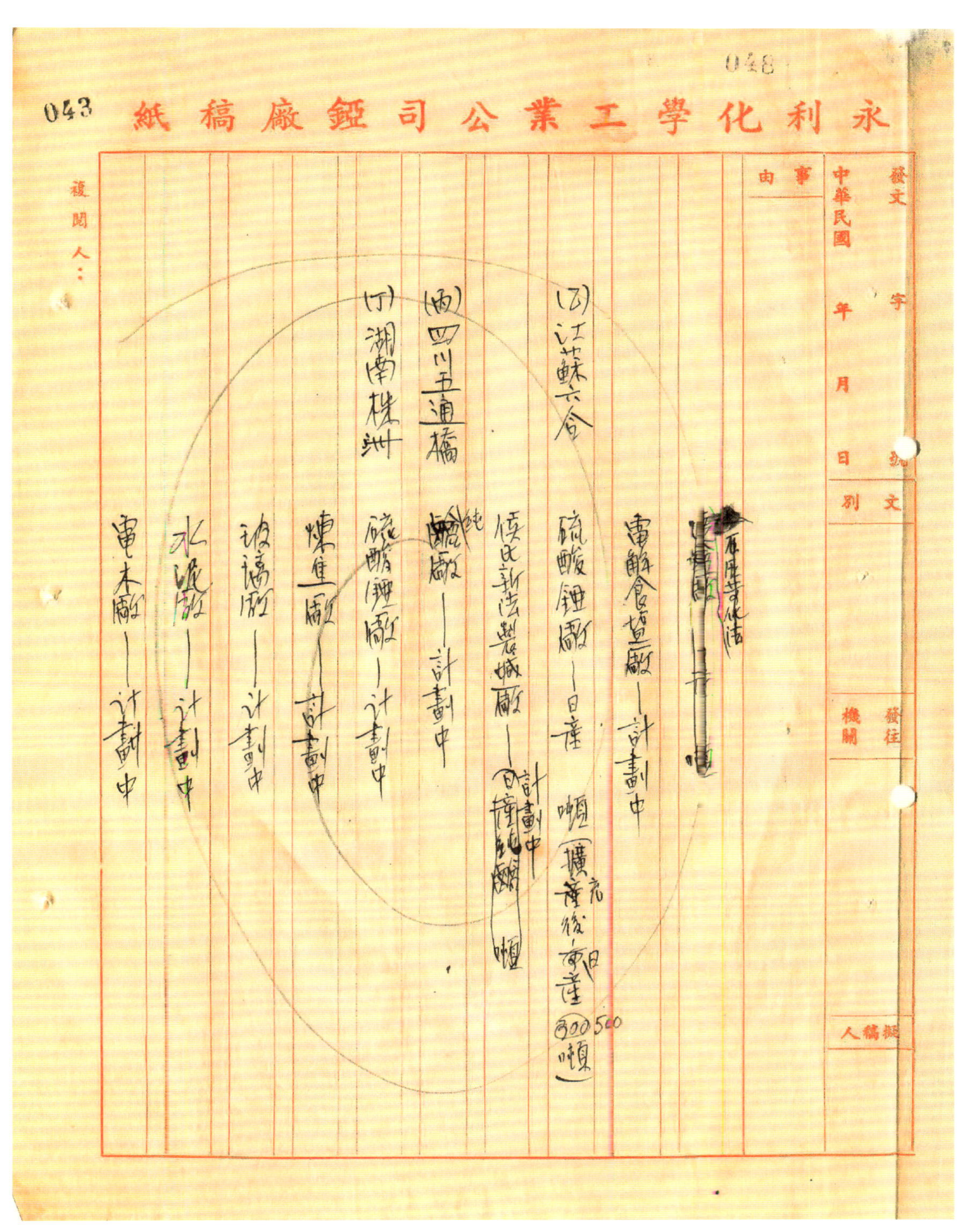

048

043　永利化學工業公司錏廠稿紙

發文　字　號

中華民國　年　月　日

文別

事由

發往機關

擬稿人

複閱人：

（不用苛化法）

電解食鹽廠—計劃中

（乙）江蘇六合

硫酸錏廠—日產　噸（擴充後日產500噸）

侯氏新法製堿廠—（日產純鹼　噸）計劃中

（丙）四川五通橋

純鹼廠—計劃中

（丁）湖南株洲

硫酸錏廠—計劃中

煉焦廠—計劃中

玻璃廠—計劃中

水泥廠—計劃中

電木廠—計劃中

永利化学工业公司铔厂管理部门概况（一九四七年一月一日）

018

永利化學工業公司錏廠稿紙

發文 字 號

事由：本廠管理部門之概況

本廠管理部門可依下列六項，作一簡畧述說：

1. 文書——本廠文書室直隸廠長辦公室，其經管事項，非常繁雜，所有內外公文之處理，命令通告之發佈，各部報告之整編，職員動態之調查，重要文件之保管等，均由該室負責執行，實不啻工廠之神經樞紐。

2. 經濟——本廠有會計處之設，下隸普通會計、成本會計、審計、統計、出納等五課，總攬本廠經濟大權，並供給各項統計，秉承廠長命令，統籌全廠財務，直接向總管理處會計部保持聯繫。

3. 地產——本廠有地產部之設，管理廠內地皮及房屋建築，並負

複閱人：

擬稿人：

019 永利化學工業公司錏廠稿紙

發文　字　號

中華民國　年　月　日

文別

發往機關

擬稿人

事由

責令購地設農場，或由該部經營其他管理工作之一。

4. 工人——本廠對於工人，注重教育訓練，不重管理干涉，故有工訓部之設。該部除經管工人動態之登記外，並設有學校與教育兩大部門，對於工人經常施以有形式的或非形式的教育，使養成良好習慣，造成良好公民。

5. 物料——本廠設有物料部，內分採購、運輸、保管、收發、等課，並附有成品庫，規模甚大，所有進出本廠之物料，統由該部經手。該部備有駁船多艘，往返搬運，至為忙碌。

覆閱人：

永利化学工业公司铔厂生产部门概况（一九四七年一月一日）

020　永利化學工業公司錏廠稿紙

發文　字　號
中華民國　年　月　日
文別
事由：本廠生產部門工作之概況
發往機關
擬稿人：[簽名]

本廠主要產品為化學農肥料，計有硫酸錏與硝酸錏兩种，但在製造此兩种產品之前，必先得液錏、硫酸、硝酸等三者以為原料。硫酸錏與硝酸錏為平時農民之必需，液錏、硫酸、硝酸則為戰時國防之利器。故本廠生產部門可合成一体，分之則為五个獨立之單位。茲將各單位之工作概況，分列介紹之如次：

1. 合成錏廠——採用N.E.C.法。其法係於水煤氣爐內燃燒焦炭，將空氣與蒸汽循環吹入，以取得含有氫氮之混合氣体，經過氧化、精煉手續，配成氫三氮一之比例，然後使受三百大氣壓力之壓縮，再通過合成塔之觸媒劑，即得錏氣，冷凝後，乃成液錏。

複閱人：

021 永利化學工業公司錏廠稿紙

發文　字　號

中華民國　年　月　日

文別

發往機關

擬稿人

事由

2. 硫酸部——採用觸媒法，燃燒硫磺或燃燒硫化鐵，得二氧化硫。二氧化硫與空氣中之氧在適當溫度之下，通過觸媒劑，乃氧化而成三氧化硫。三氧化硫得水，即成硫酸。

3. 硫酸錏廠——將硫酸與錏液送入飽和器内，同時通入錏氣及蒸汽，即有硫酸錏結晶析出，濾清烘乾，乃得成品。

4. 硝酸廠——採用白金接觸法。將錏氣與空氣混合，通過白金網燒之，使成一氧化氮，再使氧化，使成二氧化氮。二氧化氮得水，即成硝酸。

5. 硝酸錏廠——硝酸與錏化合成溶液，濃縮之，乃得硝酸錏結晶。

複閱人：

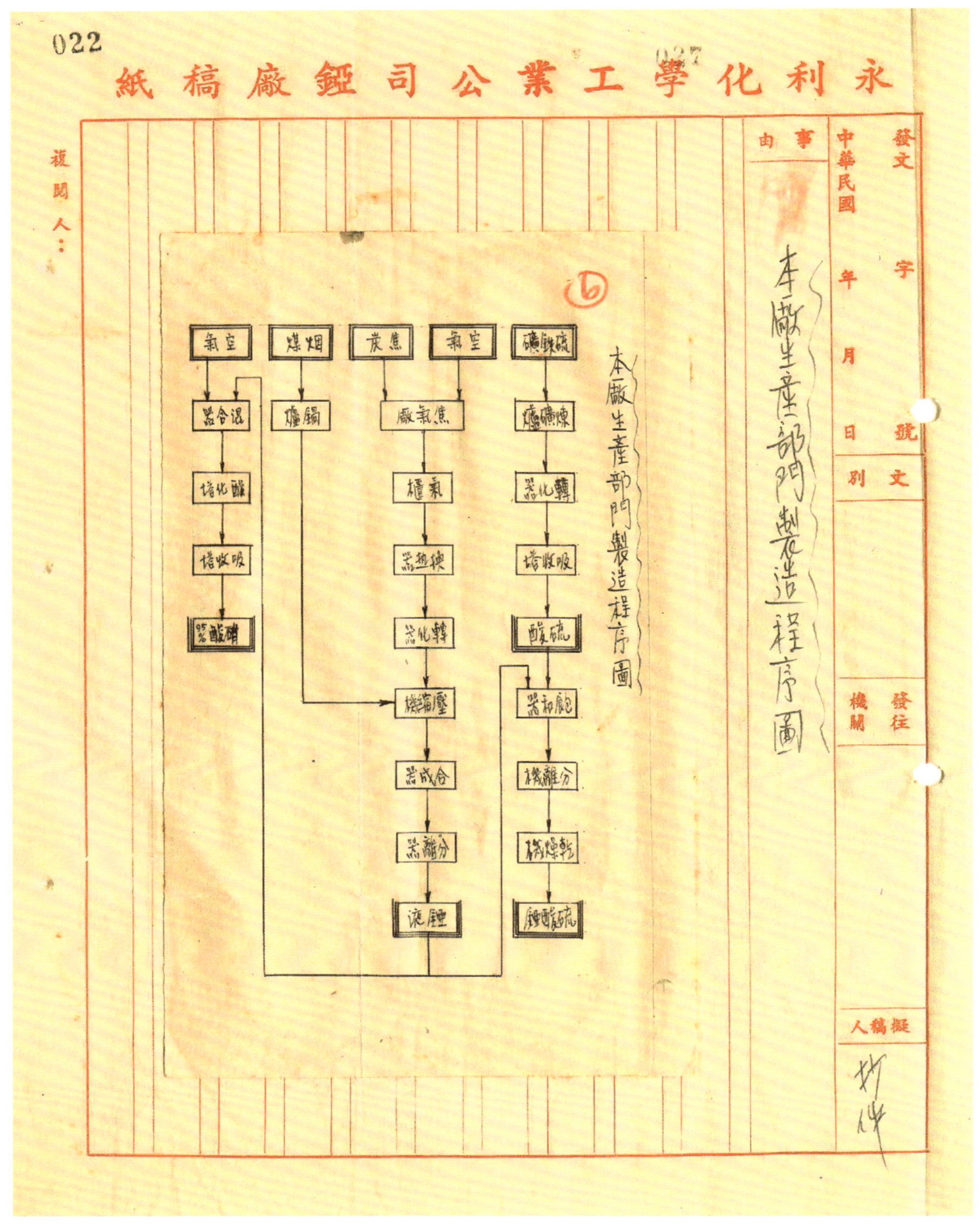

022

永利化學工業公司錏廠稿紙

發文	字 號
中華民國	年 月 日
文別	
事由	本廠生產部門製造程序圖
發往機關	
擬稿人	抄件

複閱人：

本廠生產部門製造程序圖

025　037

永利化學工業公司錏廠稿紙

發文　字　號

中華民國　年　月　日

文別

發往機關

擬稿人

複閱人：

事由：本廠工程部門之概況

本廠工程部門包括三大機構：一曰機械部，一曰電工部，一曰土木部，茲根據其經管之業務，分機械、電氣、動力、土木、給水等五方面加以簡單介紹：

(1)機械工程——由機械部專管，內設繪圖、鉗工、車工、鉚工、鍛工、模樣、翻砂、電焊、氣焊、鉛焊等各組，分佔兩大廠屋，內部均裝有二十噸電力起重機。翻砂部份所製鑄物，最重之件可達十噸，機械部之使命異常重大。工廠初創時，除一部份機器必須由國外購置外，其餘皆賴該部自製，工廠開工後，則一切機件之添配與修理，均須由其負責，並須進而製造成套機件。

026　　038

永利化學工業公司錏廠稿紙

發文　字　號
中華民國　年　月　日
文別
發往機關
擬稿人
事由

(2) 電氣工程——本廠無發電廠設備，每日用電約一五〇〇〇〇度，悉由南京首都電廠供給。本廠用電情形相當複雜，並有若干精密自動電器及儀器，如自動電話交換機及自動溫度、流量記錄儀等，非有優良技術人員，不能勝任，故電工部之組織非常龐大。

(3) 動力工程——本廠動力室有鍋爐三座，各有一千匹馬力，全具自動設備，目前不自發電，所製之蒸汽專供廠內高壓機器及化學製造之用，其蒸汽壓力為每方吋三百磅。又本廠近常因感首都電廠電力不足，電費亦貴，已擬另一萬瓩電力發電廠計劃，機器正向美國洽購中。

複閱人：

027 永利化學工業公司錏廠稿紙

發文　字　號
中華民國　年　月　日
文別
發往機關
擬稿人
事由

(4)土木工程——此項工程，概归土木部主持。所有房屋建築、深井、鐵路、道路、下水道、爐灶以及一切木瓦工程，均由該部執行。該部設有木工廠，內置鋸木、鉋板等機器多座。又有瓦工廠，製造青磚、石棉瓦及保溫管壳等。工作相當繁雜，經常僱用工人達數百名之多。

(5)給水工程——給水工程分工廠用水及住宅用水兩項。工廠用水除鍋炉水係用以深井井水加煉精充用外，其他各部之洗滌、冷卻等工作，皆用江水。江水抽水機有150馬力，每日取水一千五百餘噸（約400000加侖）。住宅用水，全用井水，由一十馬力及一馬力抽水機供給，每日取水八百餘噸（約200000加侖）。煉水部份之設備，非常新穎。

複閱人：侯德榜、吳驥侯

永利化学工业公司锰厂研究工作概况（一九四七年一月一日）

028

040

永利化學工業公司錏廠稿紙

發文　字　號

中華民國　年　月　日

文別

事由：本廠研究工作之概況

發往機關

擬稿人：[illegible]

複閱人：

本公司傳統精神，對製造與研究並重。基於此種精神，故先有塘沽鹹廠在全世界鹹業嚴守秘密中苦幹成功，後有侯氏製鹹法之艱苦抗戰期內異軍突起。本廠建立，雖係外商設計，而研究工作固仍居重要地位。茲分四方面述之於次：

(1)化工方面——本廠有化學部之設，專司化工研究，現該部暫設本廠，乃一龐大機構，內分研究與分析兩大部門，員工近百，各有專司，圖書儀器，相當完備。侯氏製鹹法之各項試驗，即均係該部所研究成。目下正着手研究製造各種觸媒劑，亦已獲得輝煌成就。本廠各部日常之化學管理以及偶然所遇之化學疑難問題，亦均由該部負責執行或研究解決之。下述三方面之研究工作，亦必得該部之協助，始可進行。

029

永利化學工業公司錏廠稿紙

發文 字 號

中華民國 年 月 日

文別

發往機關

擬稿人

事由

(2)冶金方面——化學工業之發展，端賴冶金技術為之輔。本廠各部機器所用之合金材料，種類繁多，現正由機械、化學兩部合作研究，試行自製。惟設備方面，因受抗戰影響，損失甚重，故目下尚未能積極進行，現正力求補充，如半噸Rennerfelt氏電爐，及若干精密儀器如Grating Spectrograph等，均將陸續運到，最近期內，此可展開有系統的研究工作。

(3)農藝方面——本廠闢有佔地130畝之試驗農場，分肥料、園藝、森林、病蟲害、畜牧等五組，進行研究工作。其肥料組又分全國性及地域性兩項，前者與中央農業實驗所訂有合約，合作試驗肥料各种與其對農作物之影響；後者則在本廠一帶舉行，研究硫酸錏施用方法。其他四組之工

複閱人：

030

永利化學工業公司錏廠稿紙

發文　字　號

中華民國　年　月　日

文別

事由

發往機關

擬稿人

作，屬於工廠福利範圍，僱用工人經常達百餘人之多。廠
方更另有農事討論委員会之設，主持整個設計工作，並
聘請國內農業專家，以充顧問。尤其化學方面則受本公司
化學部之指導。

(14) 地質方面——本公司事業範圍，日見擴大，各廠所需原料種類逐漸增多，須有精密
如煤、鎂、燐、鉀、鋁、硫磺、硼砂、粘土、矽砂、石膏等礦產，
均須預為勘查，以求獲得詳細確實數字，而為建廠之憑籍，故本公司有礦
產原料探採部之設立。此部現暫設本廠，長期派人分赴各
地，從事調查，或實行鑽探，採取標品，如有必要，並設

複閱人：

031

0043

永利化學工業公司錏廠稿紙

發文　字　號

中華民國　年　月　日

文別

事由

發往機關

擬稿人

複閱人：

續開採，俾應各廠之需求。

侯德榜为购大宗器材请予放行以利建造安装事致临时输入委员会主任、副主任函（一九四七年七月九日）

0087

永利化學工業公司錏廠

編號　字第五〇九號　第一頁　卅六年七月九日

敬啓者：敝公司在抗戰期間（民國卅一年至卅四年）及勝利以後，曾由美國第二次第四次各借款項下，購買大宗器材，爲復興敝公司各工廠之用。此項器材，大都由紐約世界貿易公司承購，間亦有一二由紐約華昌貿易公司代購者，其外匯業經由財政部核准在案。其價款早已付清，有收據爲憑。惟因在抗戰期間，交通工具奇缺，是以遲至今日，始陸續運滬。查去年有一部份器材，已由美裝運抵滬，乃至今仍有未蒙放行者。敝公司對於此項器材，未運回時，盼望能由美起運甚殷，既運回後，應如何積極領取裝配，以增生產。乃滯留於貴會堆棧數月，而未能取出，棧租擔負既重，而機件在堆棧銹蝕，損失更大，至堪焦慮。敝公司既非進出口商人，而所購機件，又屬技術上特殊需要者，迥非尋常商品可比。爲此懇請儘數放行，以便工

永利化學工業公司錏廠

總號　字第五〇九號第　二　頁

卅六年七月九日

廠復興工程之進行，而符政府維持工業，鼓勵生產之旨意。況此項器材，價款外匯，早已向財政部結集，其數亦已繳還國庫，此時與不當申請外匯，自與目前

貴會取締進口，節省外匯之原則，截然不同。用特懇請，統衡予以放行。再敝公司在美由華盛頓應出口銀行貸款一千六百萬元美金，現已陸續動用，在美採購器材，此項器材，爲數達數百種，均爲復興新廠，建造新廠之用，到滬時若一一依此手續辦理，則費時曠日，不堪設想。似此惟有懇請發給通用進口證，以利建造安裝之進行，不勝感企之至。

此致

臨時輸入委員會　主任委員張公權先生　副主任委員李馥蓀先生　台鑒

永利化學工業公司總經理侯德榜　印

廠址：江蘇省六合縣卸甲甸　通訊處：南京(八)頤和路二十三號　電話：三三九九六　電報掛號三四五四　南京

永利化学工业公司錏厂工厂伤亡抚恤暂行办法（一九四八年一月一日）

本廠空襲傷亡撫卹暫行辦法之擬訂，誠如小組長座談會公佈結論的弁言，和結論中所云：在空襲威脅的現況下，我們為了支援前綫和保障全廠職工生活，需要積極生產；但在另一方面，又感覺防空設備太不健全，為了防範萬一，穩定同仁工作情緒，和加強責任心起見，不得不有撫卹與獎懲辦法之公佈，而真正的希冀，還在這些辦法，可以不致於實施，所以在空襲傷亡撫卹暫行辦法的第一條便開宗明義地寫着：「本廠職工，凡遇空襲時，應各就其環境，盡力設法避免無謂犧牲，為國惜身，不可疏忽。」此其一。

在整個南京市城郊地區，同受空襲威脅的情況下，本廠為了擬訂撫卹與獎懲暫行辦法，更臻完備和合理起見，事先曾派人赴南京電廠、浦鎮機器廠、電器材料廠、有恒麵粉廠等公營與私營工廠，調查有沒有關於此類的法規，要來作參考資料；結果，僅要來南京電廠空襲傷亡撫卹規則暫行辦法一種，其他各廠，都還沒有考慮這項問題；因此本廠祗好就以南京電廠的暫行辦法作藍本，參酌本廠實際，和特殊情形，擬訂本年八月廿一日公布的錏廠職工空襲傷亡撫卹暫行辦法，和獎懲暫行辦法，南京電廠和本廠擬訂的這兩個撫卹辦法，最大的不同点，就是本廠規定給與傷亡同仁的撫卹金，每項都比較南京電廠的規定為優厚，此其二。

寫法令規章的文字，要簡單明瞭，最忌艱澀，可是人事則千變萬化，無法預作包括無遺的想定，以簡單明瞭的有限條文規定，來處理不易想像周到的事件，自然難免令人啟掛一漏萬的感覺，所以說，法律本乎人情，這意思就是一方面告訴擬制法律條文的人，不可刻薄偏頗，執行法律的人，也不可膠柱鼓瑟，應該使之合乎人情，換句話說，就是須得參酌群眾的反映，本廠擬訂的空襲傷亡撫卹暫行辦法，和獎懲暫行辦法，很顯然地未曾脫盡過去制訂法律的窠臼，既然沒有脫盡這窠臼，更談不上已竭盡言簡意賅的能事，所以希望最好不致於應用，萬一到應用的必要時，除了對死亡的已有硬性規定外，凡是受傷的，自然還得查明當時受傷情形，再行確定撫卹金多少，此其三。

在空襲時間內，堅守崗位，繼續執行任務，使工作不致中斷，及甘冒危險，奮不顧身，保全本廠重大資產，以致死亡之職工，與在其工作性質範圍

永利化學工業公司鋞廠第　次廠務會議記録　頁之三頁

内，因空襲以致死亡之職工，最大的區別，就是前者第一種被指定的職工，毫無趨吉避凶的選擇自由，如有陽奉陰違情事發生，一經發覺，不僅不予給與，還應按其情節輕重，依照廠章議處。第二種職工，置性命於度外，使本廠重大資產，賴以保存。這種自動自發的忠勇精神，實非人人所能及。而後者雖遇警報剛拉，飛機就到了頭頂，事實上儘管沒有趨避的時間，但充分保有趨避的自由，如在警報發出和飛機臨頭中間有餘裕時間的機會時，可以避免危險的人，不是都能儘量避免嗎？這一点在小組長會議紀録議程(二)結論中説得最清晰。而(一)結論中，也承認對堅守崗位，和甘冒危險，奮不顧身，保存本廠重大資產而遇難的職工，確有特別表揚和獎金的必要。依此，可見小組長們的真正意見，不是在工作性質範圍内，因空襲而致死亡的職工，和被指定在空襲時間，堅守崗位，使工作不致中斷，而死亡的職工，有無區別的問題，而是認為本廠規定分別給與撫卹標準的不够優厚，所以小組長會議紀録議程(一)結論内，開初雖認定現在一拉警報，飛機就到了頭頂，所以在工作性質範圍内，事實上與堅守崗位，並無區別，其撫卹辦法，應當相同；

而後段文字中，便說到但經各單位主管人特別指定，堅守崗位，因空襲而致死亡的職工，除照撫卹暫行辦法已有規定給與外，另應給以生產英雄的特別表揚與特別獎金，其实本廠當擬訂此項撫卹暫行辦法時，業已將撫卹金給與標準提高了；如果不信，請拿本廠擬訂的撫卹暫行辦法和南京電廠公佈的撫卹規則暫行辦法，兩相對照，就可以發現其不同之点為：

南京電廠對甘冒重大危險，堅守崗位，因空襲而致死亡之職工，僅按其死亡月份薪工半數，按月發給其遺族撫卹金，繼續至核定之年限為止（最少為五年，最多不得超過十五年）；而本廠撫卹暫行辦法第二條規定，在上述同一情形下，死亡的職工，應按其死亡時之最後一月薪給金額，逐月全數發給與其直系親屬，以五年至十五年為限。如無妻、子或女、父或母等之直系親屬者，依照本廠辦法，另不給撫卹金，卻應予公葬，與得建築紀念物；南京電廠辦法第七條規定，死亡者無遺族時，除支付報殮費外，亦給撫卹金，亦無公葬與得建築紀念物之表揚規定，對非甘冒重大危險，堅守崗位，因空襲而致死亡之職工，南京電廠無撫卹明文規定，而本廠辦法

第三條規定：對於非常危險，與被指定堅守崗位因空襲而致死亡之職工，仍給與和南京電廠辦法第三條規定，甘冒重大危險，堅守崗位而致空襲死亡職工之同等撫卹，其為優厚，無待多加解釋，此其四。

議程(四)結論中，指出撫卹金應與技術年資職位等有連帶關係，這見解是正確的，至對最低工資的工人，因致死原因，其遺族只能按月領取半薪，不能維持最低生活，希望廠方依其實際需要情形，酌予津貼，以資維持，原則上，自應完全同意，而且也曾考慮過到這一點，徒以因限於一種規章的擬訂，不宜例外太多，致引起施行時的爭執，和執行的人，得藉以挾私抵隙，上下其手，以及致使整個辦法，因受例外影響，而令應依遇難情形不同，分別撫卹等次，紊亂不清，輕重不當着想，只好付諸闕如，不過倘若遇到這種生前工資甚低，因空襲而致死亡後，其遺族只能按月領取半薪，不夠維持最低生活的情形時，若再用向同仁募捐，和其他互助互濟的方法，也未嘗不可彌補這缺陷，不用說，這種臨時性的辦法，就是今後擬訂較永久性的有關此類辦法時，在人民政府對於社会救济事業設施，未臻健全以前，對於這種特殊情况，恐怕還祇能利用私人捐贈和舉辦各項勞動保險事業用資過渡，此其五。（文字如次：

除了以上各項說明外，還有一項最重要的原理原則應請同仁大家特別注意的，那就是新民主主義政府領導下的工業政策，是在勞資兩利的前提下，怎樣培植再生產的生機，共同為發展工業而努力。本廠目前生產情形，是否已進入到可以充分從事再生產的有利階段，要顧問高明說，就是我們的成品所換來的金錢，是不是已經日有積累足以用之於再生產方面，使我們的事業向着欣欣向榮的程途邁進。如其不然，那末，相信本廠全体職工弟兄們一定會照顧到眼前資方所遭遇的困難，對於任何要求，可以自動削減。所以關於小組長會議所擬提高本廠職工遭遇空襲傷亡撫卹一点，事實上既已經比較南京寧廠的辦法提高了，希望不再提高。至關於這項辦法文字和內容，茲特就小組長會議所提出的意見斟酌修改於后，其未能完全依照小組長會議所提出的意見加以修改的地方，除逐一加以說明理由外，希望多多原諒。

 210

永利化學工業公司錏廠第　次廠務會議記錄　頁之七頁

一、原小撫郵暫行辦法第一條文字，既經小組長会議完全同意，不加修改。

二、第二條修改後文字如次：

「本廠職工在空襲時間，「服從指揮」，堅守崗位，繼續執行任務，而使工作不致中斷者，及在空襲時間發生事件，甘冒危險，奮不顧身，「其目的在保全本廠「重大」資產，以致死亡者，得由本廠「公殮」公葬，「公殮公葬」條例另定之。如遺族必欲將靈柩運回原籍安葬時，不論路程遠近，交通情形如何，由本廠按照公殮公葬辦法規定，將公葬費用全部，撥交其遺族具領，作為運柩用費」，並按下列撫郵辦法辦理」

說明：

(一)本條「服從指揮」四字，原被小組長会議删去，何以必須保留呢？因為大前提在遭遇空襲時間，希望職工們盡力設法避免無謂犧牲；但為了支援前綫，和保障全廠職工弟兄們的生活需要，乃不得不指定某些職工，堅守崗位，維持生產，很顯然的，某些應該堅守崗位的職工，是被動的，而非自動的，既是被動的，便有服從指揮的必要否則儘可自由行動，而空襲時間與懲辦法第五條的規定，便沒有存在的價值了。例，本廠可依照規定標準，臨時發給全部，發生其意義上

（二）本條內「其目的在」四字，係小組長會議所增添的，易較原來規定為寬泛。本廠可予接受，但在保全本廠重大資產的「重大」二字，必須保留，以期不違背第一條所揭櫫的宗旨「無謂犧牲」和引起應用本辦法時的過大出入。這點最為值得注意。

（三）建築紀念物，和加發半年薪給全部，作為獎金兩點，因為這辦法原來的規定，已較南京電廠的優厚得多，不能再行提高。（且與前辦法，其

（四）本來本廠既備有公墓，規定公葬，其遺族固執不願將靈柩入葬者，顯見其遺族思想之落後，吾人有進行教育，改造其思想之積極責任，不當聽之任之，甚或助長之。茲以空襲撫卹辦法，為短時期內的過渡辦法，不僅共同希冀不至應用，而且絕對相信在不久將來，華南解放後，匪機即可不再來肆虐，故為重視羣眾反映計，要擬將

（一）葬公墓公葬所需費用，於另訂之公墓公葬條例中，分別準確定標

永利化學工業公司錏廠第　次廠務會議記錄　頁之九頁

準其遺族不願將靈柩入葬公墓，必欲運回原籍者，不論路程遠近，交通是否便利，本廠可依照規定標準，將公葬費全部，發交其遺族具領，作為搬運靈柩回籍運雜費用之補貼，假如依小組長會議意見，運送因空襲殉難職工靈柩回籍費用，須全部由廠負担，不獨核定數字多少，頗為困難，易滋爭執，抑且有損改造落後思想，建立嶄新社會之國策，這點最為值得注意！

三、第二條第一項修改後文字如次

「按其死亡時之最後一月薪給金額，逐月全數給與直系親屬，其具領人之資格及次序：為妻、子或女、父或母、祖父或祖母」，「純以入廠登記表為合法證明」：撫卹年限，應斟酌其遺族「主要經濟來源」，以五年至十五年為限，其在撫卹年限內，應領全部薪給計算方法，須依照各該月份計發本廠全體職工薪資標準，同樣辦理」。

說明

（一）按其死亡時之最後一月的全部薪給金額，逐月全數給予與直系親屬，因下句既有「全數」二字，則上句「的全部」三字，似屬衍文。

(二)一切福利：就目前本廠職工現有的而言，計有(1)加工，(2)星期加班，(3)每月不請假之二天獎金，(4)工服，(5)年終放薪，(6)紅利，(7)年終考績加薪等七種，其中(1)(2)兩項須視工作需要而定，(3)項原用以鼓勵工友弟兄努力工作，不輕易請假，(7)項須待一年終了，視其全年中工作成績怎樣而定，均非職工全体無條件所能享有，(4)(5)(6)項，是為全体職工所共享，但其用意，仍因職工在工作時，服裝不免較易破爛，故配發工服，以示補貼，年終雙薪和紅利，係公司体念全体職工終年勞碌，加發一個月薪資，用申酬謝，與表示甘苦共嘗之意，並規定在本年內，如有請假情事，尚須比例扣減，所以說，這些福利，都是職工弟兄利用勞力所取得本薪以外的額外報酬。因空襲而不幸殉難的職工弟兄，自無繼續貢献勞力於本廠可言，當更無（利用）勞力取得額外報酬之理，我們對不幸因空襲殉難的職工，這種為支援前線而死，為維持本廠職工生活而死，為拓展工業奮鬥而死的精神，固然應該永

永利化學工業公司錏廠第　次廠務會議記錄　頁之一一頁

極地致最高的崇敬，但對其遺族既已給與其生前本薪全部，以維生活，似已不稱十分微薄，不宜再享受其他福利，如果死者的遺族，應有享受本廠一切福利的權利，則對繼續貢獻勞力於本廠之職工弟兄將何以處之呢？

(三)本項內「祖父或祖母」文句，係依小組長會議紀錄增添的。

(四)增添「純以本廠登記表為合法證明」一句，用意在防杜事後可能發生之糾紛，例如抗戰夫人，勝利夫人之爭執等

(五)原文為得斟酌其遺族經濟狀況句，茲依小組長會議紀錄，修改為「應斟酌其遺族「主要經濟來源」」

(六)小組長會議所提撫卹最低與最高年限，應改作十五年至三十年一點，本廠認為標準太高，因為撫卹金之給與，目的在使死者所遺直系親屬中的幼有所養，老有所終，虽死也可以瞑目九泉，假令因空襲而死亡的職工，享壽為廿歲，則就一般情形而論，其父母年齡最少亦當為四十歲，除殘廢外，正當年富力強，力足以自謀生計，

和撫育幼弱家屬，使之成長，不完全倚賴此項撫卹金，贍養全家，撫卹金給與年限，儘有斟酌縮短餘地，即令為親已衰老，子女尚在乳哺期中，其遺族又無其他主要經濟來源，但經過十五年後，老親固會老也，其子女亦可以從事輕便工作，何况在新民主主義國度內，對於養老育幼之類的社會事業，一定很快地有長足的展佈，究竟的說起，決不會有任何一人，感受生存危險的威脅，這是可以斷言的，所以希望仍維持原來「以五年至十五年為限」的規定。

（七）小組長今議提出遺族領取撫卹金時，應照當月份全體職工發薪計算標準核放一点，用意甚是周到，自應增添，不過文字上稍有修飾，和原意並無出入。

（八）死亡如無一項所規定的直系親屬，似不可由死者生前另行指定代領人，至所作確定此項代領人之資格，應為確靠本人供養之其他親屬之意，不知是否指入繼之子女，無後之伯叔父母，寡嫂孫姪，或抱養之子女而言，如果係指此類親屬關係而言，依照現代

240

永利化學工業公司錏廠第　次廠務會議記錄　頁之一三　頁

思想，凡繼人之子女，在親屬法中，將不承認其有繼承遺產權，因這種繼承辦法，係源於宗族思想，所謂不孝有三，無後為大，故為人後者為使祖先血食不至由我而絕，如娶妻不生男子，可以納妾，妾又無所出，則應入繼世代脗合的宗人子弟藉綿似續，此種和新政治精神相違謬的落後思想，似不應使其繼續存在，何況極易由此規定發生其他流弊呢。

四、第二條第二項，仍保持原文規定，不予修改

理由見上條(八)說明，不重述。

五、第三條修改後文字如次：

「本廠職工在其「工作性質範圍內」(包括因公外出者)因空襲而致死亡者，應由本廠發給喪葬費，最高喪葬費金額，不得超過領取前一日南京新民報刊登上熟米一石之時值。」並按下列撫卹辦法辦理」

說明：

(一)依小組長會議紀錄，本條「工作性質範圍內」一語，當改為「工作時間

四、「其所以仍保持原文的理由，因「工作性質範圍」，不僅不受時間拘束，其空間亦較遼廓，若依照小組長会議紀錄加以修改，則限制顯明，幅度狹隘得多了。

(二)「應由本廠發給喪葬費」，原為「得由本廠根據現行辦法，酌給喪葬費」，茲依小組長会議意見，予以修改。

(三)增加「最高喪葬費金額，不得超過領取前一日南京新民報刊登上熟米　石之時值」文字，庶以免除將來有所爭執。

六、第三條(一)(二)兩項，仍保持原文，不予修改，小組長会議紀錄主張照第二條所列辦法撫卹，歉難同意，其理由具如上述，茲不復贅。

七、第四條仍保持原文，不予修改，因職工不在工作時間內，而其工作性質與範圍，又至為明確，則在規定工作時間以外，儘有隨時設法避免空襲犧牲，為國惜身之充分準備，自不能與在工作性質與範圍內因工作而殞命者相提並論，僅能照本廠現行法規病故條規定辦理。

永利化學工業公司錏廠第　次廠務會議記錄　頁之一五頁

八、第五條本文仍舊，其餘修改後文字如次

「因空襲而致傷殘者，除醫治期內所需醫藥費，不論在本廠衛生院或送往本廠同意之南京市公私醫院醫治，統由本廠負担外，本廠於其傷愈後」，「在其工作能力可能勝任之條件下」酌給以適當工作，仍支原薪」，「如其本人自願告退，並經本廠「同意」時，得按其當時受傷原因，分別發給撫卹金」如下。

說明：

(一)本條依小組長會議修改之字句中，於「送往南京市」送往二字下，南京二字上，增添了「本廠同意之」五個字，用意在現階段中，不免有些職工，仍相信巫覡與走方及草藥醫生可以醫病的，所以其就診之醫院，受傷職工僅有選擇自由，但須本廠同意，予以限制。

(二)小組長會議紀錄於增添「於其傷愈後」，原為「得在本人同意下」七字，茲酌改為「在其工作能力可能勝任之條件下」字樣，原因在目前情況下，調動職工工作，尚不時遭遇波折，若傷愈後

十一、改派工作，必需得其本人同意，誠恐將來不無問題，故不如以其傷後之工作能力，是否足以勝任某項工作？用為酌派工作時之決定標準，較為合理。

九、本辦法第五條（甲）（乙）（丙）各項，仍維持原文規定，至（甲）項載明得撥其最後月薪一次發給二年半之撫卹金的理由，因南京電廠僅給與十個月而本廠規定增加八個月，乙項規定亦較南京電廠增多兩個月。小組長會議紀錄主張（甲）項撫卹金為三年，（乙）項為一年半，因其傷愈後本廠並非不予安插，維持其生活，以其自願告退，乃改為發給一次撫卹金，藉以表示酬答之意，似不宜再行提高

十、第六條修改後文字如下：

「本廠職工因空襲以致傷殘者，如完全喪失其一切工作能力時，得按當時致傷原因，「分別發給撫卹金」，「其」辦法如下：」

說明：

（一）本條「分別發給撫卹金」句，係依小組長會議紀錄修改。

20

永利化學工業公司錏廠第　次廠務會議記錄　頁之一七頁

十一、第六條(一)(二)兩項，仍保持原文，不予修改，理由詳前。

十二、第六條應增加一項，列為(三)，其文字如次：

「(三)合於本條(一)(二)兩項因傷喪失其一切工作能力之職工，如在受傷之日起計　年以內，因傷痕復發而致死亡，經醫院証明確實者，得斟酌其遺族主要經濟來源繼續發給其全薪或半薪，作為撫卹金，藉維其直系親屬之生活。此項撫卹金給與之年限，最少　年，最多不得超過　年。」

說明：

第六條中增加此項文字之用意，係使受傷經醫治後，不僅喪失其一切工作能力，且創痕復發，在短期間內即告死亡者，不受本條(一)(二)兩項規定之拘束，仍得繼續領取撫卹金，以維持其直系遺屬生活之權利。

十三、第七條仍保持原文規定，不予修改。

說明：

凡職工眷屬，自不能因維持生產，不得不留廠冒險工作之職工本身相比，為防杜無謂犧牲，在空襲可能繼續期內，職工眷屬以及早自行疏散為妥，即令不願及早疏散，亦儘有作隨時逃避之充分準備，其不聽勸告，因空襲而有傷亡時，本廠自不負任何責任，若依小組長會議紀錄文字增入撫卹辦法中，顯與擬訂此項辦法之原旨相違背，此點務希多加體諒！

十四、茲依照小組長會議紀錄，增改第八條文字如次：

「本廠職工因空襲而致傷亡時，其撫卹問題，經本廠根據本辦法與死亡者遺族（合於本辦法第（二）條（一）項規定中取得卹金具領人資格之直系親屬）或傷殘職工本人（或指定代表人）簽立協定後，應將此項協定，寫成一式四份，除本廠與死亡職工遺族，或傷殘職工本人，各執一份外，其他二份，應分送本廠職工會、南京市勞動局備查，以資保障」

十五、增加如下文字一段，列為本辦法第九條，全文如次：

永利化學工業公司錏廠第　次廠務會議記錄　頁之一九頁

「前項協議，如因双方發生爭執，未能順利成立時，得邀請本廠職工会負責人，居間調解，調解無效時，得由双方請求南京市勞動局進行仲裁，不服仲裁時，得訴諸人民法院裁判確定之。」

十六、本辦法第八條改為第十條，原文如舊。

十七、本辦法第九條改為第十一條，原文如舊。

十八、本辦法第十條，改為第十二條，修改後文字如次：

「本辦法經勞資双方簽署成立呈報南京市勞動局批准後，應繕寫一式四份，分別送存南京市勞動局、本公司總管理處、本廠職工会及本廠各一份備查，並公佈実施。」修改時亦如之。

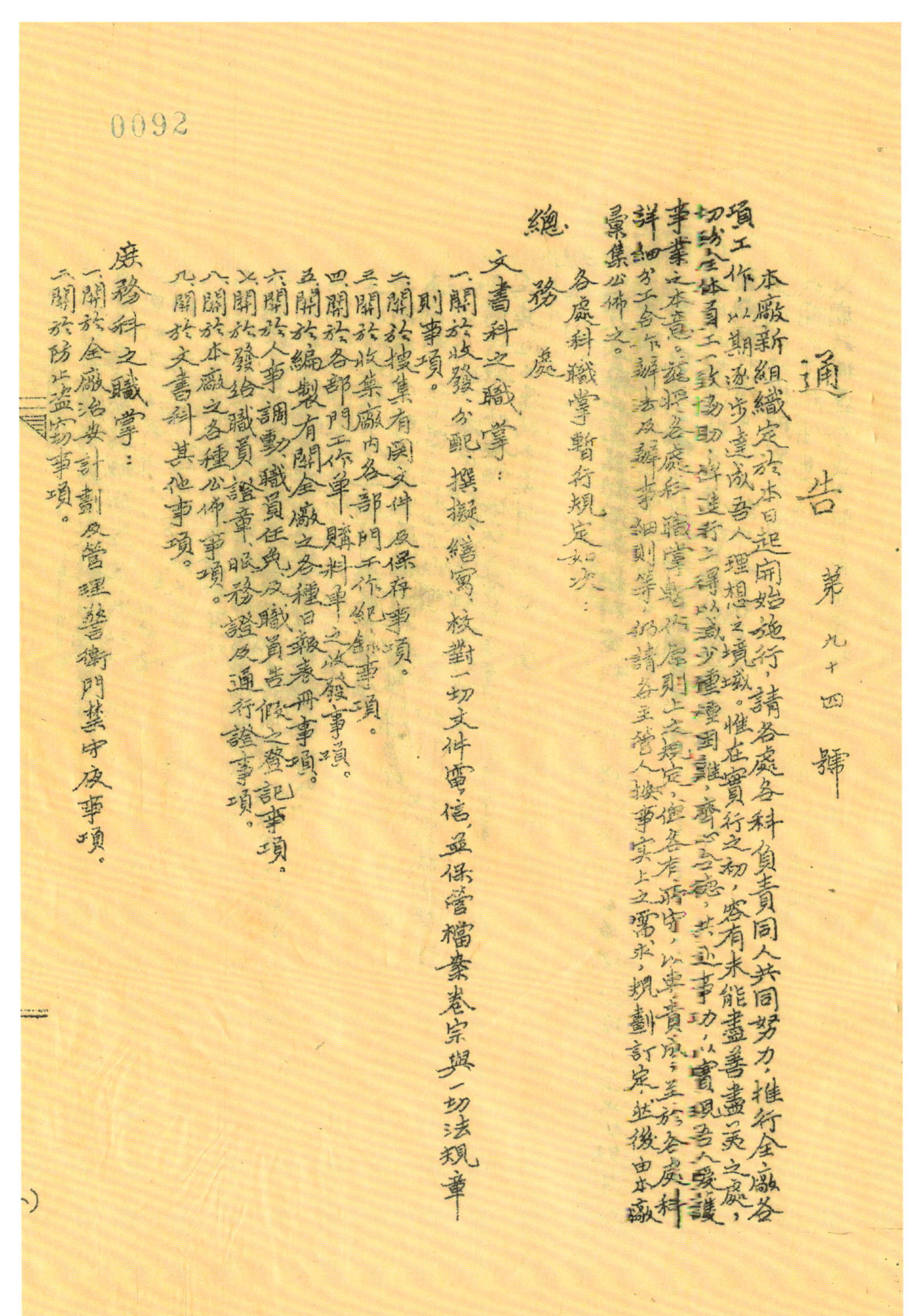

0092

通告　第九十四號

本廠新組織定於本日起開始施行，請各處各科負責同人共同努力，推行全廠各項工作，以期逐步達成吾人理想之境域。惟在實行之初，容有未能盡善盡美之處，切盼全體員工一致協助，并進行之得以逐步克服困難，齊心合德，共赴事功，以實現吾人愛護事業之本意。茲將各處科職掌暫作原則上之規定，俾各有所守，以專責成。至於各處科詳細分工合作辦法及辦事細則等，仍請各主管人按事實上之需求，規劃訂定，然後由本廠彙集公佈之。

各處科職掌暫行規定如次：

總務處

文書科之職掌：

一、關於收發、分配、撰擬、繕寫、校對一切文件電信，並保管檔案卷宗與一切法規章則事項。

二、關於搜集有關文件及保存事項。

三、關於收集廠內各部門工作紀錄事項。

四、關於各部門工作單、購料單之收發事項。

五、關於編製有關全廠之各種日報表冊事項。

六、關於人事調動、職員任免及職員告假之登記事項。

七、關於發給職員證章、服務證及通行證事項。

八、關於本廠之各種公佈事項。

九、關於文書科其他事項。

庶務科之職掌：

一、關於全廠治安計劃及管理警衛門禁守夜事項。

二、關於防止盜竊事項。

三、關於消防事項。
四、關於員工單身宿舍之分配及管理事項。
五、關於廠內各公共飯團之供應管理及改進事項。
六、關於各公共處所之燃料配送事項。
七、關於工廠傢具之保管分配及登記編號事項。
八、關於工廠文具之分配及登記事項。
九、關於工廠所有地畝之管理及保管契據圖籍事項。
十、關於戶口調查編製表冊及與地方政府鄉鎮保甲之聯絡交涉事項。
十一、關於交通船隻車輛之統籌管理及調配事項。
十二、關於招待來賓及領導參觀事項。
十三、關於突發事件之調解與處置事項。
十四、關於水電臨時發生障故之通知及準備事項。
十五、關於員工日常消耗公用物資之調查統計及編製圖表事項。
十六、關於廠內茶房雜役之管理訓練事項。
十七、關於廠內外店舖攤販之管制指導勸告等事項。
十八、其他不屬於各處科之雜務事項。

採運科之職掌：
一、關於本廠所需器材、原料、燃料、電料、化學藥品、醫藥及各種設備品等之採購運輸事項。
二、關於採運手續及付款辦法之規定事項。
三、關於採運賬目之登記及購單運單之保存事項。
四、關於行情市價之調查及比較事項。
五、關於招標購買事項。
六、關於運輸價目之調查及運輸船隻之接洽與調配事項。
七、關於搬運人工之分配及管理事項。

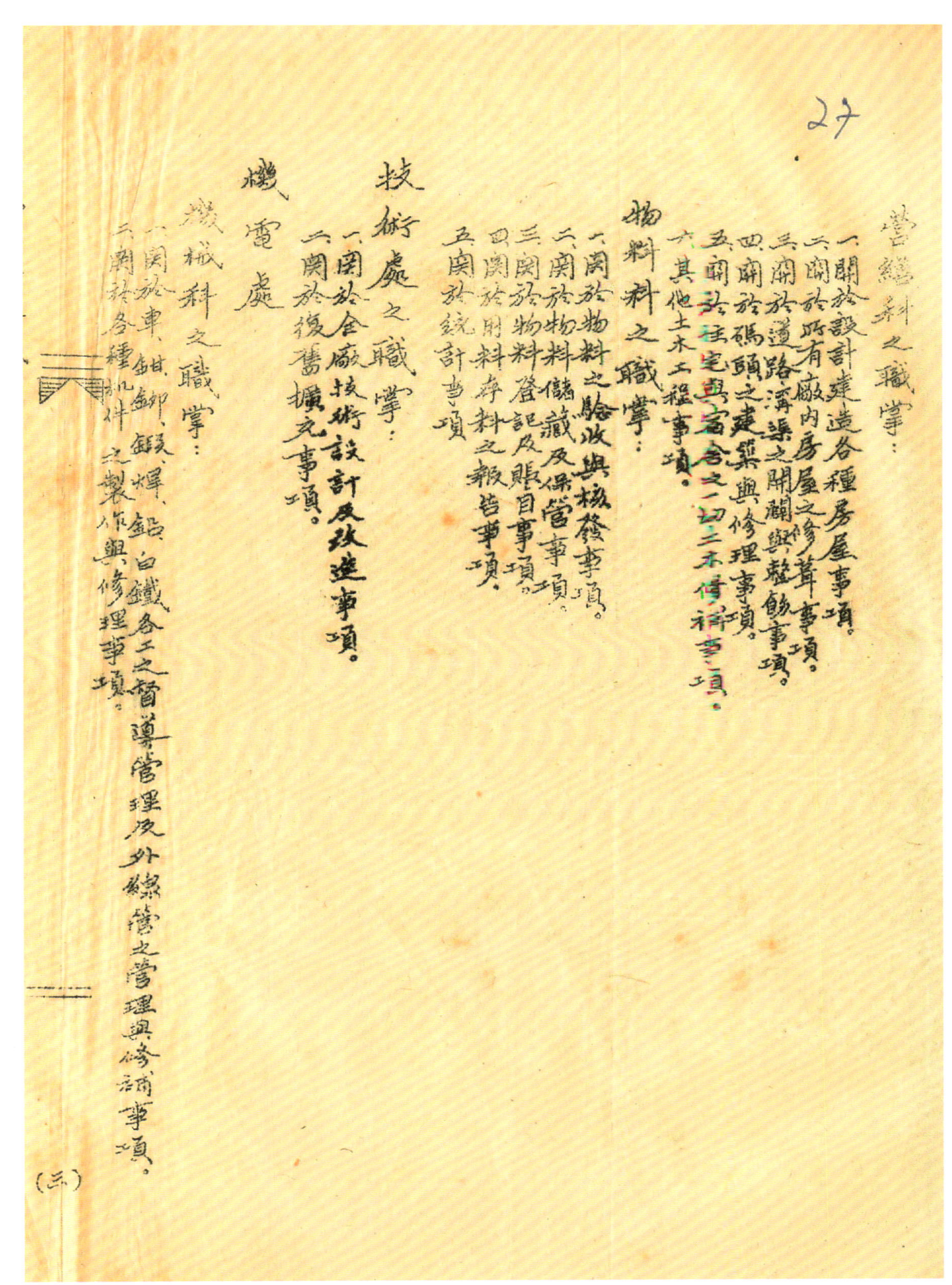

27

營繕科之職掌：

一、關於設計建造各種房屋事項。

二、關於所有廠內房屋之修葺事項。

三、關於道路溝渠之開闢與整飭事項。

四、關於碼頭之建築與修理事項。

五、關於住宅與宿舍之一切土木修補事項。

六、其他土木工程事項。

物料科之職掌：

一、關於物料之驗收與核發事項。

二、關於物料儲藏及保管事項。

三、關於物料登記及賬目事項。

四、關於用料存料之報告事項。

五、關於統計事項。

技術處之職掌：

一、關於全廠技術設計及改進事項。

二、關於修復舊損擴充事項。

機、電處

機械科之職掌：

一、關於車、鉗、鉚、鍛、焊、鋁、白鐵各工之督導管理及外線管之管理與修補事項。

二、關於各種機件之製作與修理事項。

（三）

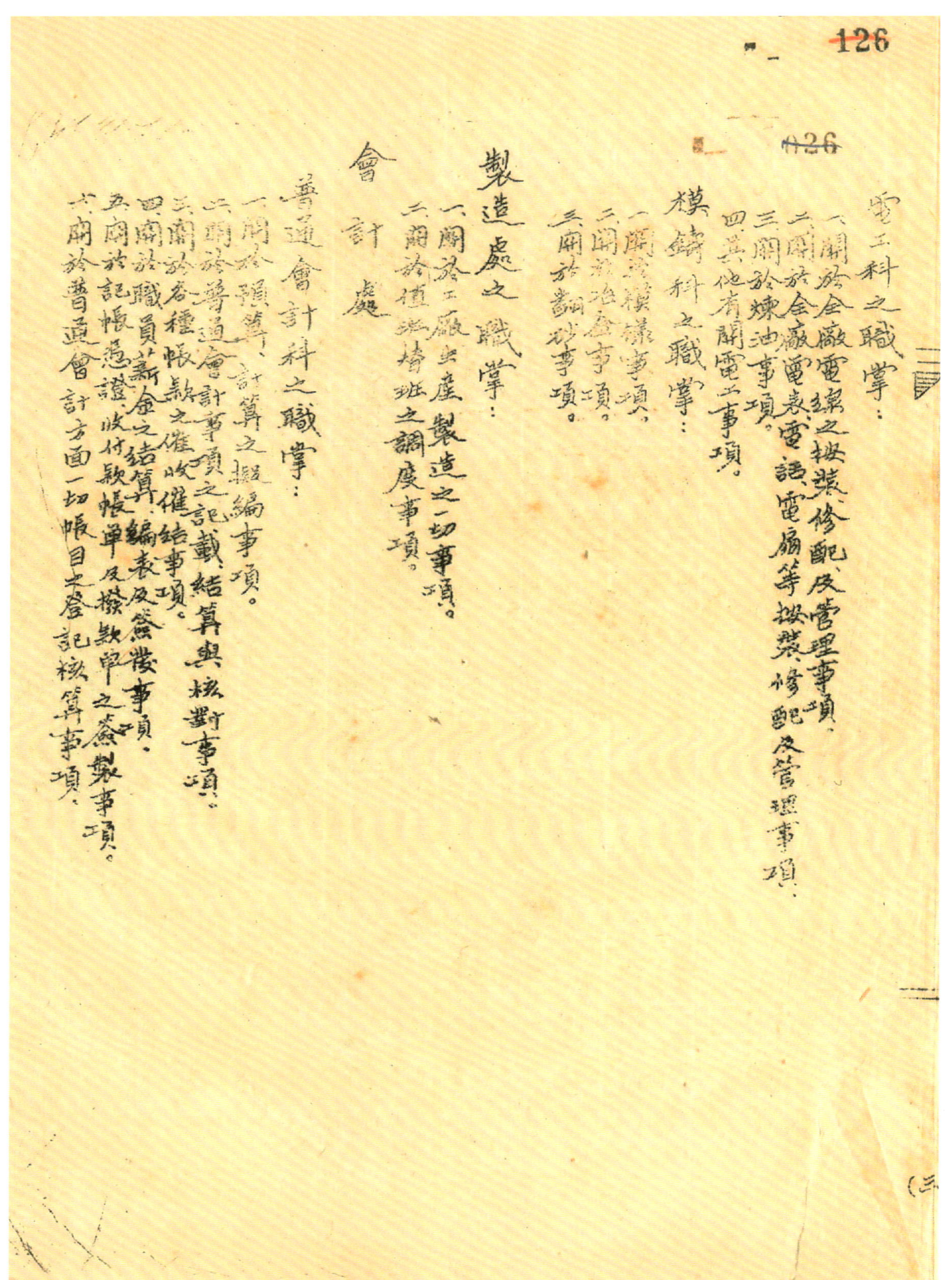

126

026

電工科之職掌：

一、關於全廠電線之按裝、修配、及管理事項。

二、關於全廠電表、電話、電扇等按裝、修配及管理事項。

三、關於煉油事項。

四、其他有關電工事項。

模鑄科之職掌：

一、關於模樣事項。

二、關於冶金事項。

三、關於翻砂事項。

製造處之職掌：

一、關於工廠生產製造之一切事項。

二、關於值班增班之調度事項。

會計處

普通會計科之職掌：

一、關於預算、計算之擬編事項。

二、關於普通會計事項之記載、結算與核對事項。

三、關於各種帳款之催收、催結事項。

四、關於職員薪金之結算、編表及發放事項。

五、關於記帳憑證、收付款帳單及撥款單之發製事項。

六、關於普通會計方面一切帳目之登記核算事項。

28

七、關於普通會計方面一切報表之編製事項。
八、關於本廠所屬業務單位會計之設計及指導事項。
九、其他有關普通會計事項。

成本會計科之職掌：

一、關於成本明細帳之登記及查核事項。
二、關於折舊之計算事項。
三、關於物料收發明細帳之登記及決算期之會盤庫存事項。
四、關於工資及薪金之分配事項。
五、關於製造費用之登記及分配事項。
六、關於工作請求單之編號及工作指定單、開工單、完工單之登記事項。
七、關於產品成本、建築成本、鑄品成本、模型成本、熔鑄成本及各項燒煉成本之登記及結算事項。
八、關於成本報告及在製品、製成品、發運暨儲存報告之編製事項。
九、關於編製年度財產目錄事項。
十、關於各地採購帳之登記及核對事項。
十一、關於各項統計圖表之編製事項。
十二、其他有關成本會計事項。

財務科之職掌：

一、關於收付全廠各種款項事項。
二、關於現金、各種票據、存摺及支票之保管事項。
三、關於現金及銀行存款收付留存之登記事項。

（四）

125

四、關於庫存表及現金收付月日報表之編製事項。
五、關於財務調度事項。
六、關於減少財務支出或增加財務收益之建議事項。
七、其他有關財務及出納事項。

審計科之職掌：

一、關於各種收支單據、記賬憑證及簿冊之審核事項。
二、關於各項預算、計算及一切帳表之審核事項。
三、關於合同、承攬之審核與保管事項。
四、關於庫存現金及備用款、預支款之查核事項。
五、關於大宗採購比價或決標時之會同審議事項。
六、關於物料驗收之監視事項。
七、關於物料、成品、半成品等盤存時之監視及核對事項。
八、關於本廠所屬業務單位會計及業務報告之審核與抽查事項。
九、關於減少不經濟支出之建議事項。
十、其他有關審計事項。

特此通告。

永利化學工業公司鋏廠 啟

廿七年十月一日

永利化学工业公司铔厂为推进员工福利设施等成立福利委员会的通知（一九四八年十月八日）

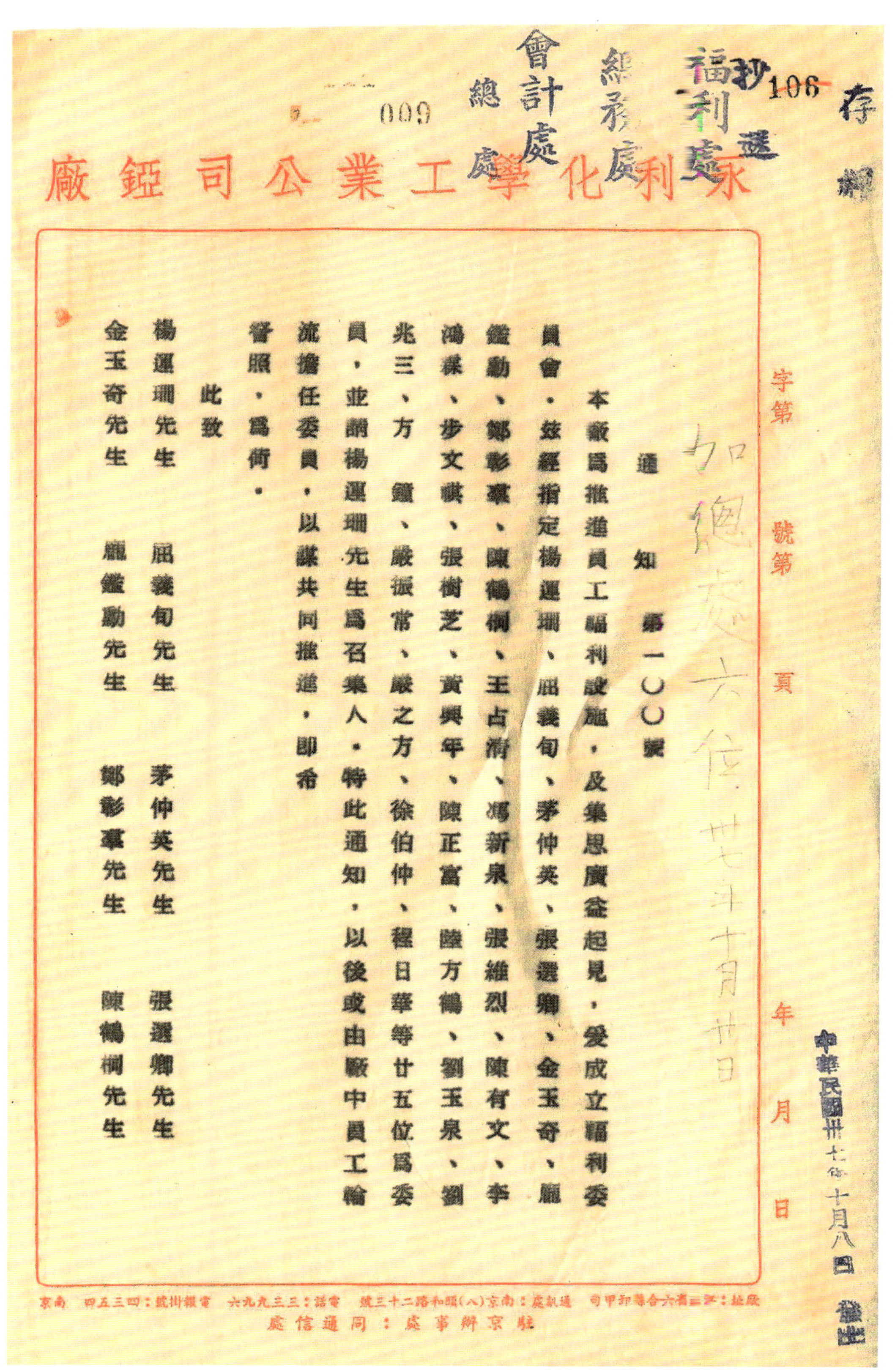

永利化學工業公司錏廠

抄送 福利處 總務處 會計處 總處

106

009

字第　號第　頁　年　月　日

通知　第一〇〇號

本廠為推進員工福利設施，及集思廣益起見，爰成立福利委員會。茲經指定楊運珊、屈義旬、茅仲英、張選卿、金玉奇、龐鑑勳、鄭彰搴、陳鶴桐、王占濤、馮新泉、張維烈、陳有文、李鴻森、步文祺、張樹芝、黃興年、陳正富、陸方鶴、劉玉泉、劉兆三、方鏞、嚴振常、嚴之方、徐伯仲、程日華等廿五位為委員，並請楊運珊先生為召集人。特此通知，以後成由廠中員工輪流擔任委員，以謀共同推進，即希督照，為荷。

此致

楊運珊先生　屈義旬先生　茅仲英先生　張選卿先生

金玉奇先生　龐鑑勳先生　鄭彰搴先生　陳鶴桐先生

中華民國卅七年十月八日

廠址：江蘇六合卸甲甸　通訊處：南京(八)昭和路三十二號　電話：三三九九六　電報掛號：四三五四　南京

駐京辦事處：同通信處

107

010

永利化學工業公司錏廠

字第　號第　頁

王占清先生
李鴻桑先生
陳正富先生
方鑑先生
程日華先生

馮新泉先生
步文祺先生
陸方禱先生
嚴振常先生

張維烈先生
張樹芝先生
劉玉泉先生
嚴之方先生

陳有文先生
黃興年先生
劉兆三先生
徐伯仲先生

李承幹啓

卅七年十月八日

年　月　日

中華民國卅七年十月八日發出

廠址：江蘇省六合縣卸甲甸　通訊處：南京（八）和平路二十三號　電話：三三九九六　電報掛號：四三五四南京

駐京辦事處：同通信處

永利化学工业公司錏厂职员、工友因故借支薪金、工资办法，员工加工暂行程序，会计处付款收款，领用物料，物料采购，验收等办法（一九四八年十一月一日）

永利錏廠職員因故借支薪金暫行辦法　卅七年十一月一日起實行

一、職員因故借支薪金，除另有規定外，概照本辦法辦理。

二、職員有下列事故之一，能提出証件或經各部門主管人之簽証者，得經廠長之核准，借支二個月以内之薪金，分四個月扣還之。

甲、本人結婚。

乙、直系親屬喪亡（父母妻子女為限）。

三、職員有下列事故之一，能提出証件或經各部門主管人之簽証者，得經廠長之核准，借支一個月以内之薪金，分二個月扣還之。

甲、本人或直系親屬疾病，本廠醫院不能治療，確需另行就醫住院或割治者。

乙、奉准給假返籍。

丙、妻分娩。

丁、本人之子女結婚。

四、上項借支扣還月份之計算，統自借支後第一次發放或預發薪金時開始計扣，並為配合半月發薪起見，應於半月預發或發薪時以半個月應扣數實扣或估扣，照規定月數扣清。

五、凡新進之職員在試用期間內者，不得享受上項借支權利。

六、職員因其他特殊事故，聲請借支，而不在本辦法規定範圍之內者，非經廠長特准，不得借予。

七、本辦法自公布日施行。

永利化学工業公司錏廠工友因故借支工資暫行辦法

卅七年十一月一日起實行

一、本廠工友因故借支工資暫依本辦法規定辦理。

二、工友如有左列情事之一，比照工廠法第四十七條之規定，得借支工資一個月之約數准予平均分二個月扣還之：

1.本人結婚；

2.父母妻喪葬；

3.為承重孫之祖父母喪葬（以本人屬承重孫者為限）；

4.本人因病不能工作，特准回籍休養。

工友因本人結婚或遭父母妻喪葬，請借工資，必須依進廠登記履歷表之記載為根據，經工作地主管人之簽章，工務處工政、工資兩科之查核登記，並應儘可能提供証件。

工友之遭祖父母之喪而為承重孫者，除照上項規定办理外，並須提供鄉保甲長之証明文件。

工友在本廠服務二年以上，以本人久病不愈，經本廠醫師之証明，確非回籍休養不可者，方得借支。

關於上項借支之扣還，為配合工資之半月發放起見，應於借支後第一次預發或算發工資時起平均分四次（即每半個月扣四分之一）扣清之。

凡居住本廠宿舍工友之父母亡故，倘因該工友之工資較低，所有借支一個月工資離屬不敷成殮者，得經廠長之特准，以加借一個月為限度，仍比照上項規定，分二個月扣還之。

三、工友如有左列情事之一，准在其工資之十五天約數範圍内酌量借支，在當月本人工資項下扣還之。

1. 祖父母喪葬（非屬承重孫者）；
2. 未成年之子女喪葬；
3. 本人父母俱亡其未成年嫡系弟妹喪葬；
4. 妻生產；
5. 本人返籍省親或接眷來廠；
6. 本人訂婚；
7. 子女婚嫁；
8. 本人父母双亡賴其生活之嫡系弟妹婚嫁；
9. 本人或其直系親屬（父母子女妻）因病經本廠医師証明確需去京治療。

工友因上項情事借支工資，除依照前登記履歷表之記載為根據，經工作地主管人之簽章，及工務、工政、工資兩科之核登記外，並應提供証件，俾資徵信。

關於上項借支之扣還，倘在預發當月半個月工資前借支者，應平均分上下半月分別扣還之，其在預發當月份半個月工資後借支，而因其當月份事病假或伙食費過

0080

爰，不敷扣還時，其不敷之數，应於次月份上半月預發工資內儘先扣還之。

四、凡工友在廠服務二年以上，其子女在中等以上学校肄業者，得憑學校之証明文件及繳費單據，於每学期開始時，向本廠貸借一学期之学宿膳費，該款自當月份起，分六個月扣清之。

五、凡工友因公受傷，必須去京治療者，应有本廠医師之証明及指定医院治療，方得酌量借支医藥費，並以該指定医院之医藥費單據实报实銷，倘無指定医院之單據者，是項借支款应由本人負担，在其下月份工資內扣還之。

六、凡工友有捏造事实，矇蔽主管人，借支工資情事，一經查明屬实，即予開除處分。

七、本办法臨時工不適用。

八、本办法自公布日施行。

永利錏廠員工「加工」暫行程序

卅七年十一月一日起實行

一、本廠各部門工作以不加工為原則。但因工作緊急須於限期內完成者，得臨時加工（包括逾時加工及例假加工）。所有加工之核准及通知計給加資手續，暫照本程序辦理之。

二、凡某項工作有加工必要時，須由該工作主管人核實認可，於加工前填寫「加工核准單」（附格式於後，請向文書科或工政科領用）；屬於職員加工者，加工核准單應送由主管處長或室主任核轉廠長定奪；屬於工人加工者，送陳主管處長或室主任核定，並轉知工政科。

上項加工核准單經核定後，仍送回原請求加工處。

三、加工如因時間關係，不及事前填寫加工核准單時，應先以口頭或電話徵得主管處長或室主任之同意（職員加工應由處長轉報廠長），隨後補具上項規定之手續。

四、加工後，應由工作主管人於加工之翌日，就實際加工時數填寫「加工證」，送主管處長或室主任核簽；簽章後，連同加工核准單，職員加工轉送會計處，工人加工轉送工資科。

五、會計處或工資科收到「加工核准單」及「加工證」後，應予核對無誤登記，核算加工薪資，依照規定之辦法發給。

會計處或工資科核算加工薪資時，應以「加工核准單」及「加工證」為憑，二者缺一，概不計給。

六、本程序公布日施行，如有未盡事項，由廠長修正之。

永利錏廠

員工加工核准單

簽單日期：民國　　年　　月　　日

處別		工作部門	
工作名稱		加工人數	
加工理由			
估計加工日數	自　月　日起 至　月　日止	估計每人每日加工	……小時
工作主管人……		處長（或室主任）……	
廠長			

附註：職員加工送廠長核定，工人加工送處長核定。

此聯存根

永利錏廠

員工加工核准單

簽單日期：民國　　年　　月　　日

處別		工作部分	
工作名稱		加工人數	
加工理由			
估計加工日數	自　月　日起 至　月　日止	估計每人每日加工	……小時
工作主管人……		處長（或室主任）……	
廠長			

此聯經核准加工後，連同加工證，職員加工送會計處，工人加工送工務處。

附註：職員加工送廠長核定，工人加工送處長核定。

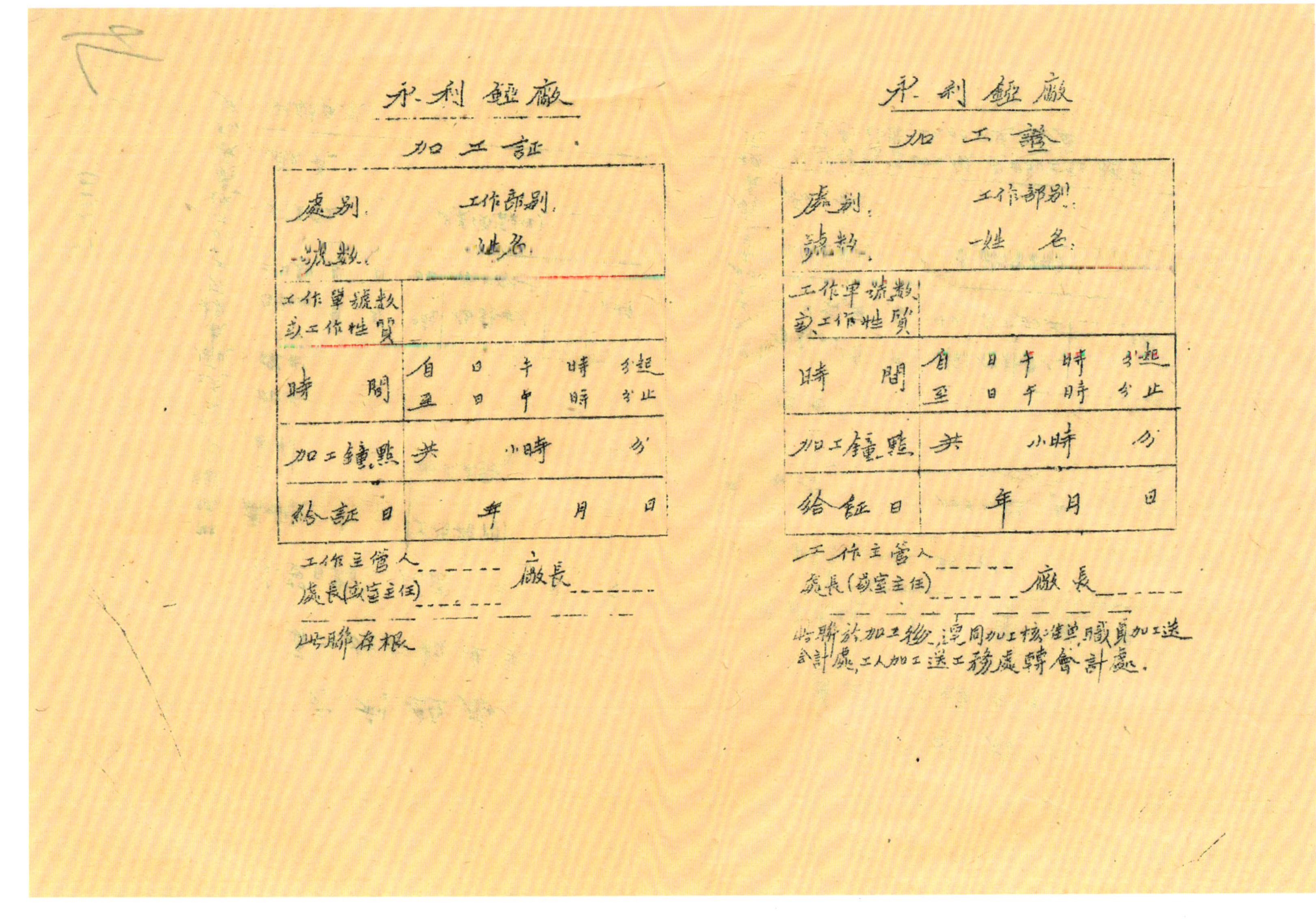

永利錏廠

加工証

處別 工作部別	
號數 姓名	
工作單號數或工作性質	
時間	自 日 午 時 分起 至 日 午 時 分止
加工鐘點	共 小時 分
給証日	年 月 日

工作主管人______ 廠長______

處長（或室主任）______

此聯存根

永利錏廠

加工證

處別 工作部別	
號數 姓名	
工作單號數或工作性質	
時間	自 日 午 時 分起 至 日 午 時 分止
加工鐘點	共 小時 分
給証日	年 月 日

工作主管人______

處長（或室主任）______ 廠長______

此聯於加工後，連同加工核准單，職員加工送會計處，工人加工送工務處轉會計處。

0083

永利铔厂会计处付款及收款暂行程序　卅七年十一月一日起实行

一、本厂会计处付收款项，概依本程序之规定办理。

二、本厂支付款项，按其性质概分为下列十项：

甲、物料采购款。

乙、包工及零星工款（包括营缮、装卸、包装、敲筛及厂内运输等）。

丙、员工薪资（包括员工薪金、工资、米代金、加班费及工友房佽津贴等）。

丁、出差费。

戊、有关员工膳宿各费。

己、各项额定税捐及依规定应付款（包括所得税、印花税及应付电费等）。

庚、员工借款。

辛、各项临时请支或借支款。

壬、本公司其他机构划拨本厂员工款项。

癸、其他厂务零星杂支。

三、关于物料采购款之支付，除该另定「物料采购及验收暂行办法」之规定办理外，会计处于收到上项附有规定各项单据并有经管人及主管人核符盖章之支款单（即代传票）后，由审计科就所附单据作数字之覆核，必要时并应作价格之抽查，经审计科核符送请会计处长核章后，再交财务科签具支票，由会计处长盖章后，连同上项支款单暨附据并送厂长核章支付之。上项采购款，不论数额巨细，应一律以支票发付，不得迳付现金。

四、关于包工及各项零星工款之支付，应由会计处审计科先就有经管人及主管人核符蓋章，並由領款人簽章及詳細註明工作件數或工數，暨單價之支款單，作書面數字之覆核，再分別有合約承攬者，就其原訂合約承攬加以覆對，無合約承攬者，審核其工作之必要及決定辦理是項工作之根據，倘有疑問，應先簽請會計處長核轉廠長決定之。由審計科核符後之支款單，經會計處長核章，交由財務科分別數，在五十金圓以下者，彙送廠長核章後，以現金支付之。其數額在五十一金圓以上者，開具支票，由會計處長核章後，連同支款單併送廠長核章後支付之。

上項支付數額之計算，倘領款人一次應領二張以上支款單，其總數在五十一金圓以上者，應合併以支票簽付之。

五、關於員工出差費之預支暨報銷，在明定單行辦法以前，均應先由請領或報銷人核實填具支款單（報銷者並應附出差旅費報告表）由派遣部份主管處長核章後，送交會計處審計科就書面予以覆核。所有員工出差費，務求撙節，在可能範圍內應儘量提供單據，方准報支。如遇特殊情況，用費過多，須事先由主管處長向廠長申述理由，核定支報。

經審計科核訖後之支款單，應連同附件，送由會計處長核章，呈請廠長最後核章後，方得由會計處財務科支付或普通會計科轉帳。所有出差費在壹百金圓以內者，概由財務科以現金支付，其在壹百另一金圓以上者，除有特殊必要者外，概以支票簽付之。

六、關於員工因故借支薪資，除照另定之暫行辦法辦理外，所有應填具職工借資書，應照規定，提附證明文件。職員部份先由工作地主管人核實蓋章。工友部份，先由工務處工政、工資二科負責核簽後，送呈廠長最後核定，再行發交會計處審核科核算登記，送會計處長蓋章後，由會計處財務科支付之。倘審計科對所填借支薪資數額有扣還月份有疑問時，得簽附意見呈廠長復核核定之。上項員工借支薪資，概依現金支付為原則，倘數額在一百金圓以上，財務科雖無充分現金足資支付時，得以支票發付之。

七、關於各項臨時發生之請支或借支款，均應由主管部門先行檢同證件或申敘詳由簽請廠長核准後，再行填開支款單，送由會計處審計科核轉會計處長核章。其應開支票者，由會計處財務科開具支票并送廠長核章支付，其應以現金支付者，由會計處送呈廠長補章後，再由財務科以現金支付之。

八、關於員工薪資、又各項額定稅捐及按規定應付款，又本公司其他機構劃撥本廠員工款項，均應由會計處普通會計科檢同應有收據或憑證，代簽支款單後，由審計科核送會計處長核章，再交財務科簽具支票，併送廠長核章後支付之。其應以現金支付者，仍應先呈廠長核章後，再行支付。

九、關於員工膳宿各費及一切廠務零星雜支，均應由主管部門簽具支款單，由經管人主管人簽章，並附具原始憑證單據，送由會計處審計科核送會計處長核章，轉呈廠長簽章後，再由會計處財務科支付之。其數額在一百金元以上者，非特殊必要，均以簽發支票為原則。又關於一切食品及器具之報損，統應由主管部門專案簽請廠長核，派人員復查及監視處置後，方得報支。非經上項手續，會計處審計科應拒絕審核。

十、一切款項非經廠長核章，會計處不得支付，其有照章應付並具特殊時間性，適廠長不在時，可先行支付，仍應於儘可能之短時間內，送請廠長補章。

（二）

一、會計處一切收款，均應由財務科掣給收據，其屬對內沖帳者，得以經會計處長蓋章者有效，其屬對外者，應以經廠長蓋章，方屬生效。

上項收據，均係正副兩聯，正聯交繳款人存執，副聯為收帳憑證。

二、會計處財務科之收付款項時間，[illegible]每日下午出納時間，概以下班前一小時為限止，逾時不再收付，以便核結當日庫存表。倘有特殊急要之收付，事實上不容稽延者，得經會計處長之核定，權准收付，次日出帳。

三、會計處財務科應以每日庫存表，經審計科複核，並會計處長核章後，附同當日收付款項憑單，限次日上午十時以前，送呈廠長批閱。

四、本程序未規定事項，除照以往成例辦理外，必要時並得由會計處簽呈廠長核定補充之。

五、本程序自民國三十七年十一月一日起施行。

永利錏廠領用物料暫行程序

卅七年十一月一日起實行

一、領用物料，應慎重估計用途，切戒浪費，並不得私人領用或借用。

二、領料時由工作負責人填寫「領料單」，送交主管處長或室主任或值班技師或處長室主任指定之人員審核簽章後，持向物料科請領。

三、填寫領料單時，除註明請領物料之名稱、數量外，若有尺寸重量關係者，應詳為註明，否則物料科得退回補註後，始能照發。

四、領料單一為三聯，一聯存根，兩聯送物料科，此兩聯中之一聯存物料科備查登帳，另一聯由物料科送會計處。

五、物料科如發覺未經主管處長或室主任或值班技師或處長室主任指定之人員審核簽章之領料單，得拒絕發料。

六、領料單如有更改數量、尺寸、重量等情事，應即退回請主管處長或室主任或值班技師或指定之人員在更改之處加蓋圖章後，始能照發。

七、領用物料，如因時間關係或夜班不及由處長或室主任或值班技師或指定之人員核簽領料單時，得開具「暫借材料單」先向物料科借料。物料科於借料後之次日，應即通知借料部門之主管處長或室主任，請其補具領料單，以換回暫借材料單。

八、領用之物料用後，設有剩存時，應即填具「物料退庫單」連同剩存物料一併退還物料科。

物料退庫單為三聯，由退料部份填寫後，所有三聯連同退料一併送交物料科。物料科照單點收蓋章後，隨即撕下第二聯存查記賬，其餘兩聯仍送還退料部份，其第一聯存根作為收據之用，第三聯由退料部份送會計處記賬。

九、領料單及物料退庫單，廠長得隨時查閱之。

十、本程序自公布日施行，並得由廠長隨時增訂。

83 0086

永利化學工業公司錏廠 （第二聯）

暫借材料單

借料日期＿＿年＿＿月＿＿日　　工作部別＿＿＿＿

品名　　　　　　　　　　　號數＿＿字第＿＿號

暫借數量	領銷數量		結餘
	日期	領單數量	

借料人＿＿＿＿　　主管人＿＿＿＿

此聯存根

（第一聯）

永利化學工業公司錏廠

物料退庫單

總號（此號由承會料編填）

退料部份＿＿＿＿　　＿＿年＿＿月＿＿日　　分號（此號由退料部份編填）

借方：	過帳符號	貸方：	過帳符號

品名：

數量：　　　單價　　　總價

原領用途（或）工作單號

附註：

物料料主管人＿＿＿＿　　點收人＿＿＿＿　　工作部份負責人＿＿＿＿

本單為三聯，由退料部份填寫後與退料一併送物料科，物料科照單點收簽字，掌下第二聯存查記帳，其餘兩聯送還退料部份，第一聯存根作為收據，第三聯由退料部份送會計處登帳。

此聯退料部份存查，並為收據。

84

（第二聯）　永利化學工業公司錏廠　總號（此号由成念料編填）

物料退庫單

退料部份＿＿＿＿　＿年＿月＿日　分號（此号由退料部份編填）

借方：　過帳符号　貸方　過帳部份

品名：

數量　單價　總價

原領用途（或）工作單號

附註

物料料主管人＿＿＿＿　點收人＿＿＿＿　工作部份負責人＿＿＿＿

本單為三聯，由退料部份填寫後與退料一併送物料科，物料科點單點收簽字，撕下第二聯存查記帳，其餘兩聯送還退料部份，其第一聯存根作為收據，第三聯由退料部份送會計處登帳。

此聯物料科存查記帳。

（第三聯）　永利化學工業公司錏廠　總號（此号由成念料編填）

物料退庫單

退料部份＿＿＿＿　＿年＿月＿日　分號（此号由退料部份編填）

借方：　過帳符号　貸方：　過帳符号

品名：

數量：　單價　總價

原領用途（或）工作單號

附註

物料部主管人＿＿＿＿　點收人＿＿＿＿　工作部份負責人＿＿＿＿

本單為三聯，由退料部份填寫後與退料一併送物料科，物料科照單點收簽字，撕下第二聯存查記帳，其餘兩聯送還退料部份，第一聯存根作為收據，第三聯由退料部份送會計處登帳。

此聯由退料部份送會計處記帳。

85 0087

永利錏廠領料單

民國　年　月　日　字第　號

（第一聯）

品名

數量

單價

總價

工作指定單號數

（或）用途說明

領用人　負責人

注意：1. 請將向庫房領出物料之品名及數量與本單所載對照是否相同。
2. 工作指定單號數或用途說明務一一請正確註明。
3. 領用之料有尺寸或重量者請詳為註明。

此聯存根

永利錏廠領料單

民國　年　月　日　字第　號

（第二聯）

品名

數量

單價

總價

工作指定單號數

（或）用途說明

領用人　負責人

材料票#　附註

此聯交物料科

（注意）請將所發物料之品名及數量與本單所載對照是否相同

86

永利錏廠領料單

（第三聯）

民國　年　月　日　字第　號	
品名	工作指定單號数
數量	（或）用途說明
單價	
總價	
領用人	負責人
材料票＃	Cr.　運P.

此聯交物料科轉送會計處

（本單暫作兩用，一為原來借料之用，二為不及核發領料單時借料之用）

永利化學工業公司錏廠

（聯一第）

暫借材料單

借料日期　年　月　日　　工作部別

品名　　號數　字第　號

暫借數量	領銷數量			結餘
	日期	領單數量		

借料人　　主管人

此聯送物料科：1. 借料全部銷清後，再向物料科索回註銷。2. 於借料之次日，向借料部份換取領料單。

永利化學工業公司錏廠
物料採購及驗收暫行辦法

卅七年十一月一日起實行

一、本廠購買物料概依本辦法之規定辦理。

前項所稱物料係指各項材料、原料、燃料、電料、化學藥品、醫藥、及一切設備品暨辦公用品而言。

二、本廠購買物料分下列三種：

甲、經常採購： 係指辦公及員工膳宿消耗品之經常需要購買者。所有辦公用品部份，由各部門根據已往消耗統計，分別品名及需要部份，按月估計月份需用量，彙列總表，於每月前十日送物料科，由物料科查明現有庫存數量，統籌開具購單，由工務處長核章，送呈廠長室核定，俟廠長核章准購後，送交總務處採運科彙編月份採購預算，是項採購預算最遲須於每月前四日送達會計處，一面並準備購買。

乙、一般專購： 係指製造及一切工程暨各部專用物料之需要購買者。關於經常需要之專用物料，應由需要部份按月於月前十日列具下月份估計需要量，開同購單，註明估計某月份所需要，送交工務處物料科查註現有庫存數量，估計月底庫存數量，及擬存儲備數量，暨依上核算之擬准購數量，由工務處長核章後，限每月前八日送呈廠長室核定，俟廠長核章准購，限每月前六日送交總務處採運科彙編月份採購預算，並準備購買。關於某一新工作單所專用或臨時發生需要即購物料，除各主管部份應儘可能先行估計併列上項月份預計內外，其確屬事先不能估及者，所有請購、核簽及核准程序仍如上述規定辦理外，總務處採運科收到上項購單時，應先以估計需要款額及約計需付日期通知會計處備款候付，應由會計處於當日簽復後再行準備購買。

丙、特種採購：係指大量或特殊情形之採購，如原料、燃料之採購，及政府配給物品之購買，概由工務處物料科簽具購單，所有按月定額之採購或配給，並應比照乙項經常需要專用物料之規定按月限期辦理請購程序，其屬事先確不能估及者，所有請購、核簽及核准程序仍如前項規定辦理外，總務處採運科收到上項購單時，並應先以估計需要款額及約計需付日期，通知會計處備款候付，應由會計處於當日簽復後，再行準備購買。

三、本廠物料之採購地點分為南京、上海及美國三地購買，請購部份應依最經濟實用之原則，選定採購地點，開填該地區之購單，倘總務處採運科對請購部份之指定地區，認有疑問或困難時，得陳由總務處長洽商請購部份同意更改之。

所有總務處採運科收到購單後，按月以預算或隨時以款額日期通知會計處時，應將採購地點分別註明，不得混淆，俾便財務上之調度。

四、總務處採運科經購在京採購之物料，除係專營或獨家經售物品暨配給品外，概依下列採購方式辦理。

甲、招標：凡整批採購之總價在三千金圓以上者，一律以招標方式辦理，所有招標辦法另定之，其開標與決標辦法與下述比價方式同。

乙、比價：凡小批採購之總價在五百金圓以上未滿三千金圓者，除有特殊必要得亦以招標方式辦理外，概應由採運科先就南京市選擇五家以上之較大商舖，開具估價單，附同樣品，由總務處長召集工務處長、工務處物料科長、會計處長、會計處審計科長及請購部份負責人暨總務處採運科長會同審議後，簽呈廠長核定採購、上列人員中之因事不克出席者，應指派人員代表出席。上項審定購買之樣品應由物料科負責保管，俟作驗收時之比照，總務處採運科於上項物料付款時並應附繳前項審議紀錄，以憑稽核。

丙、選購：凡零星採購之總價不滿五百金圓者，得由總務處採運科自行負責選購，所有選購物料之價格，以不超過當日中央日報及四聯總處發行之行情表市價為原則，倘偶有超過，應隨時陳請總務處長核准後方得辦理。

所有印刷品及器具、及器皿三件以上之採購，其總價雖在五百金圓以下，亦統應依比價方式辦理，至總價在三千金圓以上者，仍照上列規定依招標方式辦理之。

五、所有物料到廠時，統應由工務處物料科負責驗收，其屬整批購買，經招標或比價方式決定者，並應邀同請購部份派員會同驗收，又會計處派員監視驗收，驗收人及監驗人均應於物料到廠記帳通知書上蓋章負責，倘遇有品質低劣，不合投標或比價時之圖樣規範或樣品者，並應拒收退還，至數量不符者，應於記帳書及發票收據上註明實收數量暨扣算短缺數後之應付價款實數，倘所購物料非屬全部到達，不能使用，或所缺部份無法單獨補購者，應俟其全數到達或補足時，再行驗收，暫由物料科負責保管。

六、一切物料非經驗收，不得付款，至決標或審定比價時，事先約定及情形特殊經總務處長會同會計處長審定確有先行付款之必要者例外，關於付款之方式，規定如下：

甲、所有以招標及比價方式採購之物料價款，統應於驗收竣事後由總務處採運科檢同經驗收蓋章後之物料到廠記賬通知書及發票收據，繕具支款單（即代傳票）送請總務處長核章後，轉送會計處核發售貨商舖頭之支票直接付與。

乙、會計處應預撥採購備用金元（白金圓），交由總務處採運科作為零星購置週轉之用，採運科應於每次經購零星物料到廠驗收後，隨時以記帳通知書及發票收據繕附支款單送由總務處長核章後，轉交會計處發付價款，補足其備用金，所有上項備用金，採運科應除酌提一部份現金備用外，餘存指定銀行，其支付貨款，亦以儘可能發付支票為原則，每月應以銀行之對帳單送交會計處核對，利息由廠收賬。

丙、所有因事先約定及特殊情形之預付貨款，統憑售貨人之收據由總務處採運科發付支款單送由總務處長核章後轉送會計處核發售貨人抬頭之支票，直接付與，不得由採運科具領轉付。

七、總務處採運科應經常備具下列有關採購之資料及帳表：

甲、南京各業大商行鋪分類調查簿

（應分欄註明其營業範圍、商譽情形、地址及門牌號數、電話號碼，負責人姓名。）

乙、各物行情市價表

（辦理決標或比價時，上項市價表應由該科提供參考，並應逐月裝訂成冊，妥為保管，俾便查核。）

丙、購物總簿

（凡該科經購一切物料均應登載，並自收到請購單起按採購之程序、付款之分析，隨時逐欄登記，俾便查考與自行提示。）

丁、備用金登記簿

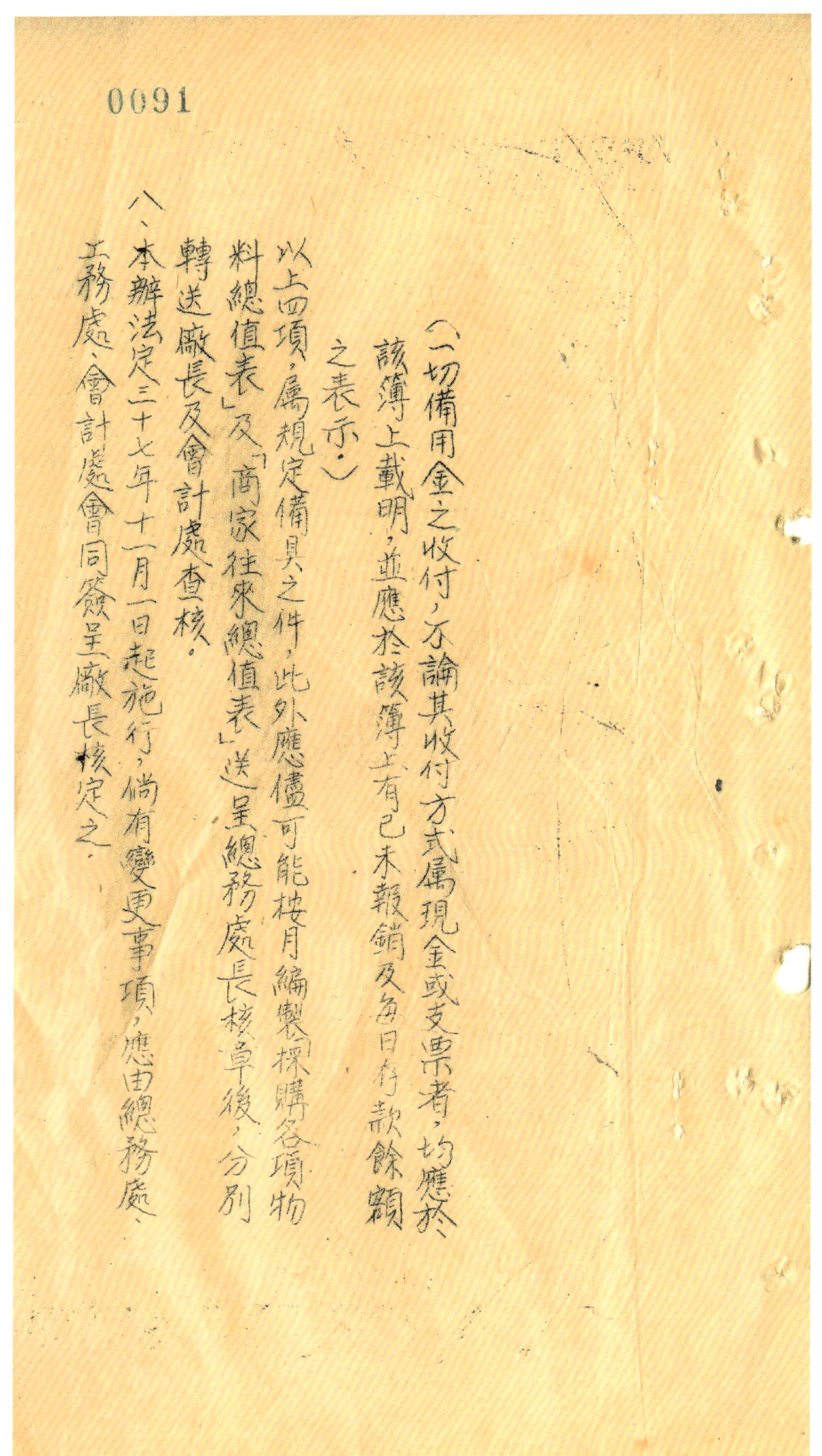

（一切備用金之收付，不論其收付方式屬現金或支票者，均應於該簿上載明，並應於該簿上有已未報銷及每日存款餘額之表示。）

以上四項，屬規定備具之件，此外應儘可能按月編製「採購各項物料總值表」及「商家往來總值表」送呈總務處長核章後，分別轉送廠長及會計處查核。

八、本辦法定三十七年十一月一日起施行，倘有變更事項，應由總務處、工務處、會計處會同簽呈廠長核定之。

永利化學工業公司錏廠職工出差差費支給暫行辦法

1. 本廠職工因公出差，支報差費，依本辦法辦理之。

2. 出差分長程、短程兩種：在南京市區（包括浦口）範圍以内者為短程，以外者為長程。

3. 職工出差必須經主管派遣，並填寫公差証（長程、短程一律使用），經各級主管蓋章，差畢後支報差費時隨同出差旅費報告表送會計處備查。

4. 本廠職工短程差（公差）費規定如下：

一、乘商輪者，始得支報船費。

二、車費、郵電及雜費，實支實報（在南京市區以乘公共汽車為原則）。

三、每日伙食費，早餐費半個折實單位，中晚餐各壹個折實單位，京處無宿不供食。

四、在南京市區出差，如須留宿，以住辦事處宿舍為原則，如必需住宿旅館者，得支報宿費，以旅館賬單為憑。

5. 本廠職工長程公差差費規定如下：

一、乘火車以二等或三等，輪船以房艙或統艙為原則。

二、每日支給伙食費四個折實單位，宿費四個折實單位，雜費一個折實單位，住公司宿舍者不得支報宿費。

三、車費、郵電及雜費實支實報。

6. 因公出差，得預先向廠借支差費，由各工作部門主管核定蓋章後，送請廠長核准蓋章，始得向會計處支款。

7. 差畢返廠在三日以内，必需將差費填具出差旅費報告表，連同單據及公差証，向會計處報銷。折實單位按出差日期照銀行折實牌價逐日計算。

8. 公差証向文書科領取。

9. 本辦法自公布之日起施行。

四年十月十六日發出

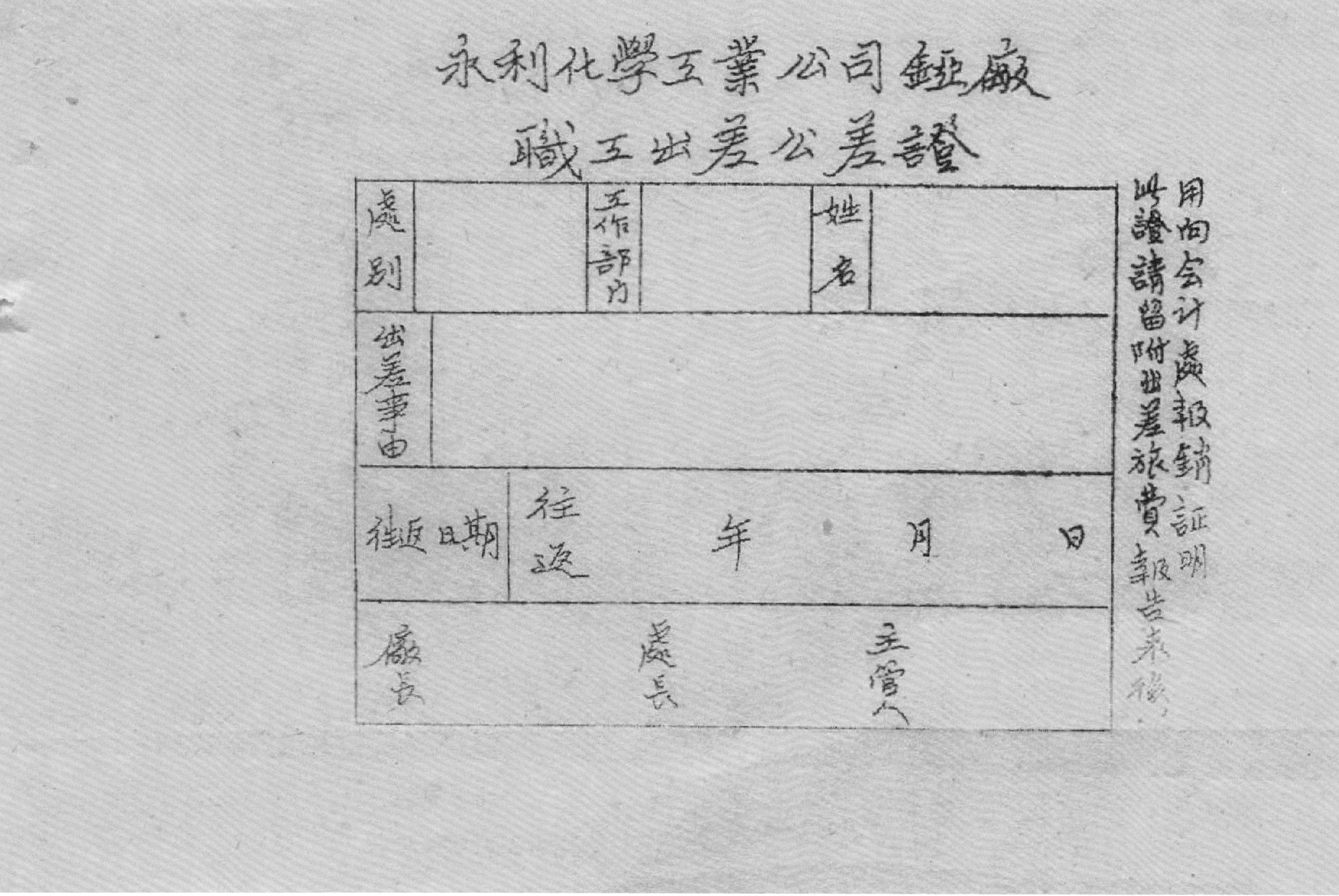

永利化學工業公司錏廠
職工出差公差證

處別		工作部门		姓名	
出差事由					
往返日期	往返 年 月 日				
廠長		處長		主管人	

此證請留附出差旅費報告表後
用向会计處報銷証明

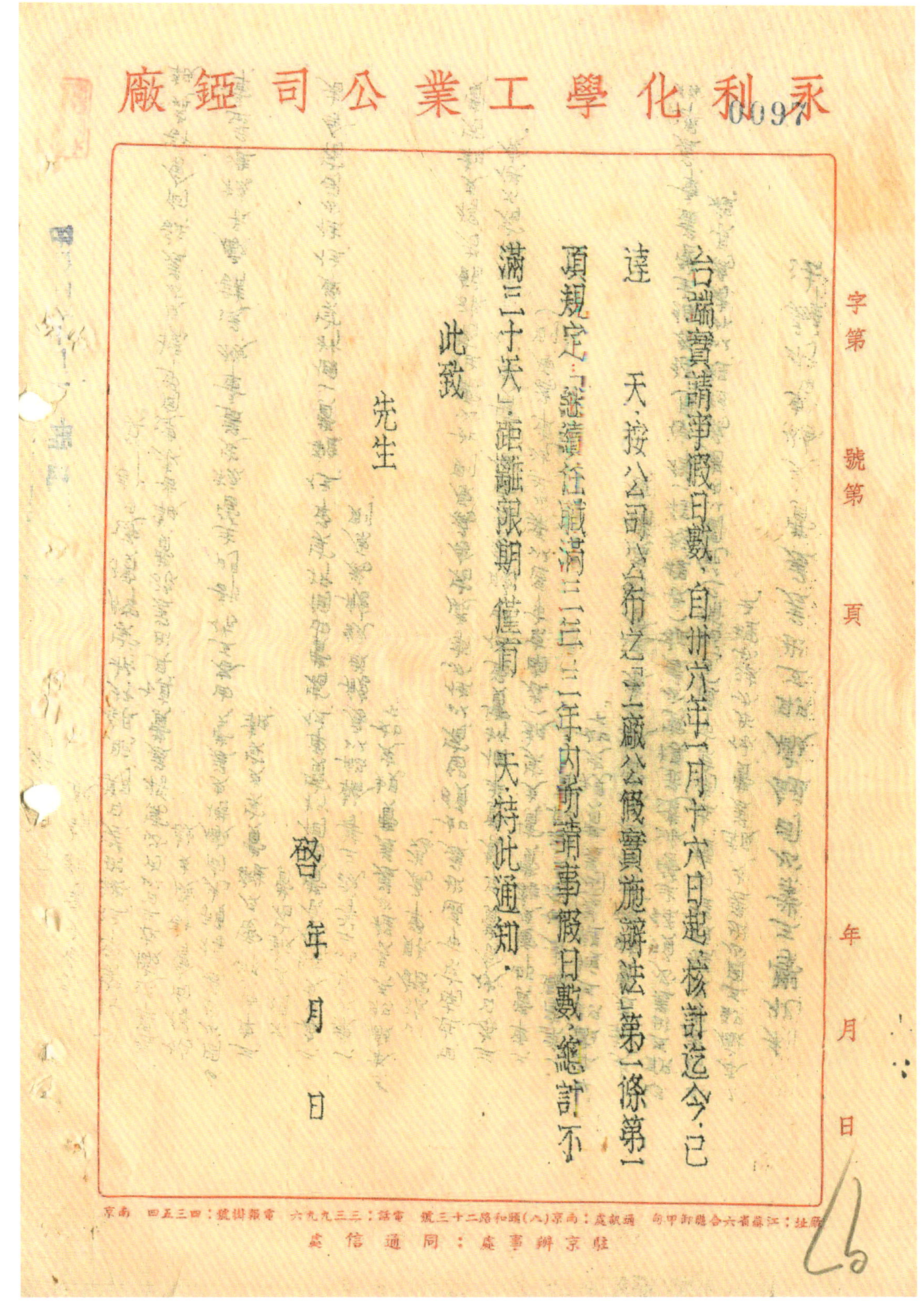

永利化學工業公司錏廠

0097

字第　號第　頁　年　月　日

台端實請事假日數，自卅六年一月十六日起，核計迄今，已達　天，按公司公布之「工廠公假實施辦法」第一條第一項規定：「繼續任職滿三「三」三年內所請事假日數，總計不滿三十天」，距離限期，僅有　天，特此通知。

此致

先生

啓　年　月　日

廠址：江蘇省六合縣卸甲甸　電報處：南京（八）高　電話：三三九九六　電報掛號：四三五四　南京

駐京辦事處：同通信處

有限责任永利铔厂消费合作社章程（一九四八年十一月一日）

有限責任永利錏廠消費合作社

第一章 總則

第一條 本社定名爲「有限責任永利錏廠消費合作社」

第二條 本社以辦社員日用物品供社員之需要並供給社員低利資金及收受社員之存款與儲金並謀全體社員生活上之改善在可能範圍內兼營生產實行自製自消

第三條 本社爲有限責任組織各社員對本社債務以其所認股額爲限

第四條 本社暫以永利錏廠爲營業範圍

第五條 本社社址設於本廠內

第六條 本社應公告之事項在本社揭示處公佈之

第二章 社員

第七條 本社社員之資格如左

1凡在永利錏廠工作之職員工友均須一律參加

2凡本社業務範圍内之職員及工友年滿二十歲而不吸食鴉片或其他代用品並未受破產及褫奪公權之宣告者爲合格

第八條 本社社員有左列情事之一者喪失其社員資格

1死亡

2辭退或被辭退

3有破壞本社名譽行爲者

第九條 本社社員中途退社經理事會核准時本社即將其股金退還但不另給官息及紅利

第十條　本社社員有左列情事之一者得經社務會出席理監事四分之三以上之決議予以除名並報告社員大會以書面通知被除名之人

1不遵照本社章則及社員大會決議履行其義務者

2有妨害本社社務業務之行爲者

3有犯罪或不名譽行爲者

第三章　社股

第十一條　本社社股每股國幣貳元每人至少須認購壹股但至多不得超過拾股

第十二條　社員認購社股均須一次繳清

第十三條　社員不得以其已繳之社股金額抵銷其對於其他社員之債務

第十四條　社員股金利息定爲年利六釐

第十五條　股金轉讓以本公司職工爲限並須事前聲請理事會登記過戶

第四章　職員

第十六條　本社設理事五人組織理事會執行本社社務設監事三人組織監事會監査本社社務理事及監事均由社員大會就社員中選任之

第十七條　前項理事之任期爲二年監事之任期爲一年均得連選連任

理事會設主席一人由理事互推任期一年連舉得連任

第十八條　理事主席總理社務代表本社理事會之辦事細則另定之

第十九條　監事會設主席一人由監事會互選之

第二十條　監事會監査本社財產狀况及業務執行狀況當合作社與其理事訂立契約或爲訴訟上之行爲時代表合作社監事爲執行前項職務認爲必要時並得召集臨時社員大會

監事會之監査細則由監事會另定之

第廿一條　監事不得兼任理事會任理事之社員於其責任未能解除前不得當選爲監事

第廿二條　本社理事監事皆係義務職

第廿三條　理事監事因辭職或其他事由缺額時得召集臨時社員大會行補缺選舉補缺選舉所產生之理事監事以前任之任期爲任期

第廿四條　本社出席聯合社之代表由理事會提出於社員大會推舉之其任期爲二年

第廿五條　本社業務之執行由理事會聘請經理一人主持之在必要時得加設副經理一人其餘各職員由經理薦舉理事會僱用

第五章　會議

第廿六條　本社社員大會分通常大會及臨時大會兩種

通常大會於每一業務年度終了後一個月內召集之臨時大會因下列情形召集之

1 理事會認爲必要時

2 監事於執行職務上認爲必要時

3 社員全體四分之一以上以書面記明提議事項及其理由請求理事會召集時

前款請求提出後十日內理事會不爲召集之通知時社員得自動召集

第廿七條　社員大會之召集應於七日前以書面載明召集事由及提議事項通知社員臨時社員大會以臨時通知召集之

第廿八條　社員大會應有全體社員過半數之出席始得開會出席社員過半數之同意始得決議但解除理事監事職權之決議須有全體社員過半數之同意始得決議解散本社或與他社合併之決議應有全體社員四分三以上之出席出席社員三分之二以上之同意

第廿九條　社員大會開會以理事會主席爲主席理事主席缺席時以監事主席爲主席社員召集大會臨時公推一人爲主席

第三十條　社員大會開會時每一社員僅有一表決權社員不能出席社員大會時得以書面委託其他社員代理但同一代理人不得代表二個以上之社員

第卅一條　社員大會開會時須作成決議錄載明開會日期社員總數出席社員數及會議始末由主席記錄及二個以上之出席社員署名蓋章交由理事會保存

第卅二條　社員大會流會二次以上時理事會得以書面載明應議事項請求全體社員於一定期限內通函表決但此期限不得少於十日

第卅三條　本社每年一月四月七月十月各召集社務會一次

第卅四條　社務會由理事會召集之其主席由理事監事互選之

社務會應有全體理事監事三分二以上之出席始得開會出席理事監事過半數之同意始得決議

社務會開會時經理及營業員得列席陳述意見

第卅五條　理事會及監事會由各該會主席召集之

理事會監事會應各有理事監事過半數之出席始得開會出席理事監事過半數之同意始得決議

第六章　業務

第卅六條　本社營業分消費生產信用運銷四部其營業規則另訂之

第卅七條　本社購進物品轉賣於社員皆以日常家用必須品爲主

第卅八條　本社得購進原料品自行加工或製造之

第卅九條　本社售貨價格以附近一般市價爲準由理事會定之

第四十條　本社售貨以現金交易爲主如遇有困難情形者可通融記帳但不得超過其

本人應有薪額四分之一於月底發薪時由會計處按數扣還

第四一條　凡社員向社訂購貨物須預交代價之一部或全部

第四二條　本社得因需要之可能陸續籌設合作食堂合作加啡店合作電影場合作茶園合作旅社合作洗染店合作農場等其辦法分別另訂之

第四三條　本社信用部放款以社員爲限存款不限於社員

第四四條　本社存款利率以月利計由理事會決定之但至多存款不得超過一分放款不得超過一分六釐

第四五條　收付款項之票據須經理事會主席及經理連署方生效力

第四六條　關於存款放款代收代付款項辦法另訂之

第四七條　本社得因事實之需要陸續增辦相互保險及滙兑等業務其辦法另訂之

第七章　結算

第四八條　本社以國曆一月一日至十二月三十一日爲一業務年度理事會應於每年度終了後一個月内社員大會開會之七日前造成財產目錄資人閱覽並另繕一份交由監事會審查後報告社員大會

第四九條　本社年總結算後有盈餘時除彌補累積損失職員薪水雜費及付股息等外其餘額平均分爲一百分按照下項規定辦理

1以百分之二十爲公積金

2以百分之二十爲職員酬勞金

3以百分之六十作社員分配金按各社員之購買額比例分配之

第五十條　本社結算後有虧損時以公積金股金順次抵補之

第八章 解散

第五一條 本社解散時清算人由社員大會就社員中選充之

前項清算人應依照合作社法規定清理本社債權及債務

第五二條 本社清算後有賸餘額時由清算人擬定分配案提交社員大會處理之

第九章 附則

第五三條 本章程經社員大會通過呈准主管機關登記後施行

赵同誉就厂务事项致镇方兄的函件（一九四九年六月二十九日）

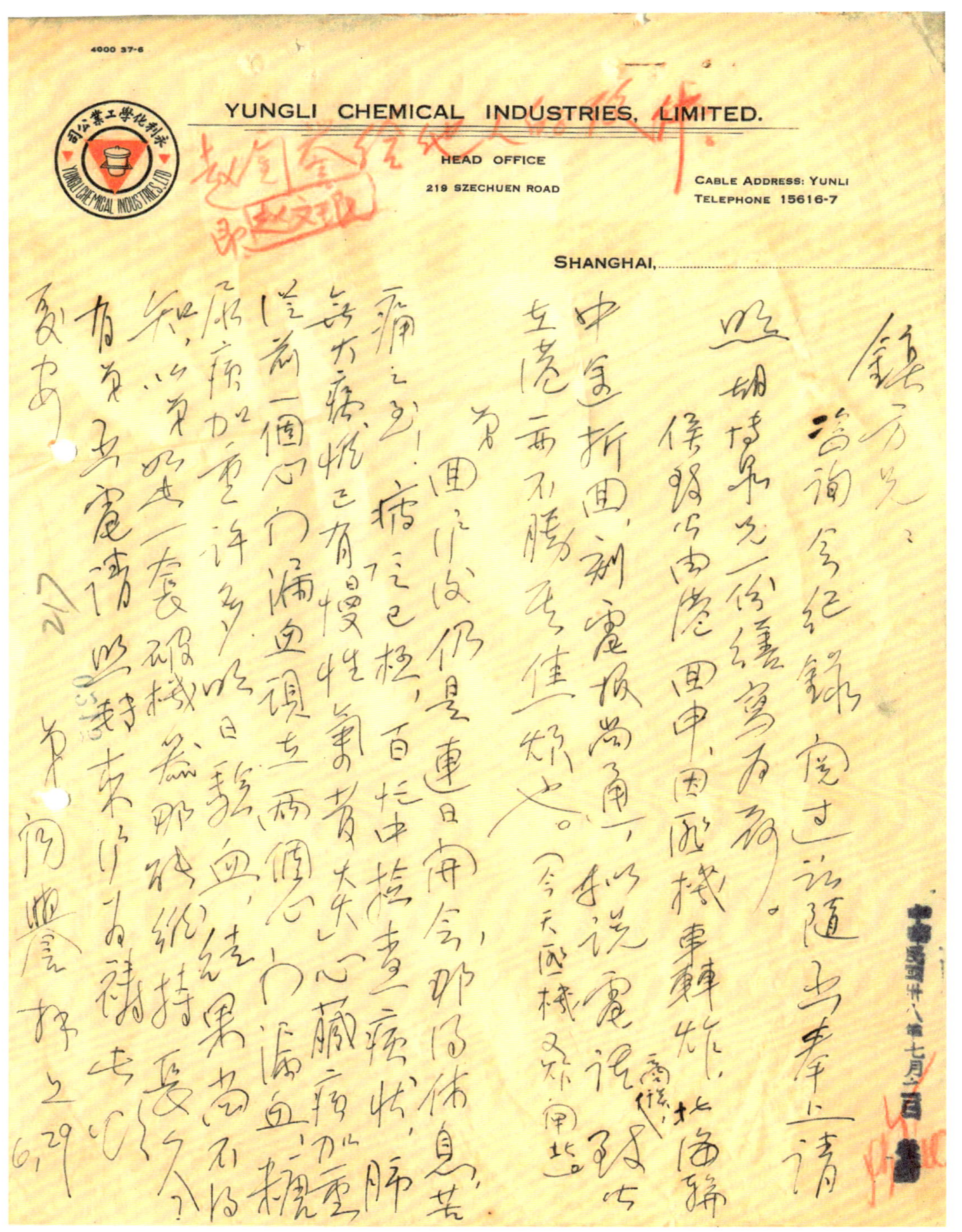

4000 37-6

永利化学工业公司

YUNGLI CHEMICAL INDUSTRIES, LTD.

YUNGLI CHEMICAL INDUSTRIES, LIMITED.

HEAD OFFICE

219 SZECHUEN ROAD

CABLE ADDRESS: YUNLI

TELEPHONE 15616-7

SHANGHAI,

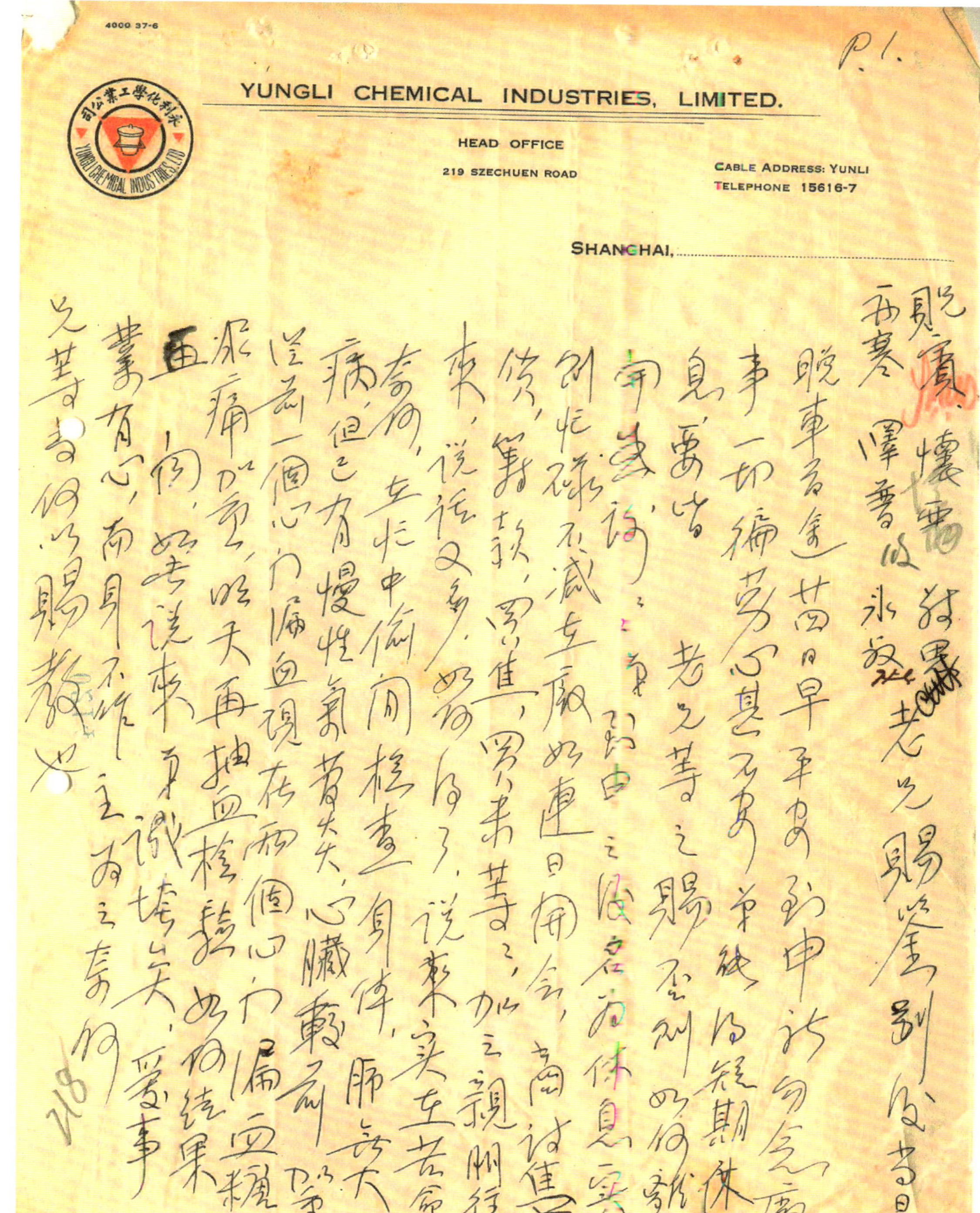
4000 37-6

P. 1.

永利化學工業公司 YUNGLI CHEMICAL INDUSTRIES, LTD.

YUNGLI CHEMICAL INDUSTRIES, LIMITED.

HEAD OFFICE
219 SZECHUEN ROAD

CABLE ADDRESS: YUNLI
TELEPHONE 15616-7

SHANGHAI, ...

覺寅、懷霖、致果 老兄賜鑒：別後當日
雨寒、澤普、以永、敬

晚車首途，廿四日早平安到申，於公於廠
事一切偏勞，心甚不安，弟總欲早期休
息，要皆 老兄等之賜，不然則如何能
南來詢之：弟擬由之陳君為休息安
則忙碌不減在廠，如連日開會，商討售
貨，籌款，買煤，買米等等，加之親朋往
來，說話又多，如何得了，說來實在苦命
奈何。在忙中偷閒檢查身體，肺無大
病，但已有慢性氣管炎，心臟較前略重
從前一個心門漏血，現在兩個心門漏血，糟
深痛加劇，昨天再抽血檢驗，如何結果
再詢，好在說來本識培矣。愛事
業有心，而身不能主，奈之奈何。
兄等有何賜教。

208

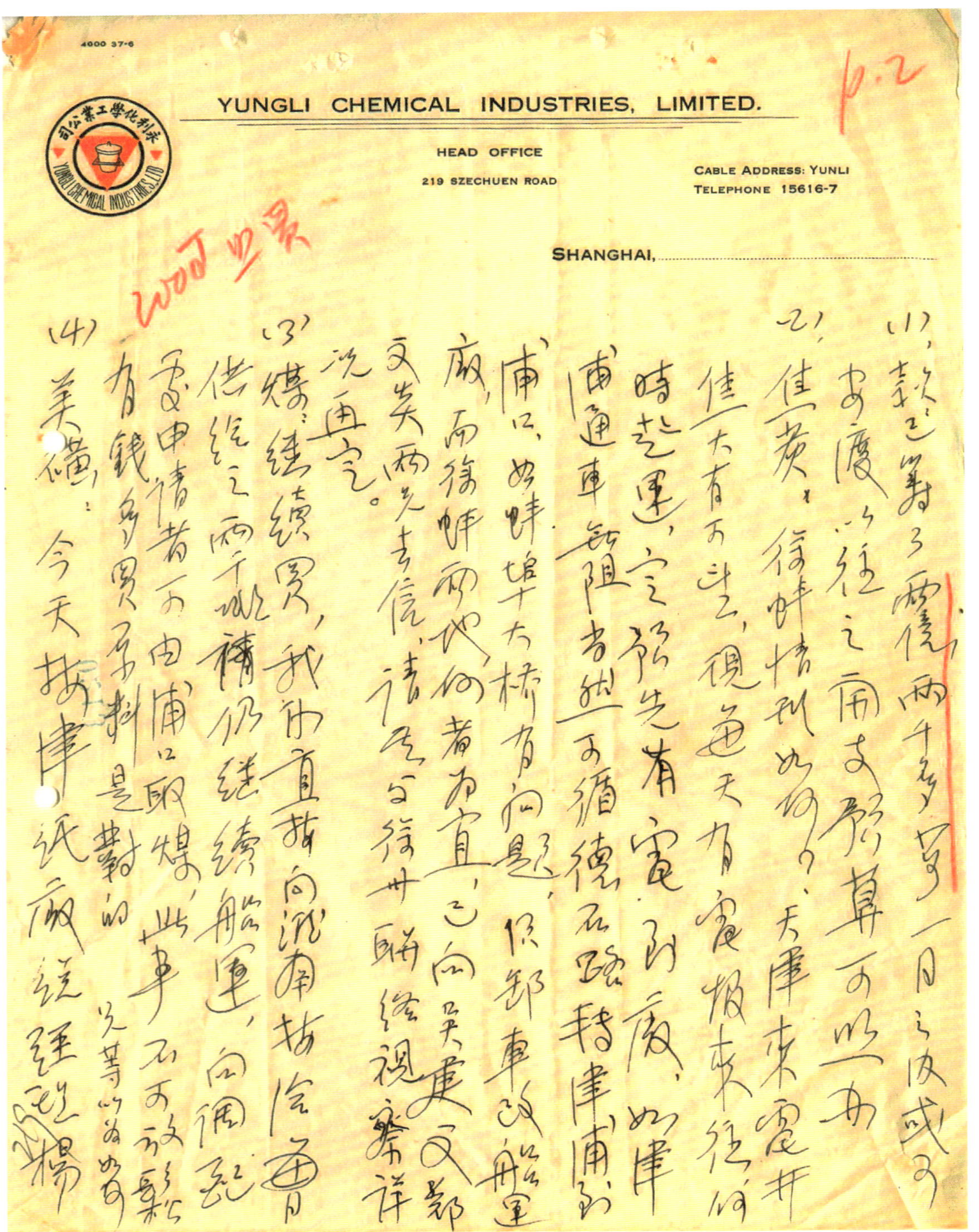

(1)款已筹了两亿两千多万，一月之次或可安度以往之开支，预算可以如佳矣。徐蚌情形如何？天津来电，并注大有不安，现每天有电报来往。

(2)时赶运，定额先有电到厂，如津浦通车无阻者，然可循德石路转津浦到浦口，如蚌埠大桥有问题，须部车改船运厂，而徐蚌两段何者为宜，已向吴建文部长、英两处去信，请其与徐州联络视察详况再定。

(3)煤，继续买，我们直接向淮南接洽每月供给之两千吨，请仍继续船运，向两路交申请若干由浦口取煤，此事不可放松，有钱多买原料是对的。又等以为如何

(4)美储：今天接津纸厂徐经理

YUNGLI CHEMICAL INDUSTRIES, LIMITED.

永利化學工業公司 YUNGLI CHEMICAL INDUSTRIES, LTD.

HEAD OFFICE
219 SZECHUEN ROAD

CABLE ADDRESS: YUNLI
TELEPHONE 15616-7

SHANGHAI, ...

4000 37-6

p.3

君來電，即派人去廠面商」，弟擬去電
不必來人，告以廠價，錢當筆匯，焦豈不甚
好？硫礦廠係每噸四十五元，我共有（6 庫存，6+2+2 廠存，2+2 永業存）
一百一十噸，所得無能力再大可買焦。
(5) 搞雙方廠搜買焦炭，我們有些但無
能力，目前最好我們去繼續購買中。
(6) 工資小組：進行如何？此事請儘早
早日得有結論，為禱為禱。
(7) 復戰問題：是大家所注意的事，竟專函
本事請公司職工會籌備會成立一小組討論
早日實現，原則上如搞要之開討結果
咸贊成，弟意：(A) 以目前各方課之需要
由主管人提名，(B) 提名之後，調查其戰前戰時
先作早晚先後之決定，如 (a) 逾六天的，(b) 33天的，自動離職

七三三

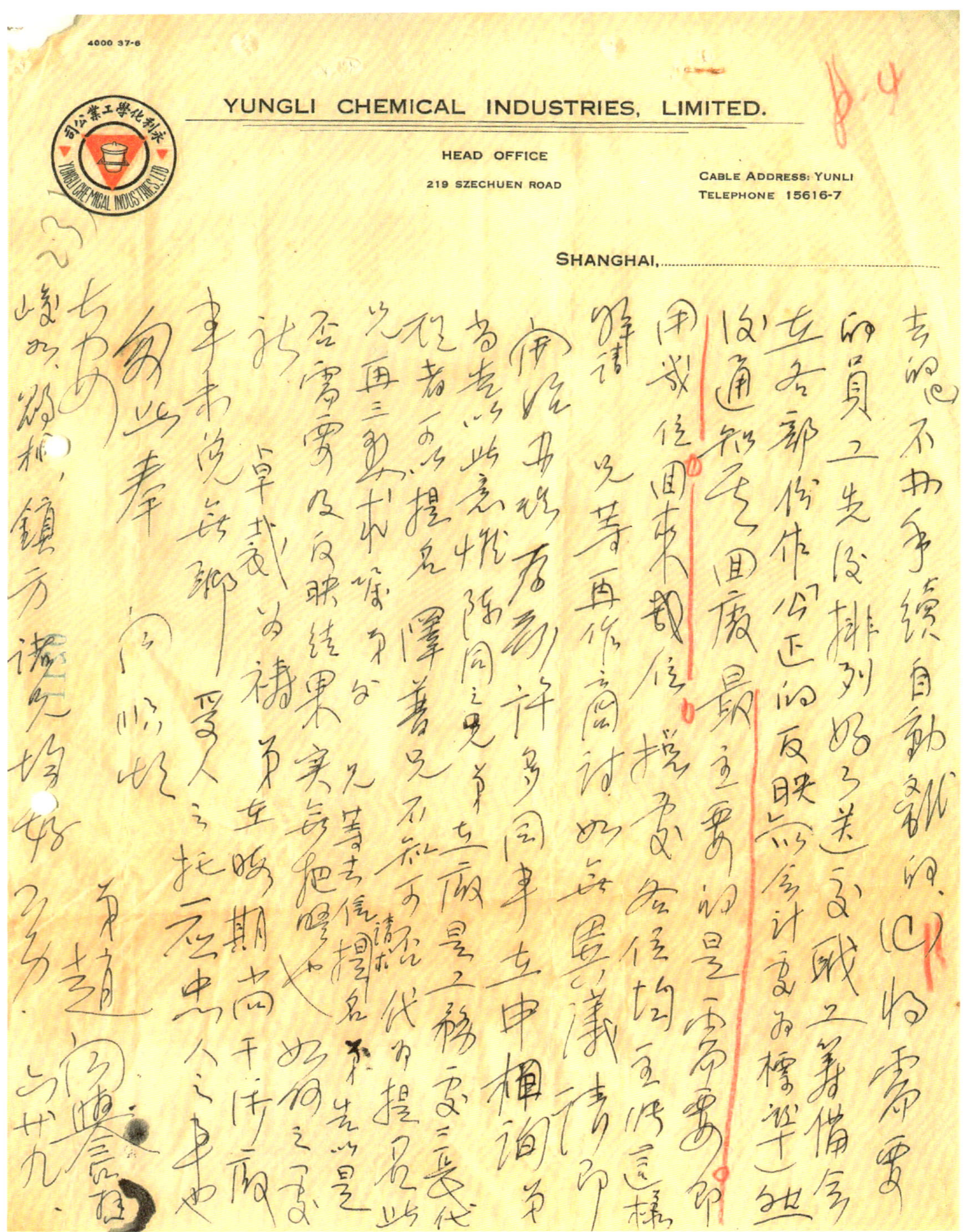

4000 37-6

永利化学工业公司 YUNGLI CHEMICAL INDUSTRIES, LTD.

YUNGLI CHEMICAL INDUSTRIES, LIMITED.

HEAD OFFICE

219 SZECHUEN ROAD

CABLE ADDRESS: YUNLI

TELEPHONE 15616-7

SHANGHAI, ……

8.4

去冬不如手续自动乱的。（一）将需要的员工先后排列好了，送交战工筹备会并各部份作公正的反映，以公计划为标准，然后通知各□最主要的是需要即用或候回来载信，据实公信均直供这样办法。请兄等再作商讨，如无异议，请即实行。若能务许多同事在申探询弟者，以此意慨陈同之兄弟在厂是工务处之长，代提者可以提名，择善兄不能，可请代为提名，此兄再三恐不妥，弟不当兄等去信提名，请于不去以是否需要及反映结果实无把握也。如何之处，祈卓裁为祷。弟在晚期尚干涉厂事，未免无聊。吾人之托一应出人之本也。匆此奉询，顺颂

大安

弟赵□□启

峻如、鹤柏、镇方、谦光、培□各兄

六、廿九、

永利化学工业公司錏厂与卖地农民协议书、契约（一九四九年十二月十九日）

0177

協議書

關於民國廿三年，以田業出賣與永利公司建立錏廠之四十八家原業主龔明山等，根據當初曾有每戶得有一人入廠工作之協議，聲請錏廠給予工作一案，經雙方報由南京市人民政府勞動局派第三科科長李雲青蒞廠，會同六合縣人民政府大廠鎮鎮長侍幹，了解本案眞相以後，認爲錏廠履行協議，固有予該原業主等每家一人以入廠工作之機會；惟鑒於錏廠實際困難情形，實無增添新人之必要。該原業主根據協議，固有要求入廠工作之權利；但根據該請求人塡送之調查表予以分析，四十八家中已有十六家有人在廠工作，五家業已絕嗣，兩家當時聲明，不願入廠做工，尚無人入廠工作者，僅二十五家，而此二十五家，在錏廠自建立至抗戰勝利復工，曾數次佈告招工時間中，不請求入廠作工，不能謂非自行放棄機會。再就各家現況而論，確能遣人入廠工作者，不過寥寥數人，而貧苦無力謀生者，有八家之多。爲照顧雙方困難，擬定處理辦法兩項如次：

一、自願放棄出賣田業時附帶協議規定，嗣後完全斷絕向錏廠請求入廠工作關係，由錏廠一次給與白米柒石，助其作從事其他生產之資金。此項白米，得按照發給前一日南京新華日報登載之中熟米價，折發人民幣。

二、業已有人在廠工作之十六家，應互相砥礪，努力工作；如有因立場或事故，違反勞動紀律與廠規。。。。受開革處分時，因出售田業附帶每戶得有一人入廠作工之協議，即告失效，不得再向錏廠提出任何要求。

上列兩項辦法，經提交當事人反映後，雙方完全同意，請憑南京市勞動局李科長雲青，六合縣大廠鎮鎮長侍幹，簽立協議書。此項協議書，計一式三份，除雙方當事人各執一份外，其餘一份，呈請南京市人民政府勞動局備案。

0178

六合縣大廠鎮鎮長侍 幹

出賣田業四十八家合於本辦法第一條原業主代表

陳德潤　吳發祥　芮明禮　芮明瑞　芮明山

舒十林　舒恆山　劉守業　劉德源　劉德才

李國源　韓長祥　陳發榮　陳發祿　李修全

劉其沖　張春年　張有仁　李朝松　李朝剛

張有祿　張有貴　舒德炳　張春懷　張有亮

出賣田業四十八家合於本辦法第二條原業主代表

李國金　李國和　李登高　芮明河　陳如洲

舒德金　潘傳昇　李朝頂　李國仁　李國

韓長福　韓慶 美 豐　朱永康　朱永源　張春

揚 相 明 炳

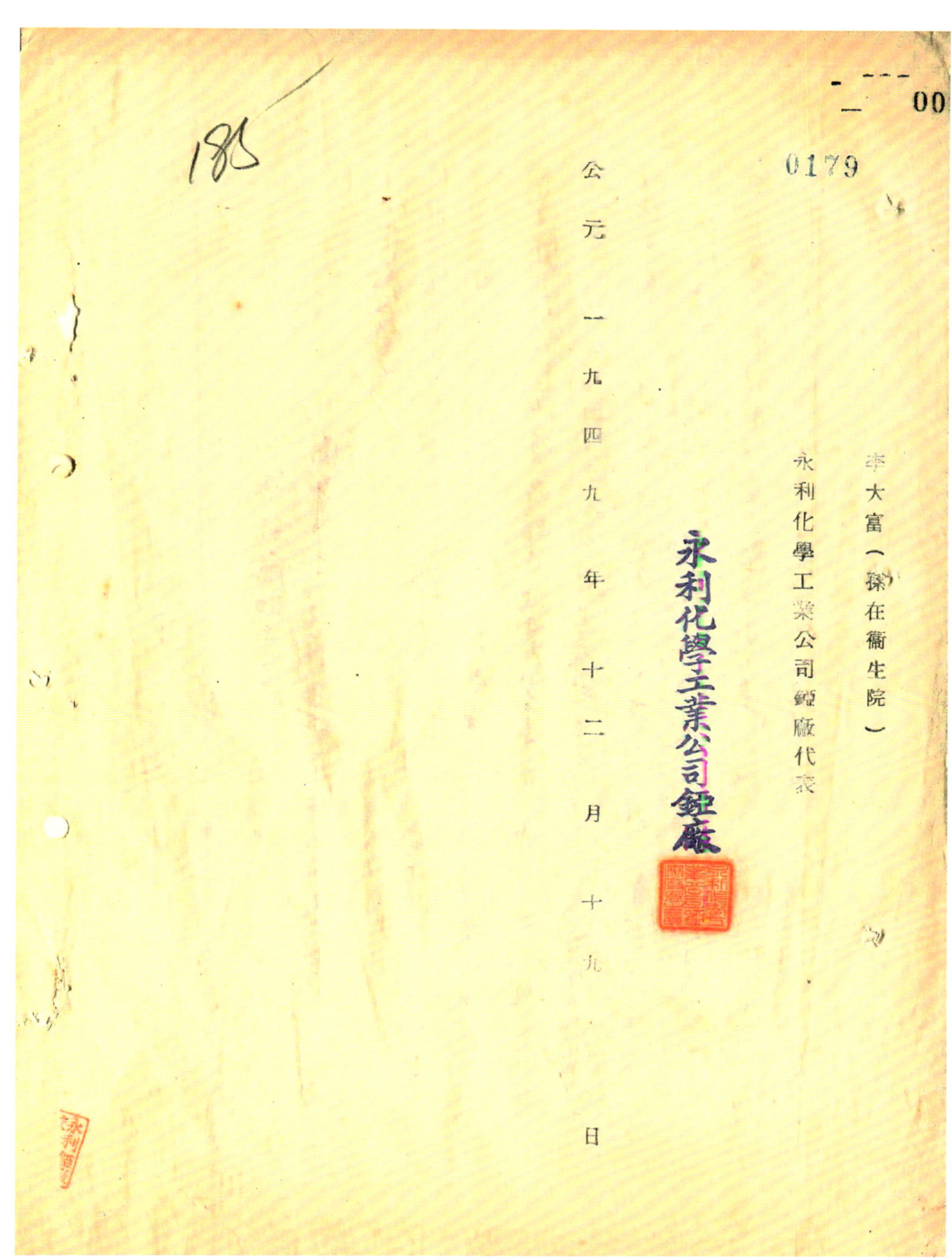

0179

李大富（係在衞生院）

永利化學工業公司錏廠代表

永利化學工業公司錏廠

公元一九四九年十二月十九日

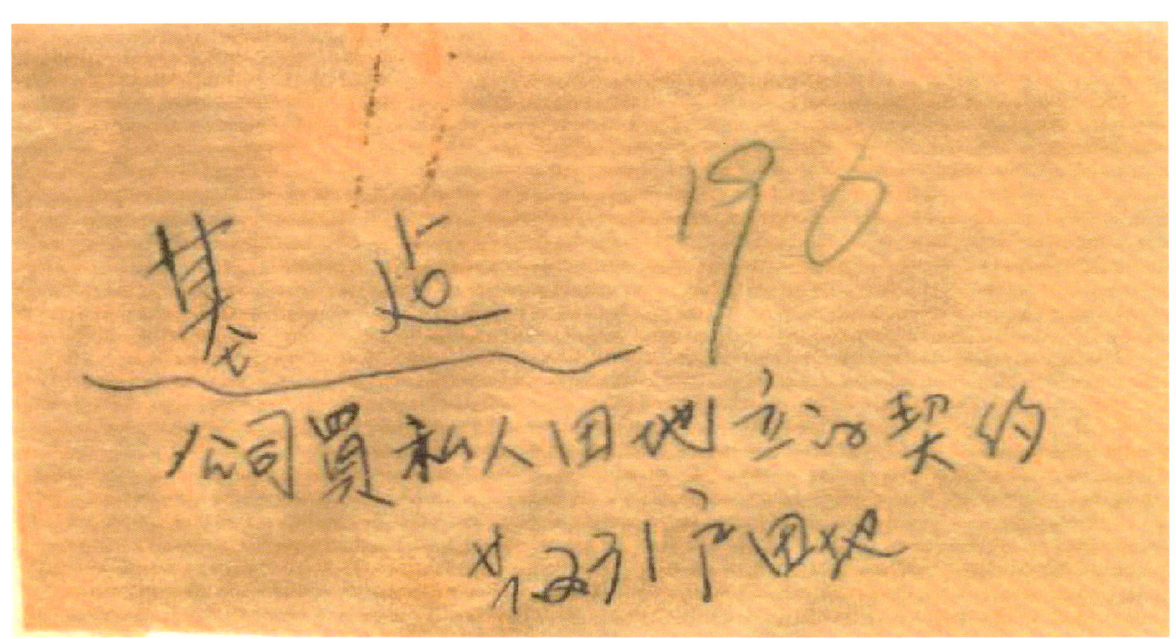
基建　190

公司買私人田地立訂契約

共1231户田地

0180 042

191

範圍內尚有五達公司一戶未成交[illegible]戶田歸

永利化學工業公司湘廠籌備處

字第　號第一頁　民國　年　月　日

立絶賣田地總契代表人楊子吉賀養生等貳百叁拾壹戶今因永利化學工業公司於民國二十七年抗戰初期呈奉 政府令在株洲白石港復興重化學工業測量繪圖徵購廠址復國以來着手建設子吉等願將株洲鄉原株洲鎮第八保白關鄉第十九保賀家土等處其地段從毛家坡江岈起直上採一直線穿過樟樹坡抵粵漢鐵路西折沿鐵路：基抵白石港心再循白石港心出港抵湘江再沿湘江至毛家坡止範圍界內所管田業等根據土地陳報處劃編(一)原白關鄉白字第一段自第一號起至六三三號止內除50至54號57至60號83 86 89號485至488號493號至499號532號至535號126 127 138 139號計叁拾壹坵號外實在陸百零二坵號再內124號摘六分之五125號摘三分之一127號摘二分之一(二)白字第二段自五〇號起至六三四號止內除63至84號計貳拾貳坵號外實在五六三坵號再內50號摘十分之九55號摘七分之六56號摘四分之三57號摘八分之五58號摘三分之一

東西廠界係採直
綫截收，板子戳有
戳字樣

043

191

0181

永利化學工業公司湘廠籌備處

字第　號第二頁　民國　年　月　日

61號摘六分之五62號摘五分之四85號摘六分之一86號摘六分之五89號摘十分之九94號摘十分之九95號摘三分之一97號摘五分之三（三）原株洲鎮株字第二段375號摘五分之四376號摘四分之三377號壹坵計三坵號以上三段合計壹千壹百陸拾捌坵號按計時熟高水田壹千四百叁拾叁畝伍分壹釐低水田陸拾玖畝捌分菜園熟土壹百柒拾捌畝伍分叁釐山坡熟土貳拾畝零捌釐房屋基地柒拾四畝零捌釐大小水塘叁零四口計叁百四拾柒畝捌分柒釐竹樹山捌拾九畝伍分柒釐落山伍百叁拾柒畝貳分玖釐以上八項共計面積貳千柒百伍拾畝零柒分壹釐所載未載毫不存留一概掃售與永利化學工業公司接管為業此係遵照二十七年八月二十七日及三十五年九月二十五日雙方兩次協約憑湘潭縣政府派委員黃鑫賡監證總計業價洋玖萬零柒百貳拾柒元伍角玖分及拆屋遷墳搬家等費當由各户親手領訖出具印契約貳百玖拾四紙裝成

廠址：湖南株洲白石港　電報掛號：四三五四株洲

192

0182

044

永利化學工業公司湘廠籌備處

字第　號第三頁　民國　年　月　日

三冊並印領結存證又田賦正供計壹拾四兩伍錢柒分玖釐冊名詳列於後任聽公司更名輸稅至界地所有產業此日憑中折楚買清賣明絕無異言倘有不清全歸絕賣人理落今欲有憑立此總契一紙并檢出新老契壹百七十二紙縣府頒發四都無契證明書七十壹紙一併交與永利化學工業公司永遠收執為據

計批本契管原田賦載三都二甲周甫林三錢八分八釐賀振宇二錢四分劉炳藩九錢九分九釐賓南雲一錢八分五釐劉志源一錢二分邱致中五錢七分嚴雲祥五錢〇七釐賀賢三叁錢賀仲恩五分七釐劉邦敏九分賀天和一錢三分六釐賀有高七錢二分賀三佑三錢三分周大章二錢周甫文二錢周錦盛三錢七分周樹棠三錢七分周丞階一分黃義學三錢三分五釐李正良六錢三分賀自清五分八釐徐光祿一錢九分五釐余秀林一錢〇八釐湯振清一分五釐謝國基二錢四分江天義一錢江天義六錢三分八釐

廠址：湖南株洲白石港　電報掛號：四三五四株洲

193

0183　045

永利化學工業公司湘廠籌備處

文沈氏二錢五分七釐言樹臨五分三釐賀秀田一錢九分二釐葉廷書五釐熊
席富六錢五分六釐劉湯氏一錢五分周甫林三錢余明德六分八釐賀榮
盛一錢七分三釐易慎恭一錢鍾上珍一錢六分五釐劉慶輝六錢三分五釐
賀昇平二分七釐晏正東一錢七分八釐黄遠聽一錢沈作新一錢二分三釐
沈桂亭六錢〇七釐沈玉林四錢六分五釐晏會溪公二錢四分沈庚直四分
四釐程達永一分黄文序五錢五分余登南公一錢五分三都一甲葉德明
五分以上共壹拾四兩五錢七分九釐又三都二甲楊時中三錢一分沈奉
先一錢四分五釐黄文亭一兩一錢余善謨三錢一分生〻公司一錢七分
六釐長左一屯生〻公司一錢二分賀傑英五錢一分二釐晏又音如鎰二錢
四分再前載張崇富一錢晏會溪公二錢四分沈庚直四分四釐程達
永一分黄文序五錢五分余登南公一錢五分共壹兩〇九分四釐計六
名係誤載應剔除以上除剔除實計五十六户共餉銀壹拾陸兩

字第　號第　四　頁　民國　年　月　日

廠址：湖南株洲白石港　電報掛號：四三五四株洲

194

0184　046

永利化學工業公司湘廠籌備處

字第　號第　頁　民國　年　月　日

叁錢玖分捌釐整此批

立總契代表人　楊子吉㊞
賀春生㊞

縣府監證人　黃鑫廣㊞

保　長　熊漢榮㊞

鄉　長　邱嶽㊞

白陶鄉鄉長　聶漢卿㊞

照章以每畝二分三釐科賦应另升科壹拾捌兩壹錢七分捌釐合計叁拾四兩伍錢七分陸釐正查湖南省政府民卅七年元月廿二日長府財四字第493號代電核示課征税額

中華民國三十五年十一月廿五日楊子吉立筆

廠址：湖南株洲白石港　電報掛號：四三五四株洲

永利化学工业公司湘厂筹备处与永利化学工业公司铔厂就征地事宜的往来函件（一九四九年十二月十九日）

會
佈

0186
049
197

永利化學工業公司湘廠籌備處

長京總(37)字第一號 第全頁 民國卅七年三月三日

逕啓者：茲寄奉湘廠〻地總契照片一幀，即希
察收備存為荷。
此致
鋞廠

附照片一幀

永利化學工業公司湘廠籌備處啓

電報掛號：四三五四長沙
地址：長沙落星田九嘉巷

中華民國卅七年三月七日
收文 湘 字第1號

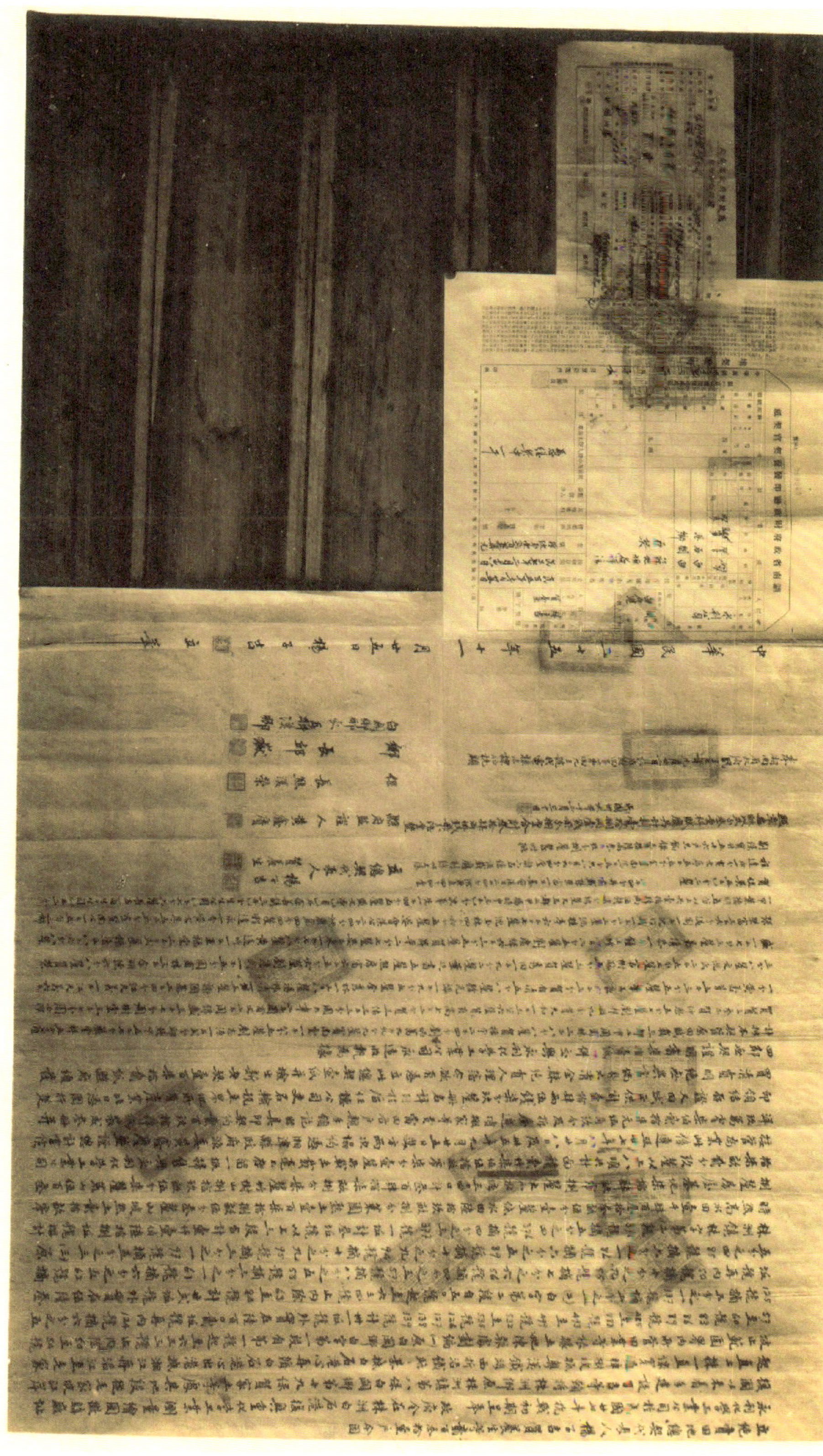

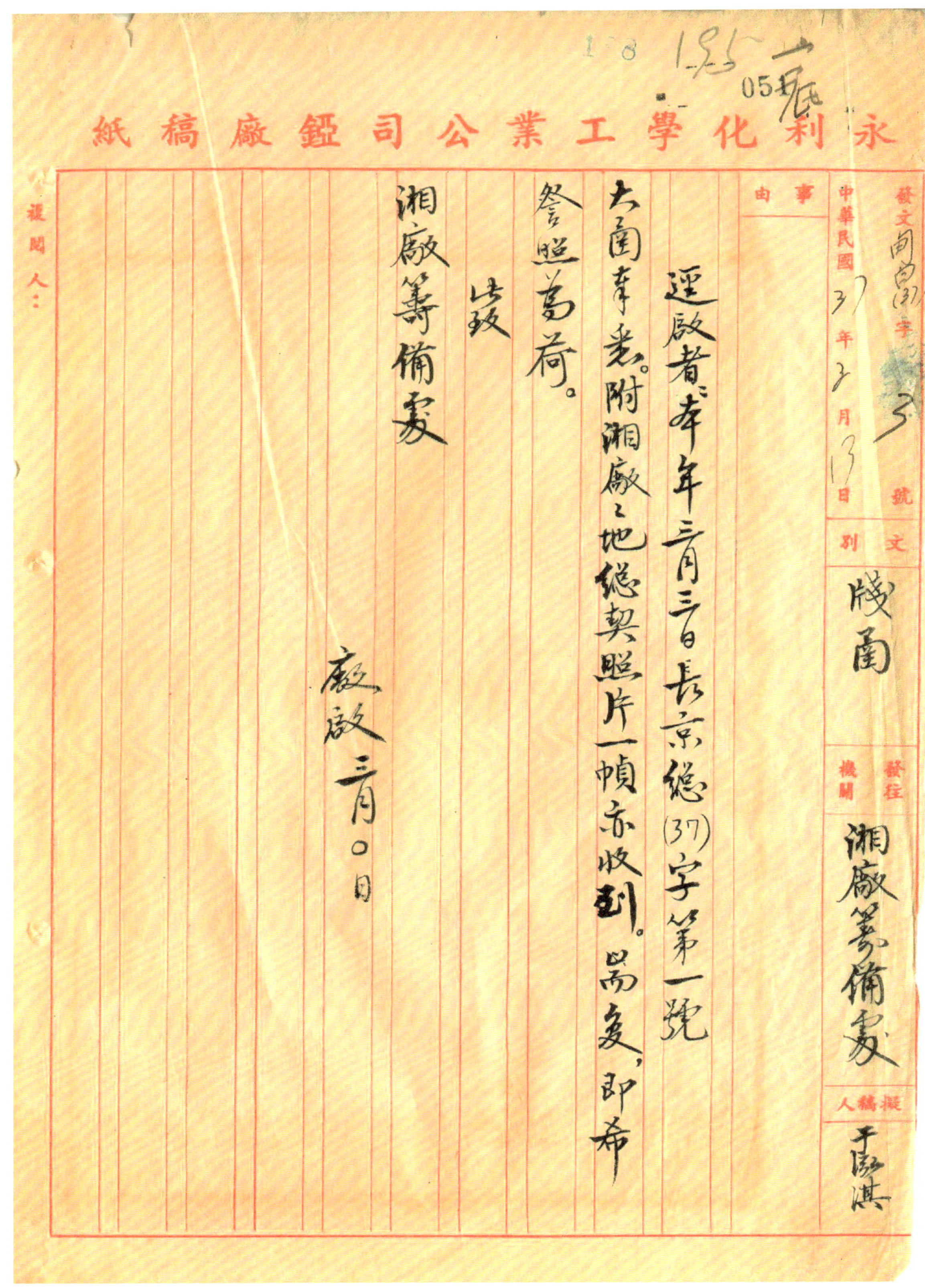

永利化學工業公司錏廠稿紙

發文 甯(37)字第 3 號

中華民國 37 年 3 月 13 日

文別：牋函

發往機關：湘廠籌備處

擬稿人：于[illegible]淇

事由：

逕啟者：本年三月三日京總(37)字第一號大函奉悉。附湘廠之地總契照片一幀亦收到。耑复，即希詧照爲荷。

此致

湘廠籌備處

廠啟 三月〇日

第一頁

永利化學工業公司錏廠目前概況

一、廠址—位在江蘇六合縣的卸甲甸和關門橋的中間，三面有圍墻，一面臨江，佔地約二千畝，面對八卦洲和南岸燕子磯遙遙相望。

二、性質和成立的意義—本廠是純粹民營的重化學工業，現時出品只硫酸錏一種，硫酸錏是肥料的一種，俗常叫做「氮肥」或者「肥田粉」，它是由硫酸和氨化合而成的，主要的用途在於肥田，是農業增產必需的肥料。本廠的成立，奠定了我國重化學工業的基礎，對國計民生具有重大的意義：

(1)在本廠未成立以前，我國沿海各省所用的肥田粉，都是由英、德兩國供給，每年進口約三四十萬噸，價值美金三千餘萬元，偌大數字的損失實在驚人，本廠成立以後，才把這漏卮杜塞了一部份。

(2)我國是一個以農立國的國家，農民佔到全國人口十分之八，農業生產在全國生產總額中要佔到頭等重要的地位。我們的出口貿易，主要也是以農業品為大宗，可是因為我國農業技術不求進步，生產力小，往往要依賴洋米的接濟，這真是奇恥大辱。本廠出產肥田粉，用意在提高農民的工作

0004 ~~010~~ 032

第二頁

效率，使農產品產量普遍增加，提高人民生活，增進人民福利。

(3) 為了適應新民主主義的社會的要求，我們一定要走上普遍工業化的道路，將來城市內的工商業愈發達，集中居住的人民也愈多，衛生設備也更求完善，因此，糞便多放入下水道，不再收回，天然肥料逐漸消減，乃是必然的趨勢，假使沒有充分的化肥來彌補這缺陷，這對於促進農業，當然是極不利的。而且我國農家所用肥料一向沿用人畜糞便、草灰、獸骨等維持土壤的生產力。但耕種多年，地力衰竭，每畝的產量遠不能和歐美農業先進國相比，這確是嚴重問題。為了補充天然肥料的不足和增加生產，化肥工業的興辦確是刻不容緩的工作。

我們的先總經理范旭東先生的確不愧為中國化學工業的偉人，他除於塘沽早已創辦了鹼廠以外，又於民國廿三年担起了創辦錏廠的重任。他一方面籌措資金、勘察廠址，一方面由他的合作者侯德榜博士渡美設計。克服了重重的困難，嘗盡了創業的辛苦，終於在廿五年年底完成建廠工程，於廿六年二月正式出貨，為我國化工建設開一新紀元。這是人民幸福的開始，也是中華民族的光榮。

三、硫酸錏的產量和銷場：

(1)產量——現在產量，每年約三萬公噸，以每斤硫酸錏平均增產農作物三斤計算，三萬公噸的硫酸錏，每年可增產農產物約九萬公噸。現在本廠正打算擴充設備，將來工作完成，每年可產硫酸錏約十七萬公噸，即每年可增產糧米約五十一萬公噸，就目前情形而論，我國尚須繼續添設與本廠產量相同的化肥工廠至少五十個，才可以供應全國農業增產的需要。

(2)銷場——本廠硫酸錏從前的銷場為江蘇、浙江、福建、廣東、台灣各省。

四、製造硫酸錏的原料和程序：

(1)原料——為煤、焦及磺鐵礦石三種。煤焦在抗戰前都由棗莊中興煤礦供應，自該礦受戰事影響廢棄以後，本廠所需煤焦都是從川、湘等地運來。磺鐵礦石是南京上游馬鞍山的產品。今後津浦路通車，北方煤產南運，本廠原料的供應，當不至再成問題。

(2)製造程序——大要分為三部：(一)從空氣和水蒸氣裡攝出氮氫二氣，經過高压高溫而成阿母尼亞；(二)將磺鐵礦石燒煉三氧化硫，加水成硫酸；(三)將阿母尼亞

第四頁

和硫酸配合即成白色粉狀結晶物—硫酸錏。

本廠並不製造硫磺。

五、本廠主要機器設備，均係美、德各大工廠精製的，其重要項目及數量如下：

煤氣發生炉 二套
洗氣塔 一座
水洗塔 一座
銅液塔 一座
高壓機 二套
循環機 二套
合成器 一座
礦磺炉 四套
吸收塔 一座
轉化器 四座
涼酸管 四套

飽和器 三座

乾燥器 一座

鍋炉 四座

發電機 三座

柴油發電機 一座

各種水泵及馬達 數十套

六、交通運輸工具——本廠原有機船為永利、永大、永鋥及安豐共四艘，木船有長齊及永利一號至六號共七隻，均於本年二月初為國民黨偽政府首都衛戍總司令部船舶管制處强迫徵調，封泊下關碼頭。後永利輪開沪修理，現仍留沪。這次南京偽政府撤退時，竟將本廠永大輪燒壞及木船數隻燒去，幸他其船隻未遭波及。

七、員工數目——去年十月間有職員二百四十七人，工友二千一百四十三人，現有職員一百八十五人，工友二千零二十三人，連職工眷屬不下六千餘人。

八、目前財務狀況——本廠專負責製造工程，關於財務的籌措調度和產品運銷

第六頁

各事，都由本公司上海總管理處所屬的財務、營業、運輸等部門負責處理。所以本廠每月經常的開支和消耗物料等款，向都由總處財務部撥匯南京各銀行收存提用。歷年以來，并沒有感到不方便。不過，自從今年一月中旬長江被封，交通斷絶，致原料及燃料等無法運廠。不得已自一月十九日起停工待料，到現在已將近四个月了。在這個時期，除了薪資照常發給外，對其他費用，只好極力節省。總處為了護廠和維持員工生活，確曾煞費苦心，對財務調度，極感困難。尤其最近受金圓券貶值和物價動盪的影响，已經到了一籌莫展的地步。現京滬交通還待恢复，為了急切要復工，才可以把六千以上的員工暨眷屬的生活，繼續維持下去，所以希望政府能給我們以充分的幫助。

九、尚待興辦的事業——本廠除了製造硫酸錏以外，另有硝酸廠的設備。在抗日戰爭時期，曾被日寇搬走。勝利以後，經過三年的交涉，才於去年運回本廠。現在尚未安裝就緒，而且缺乏零件，不能出貨。

永利事業在計劃中的還預備出產硝酸錏、硝酸鈉、硝酸碳等各種製品，添設煉礦廠和煉焦廠，更想擴充到燐肥和鉀肥的製造，燒鹼廠的建設

0009

第七頁

這些都是先總經理范旭東先生未完成的事業。今後全國解放，和平來臨，我們永利同仁一致相信在侯德榜博士的領導下，依舊可以繼續完成范先生的遺志，並且發揚光大，爲千千萬萬需要我們的人造福！

1946